THE PUBLIC LIBRARY IN BRITAIN 1914-2000

THE PUBLIC LIBRARY IN BRITAIN
1914-2000

Alistair Black

The British Library

First published in 2000 by
The British Library
96 Euston Road
London NW1 2DB

British Library Cataloguing in Publication Data
A catalogue record of this title is available from The British Library

ISBN 0-7123-4685-6

Printed in Great Britain by St Edmundsbury Press, Bury St Edmunds

Frontispiece illustration:
The public library (mid-1950s) as oasis of tranquility and haven of the self.
Keighley Public Library.

For Yolanda, Jasmine and Sammy

Contents

Sources of Illustrations

Cover illustration: Bradford Public Library, Local Studies Department
Frontispiece illustration: Keighley Public Library, *Annual Report* (1956-7)

Plate

1   *City of Nottingham Public Libraries and Natural History Museum 1886-1928*
      (Nottingham, 1928), Nottingham Public Library, Local Studies Department
2   Bradford Public Library, Local Studies Department
3   Bradford Public Library, Local Studies Department
4   Herefordshire County Libraries, *Annual Report* (1937-8)
5   Papers of William Benson Thorne, Library Association Archive
6   *Library Association Record* 47 (April 1945)
7   Edinburgh City Libraries
8   The British Library
9   *The Stack: Magazine of the Nottingham Public Library Staff Guild*
      (Summer, 1952) Nottingham Public Library, Local Studies Department
10   Bradford Public Library, Local Studies Department.
11   Bradford Public Library, Local Studies Department
12   Brighton Local Studies Library
13   Brighton Local Studies Library

Abbreviations

CUKT	Carnegie United Kingdom Trust
LANC	Library Association News Cuttings, The Library Association Archives
LAR	*Library Association Record*
MOA	Mass-Observation Archive, University of Sussex
PRO	Public Record Office
PWBT	Papers of William Benson Thorne, The Library Association Archives
SRO	Scottish Record Office

Preface and Acknowledgements

If asked, most writers would probably claim that their work could have been much improved had they been afforded more time to complete it. I have no hesitation in grasping this excuse! The first Public Libraries Act received royal assent on 14 August 1850, and so it is appropriate that this study appears now, 150 years after that date, to mark the occasion. Meeting this 'anniversary deadline' has meant being self-disciplined in choosing which avenues of investigation to pursue and which, however intriguing and attractive, to ignore. I apologise in advance, therefore, to those readers who discover that certain of their interests are either treated too briefly or passed over completely. I ask them to understand that this is not a 'total' history of the public library since 1914. It is, rather, an interpretation of its history, drawing more on aspects, as opposed to a detailed chronology, of the public library's twentieth-century past.

I began researching the history of the public library fifteen years ago. Although during the course of my work on the Victorian and Edwardian public library (my thanks in this respect to the ESRC for awarding me a doctoral competition award between 1985 and 1988) I was naturally tempted to look at aspects of public library development well into the twentieth century, research on the period since 1914 only began in earnest in 1998 with the award of a Social Science Fellowship from the Nuffield Foundation, for which I remain extremely grateful.

I am indebted to the staff of the several institutions that I have visited in the course of my research: the Public Record Office, the Scottish Record Office, the Library Association and the local history departments of public library authorities in Bradford, Bournemouth, Brighton, Croydon, Edinburgh, Glasgow, Greenwich, Harrogate, Leamington Spa, Leeds, Newcastle-upon-Tyne, Norwich, Nottingham, Oldham, Sheffield, Tower Hamlets and Winchester. The type of documents examined in these repositories is noted in the book's Introduction.

Commentaries by public library users presented in the book are drawn mostly from the Mass-Observation Archive, University of Sussex, whose volunteers provide such raw and exciting biographical material relating to everyday life in Britain (again, for more information, see the Introduction). I very much appreciate the care and attention given to me by Dorothy Sheridan and her staff, as well as the funding by the Library and Information Commission (and the guidance of the Commission's Margaret Croucher) of an Archive 'directive' to its volunteers, on the topic of public libraries, in 1999.

I would also like to thank Leeds Metropolitan University for its support, firstly in terms of the programme of research leave it has recently commenced, of which I have recently been a grateful beneficiary; and secondly, for its funding in the mid-1990s of a research project on late twentieth-century public library policy (specifically community librarianship), which inevitably entailed an investigation of certain themes of public library provision throughout the period covered here.

Photographs and other illustrative material were provided courtesy of the following: Bradford City Libraries, Brighton Local Studies Library, The British Library, Edinburgh City Libraries, Heredfordshire Libraries, The Library Association, the Library History Group, Nottingham City Libraries and Winifred Thorne.

But it is always more pleasing to express one's gratitude to individuals. My thanks go to: Peter Hoare, for reading the manuscript in full and passing detailed comment; to Dave Muddiman, Melvyn Crann and Keith Manley, for reading sections of the manuscript and giving me the benefit of their critical opinion; to Sheila Murphy, for her careful proof-reading; to Brian Livesey, for his technical support; to Belle Hepworth (at 'Just a Sec', Ilkley) and Vicky Chappelow, for their accurate and speedy typing; and to David Way and Lara Speicher at British Library Publishing, for their friendly guidance and encouragement. Finally, a very special 'thank you' goes to Winifred Thorne, for allowing me to examine the papers of her father, William Benson Thorne, before depositing them with the Library Association. Listening to her memories of her father's career, and examining the documents he left in her care, was one of the most memorable and enjoyable aspects of my research.

Alistair Black
Ilkley
March 2000

CHAPTER ONE

Introduction

Themes and Sources

This is the time of the 'new': new technology, a new World Order, new man, a new age (including its new-age travellers), a new millennium, new-wave 'this and that'. In the context of a New Britain, we have seen in recent years the emergence of New Labour (offering a New Deal for the unemployed). The people of Britain have also been promised a 'new library network'.[1] We appear, therefore, to be experiencing a major break with history. At least this is what we are told by various advertisers, public relations professionals, spin doctors, technological entrepreneurs, politicians and academics.

Upon closer inspection, however, it might be seen that continuities vastly outweigh changes – social, economic, political, cultural – which we might wish to describe as 'new'. This is certainly the case in respect of the public library in Britain, in terms of both its roles and meaning. Despite the best efforts of the institution's providers and supporters, including librarians and cultural commentators, as well as the promise to harness the latest information and communication technologies to construct a 'new library' system representing a 'people's network',[2] there is too little that is *radically* new – as yet at any rate – about today's public library. As a recent authoritative, independent voice declared, the public library is transparently 'due for renewal'.[3] New measures are deemed necessary to realise the dream of a new public library.[4]

Notwithstanding heightened activity and innovation in library work – the implementation of 'customer care' programmes and 'total quality management', the computerisation of circulation, bibliographic and information systems, the provision (though by no means everywhere) of modern buildings and bright interiors, the enthusiastic endorsement (by some) of popular culture, and the promise of advanced 'information superhighway' status – the fact remains that for too many people public libraries and their librarians retain a dated, historic image, as relatively inaccessible 'temples of knowledge' and as cultural backwaters frozen in the time of a bygone age, out of touch with many of the needs and cultural rhythms of modern society. Nearly half the population does not possess a library ticket (a remarkable proportion for a free service) and around another 30% can be classed as infrequent users. Moreover, use of the public library is warped in terms of social class, for while the predominant feature is a 'broad spread of ticket ownership across all social grades, the proportion of AB/C1s [professional and white-collar workers] who have tickets is consistently higher than the proportion they represent of the population as a whole'.[5]

The Public Library Observed

Public libraries are 'places we know and trust', but they are also viewed as institutions that are run down; in a sense they are 'our forgotten treasures'.[6] The divergence of public opinion over the current state of public libraries is clearly illustrated in the responses of volunteers to a recent survey conducted by the Mass-Observation Archive.[7] Some volunteers wrote of the public library in glowing terms:

In my opinion there cannot be many assets that a city or town council can offer that can be of more value and beneficial to the community than a good public library service.

My overall feeling is that public libraries are AMAZING WONDERFUL PLACES ... They are an important part of our heritage from our Victorian do-good forbears and should be cherished at all costs.

I have a very positive image of public libraries; they are places I have always enjoyed being in, whether to browse about or choose some fiction, or to look for a specific topic or fact, or to find out about the area, local events etc.

Another observed succinctly that: 'Libraries have kept up with the times.'[8]

Other volunteers diverged from these positive perceptions and experiences. 'My impression of a public library is one of yesteryear', wrote one critic, adding that the libraries he knew were staffed on the whole by people who were not 'with it'. A further contribution echoed the dated image:

There needs to be more marketing and promotion generally to make libraries appear 'trendy' and attractive, part of the modern world not historic artefacts from a bygone age ... They need to be given more money to modernise and improve their image as exciting and fun places for everyone.

Another observed that although she thought libraries were 'a very good thing in theory', her local library was 'slightly shabby, not very well organised and stocked with hardbacks in the main'. Looking forward ten years, she hoped they would by then provide a much more flexible service in terms of accessing stock, to have better informed librarians to assist users, to be much better resourced and to have improved new technology systems.

Attempting to explain the critical view of libraries many people obviously hold, one perceptive volunteer suggested that 'our tendency to denigrate libraries and librarians is all part of our national inability to take intellectuals and learning seriously'.[9] If this contributor to the survey is correct, then the task that lies ahead for public libraries remains an arduous one.

Museums of Modernity

'The most old-fashioned thing about libraries', in the opinion of one cultural commentator 'is the way we think about them'.[10] What explains the continual recycling – despite strenuous and sometimes successful efforts to modernise and develop services – of the dated, detached and irrelevant image of public libraries? Popularly conceived, the past and the public library are contingent subjects, indissoluble by virtue of the traditionalism and notions of continuity and inherited knowledge associated with each. Public libraries have often been portrayed and perceived, by their providers and users, as museums of literary culture. J.W. Clark, the nineteenth-century historian of medieval libraries,[11] suggested that: 'A library may be considered from two very different points of view: as a workshop or as a museum.'[12] In 1930, against a backdrop of criticism of the inadequacy of the book stock in Gloucester Public Library – said to be brimming with 'shelf after shelf of dead and forgotten books, which nobody ever dreams of reading' – users were told that:

Modern young men and women … have little use of the City Public Library, which they consider to be very out-of-date. Hence the flourishing business done by the lending libraries attached to the stationers' shops and the big stores. It is complained by the 'Modern Miss', that the Public Library is more like a *museum* [my emphasis] where old and musty volumes are stored away rather than as a source of recreation for the ratepayers.[13]

Just as regular museums collect, conserve and display objects of material culture, libraries perform the same function, often with the additional responsibility of lending items, in respect of recorded culture (although the book and other information products are also, of course, very much part of the world of material culture in their own right). Thus, the book-rich public library will always find it difficult to present itself as, in the popular sense of the word, 'modern'; as pertaining essentially to the present, as being 'of the age'. Despite their computer terminals and collections of audio-visual materials, as well as the general attempts to upgrade the user experience by means of modern design and organization, the image and perceived raison d'être of libraries is, to a large degree, rooted in the remote, not the recent, past. Employed in a 'public' setting – as opposed to the specialized, 'private' sphere of university, business enterprise, voluntary organization or government – the word 'library' continues to generate connotations of conservatism and custom: at face value the word is anti-modern in its social orientation.

Yet the modern forms of social organisation and governance to which Western societies have for the most part aspired over recent centuries are patently dependent on dialectical struggles of the past. Notwithstanding the revolutionary discontinuities of history – the radical 'jumps' of history – that which is regarded as modern is inevitably the product of earlier struggles for intellectual and social progress. Modernity is inherently a history-laden concept. Its dominant, guiding discourse revolves around ideas of improvement upon past failings and deficiencies and of the incessant pursuit of revisable truths. This generates a geological analogy of 'layered' advance, each statum representing in itself the modern form of its age. A strong case can be made, therefore, for the public library to be viewed as a modern, advancing institution. Public libraries have been, at once, warehouses of the cultural record and persistently forward-looking institutions. Like modernity itself, they synthesize the historic and the new, with a view to satisfying the systematic planning that characterises the instrumental rationality of modern societies. As such they might readily be termed 'museums of modernity'. This description acknowledges the popular, 'retro' perception of libraries. It also accommodates both the intellectual definition of modernity as a project of progress and the proposition that museums – in this case museums of literary and recorded culture – are fundamentally progress oriented.

The Victorian and Edwardian Legacy

Public libraries emerged in Britain, from 1850, as *modern* institutions, serving as both workshops of scientific inquiry and citadels of cultural elevation.[14] As prominent civic institutions, public libraries operated as agencies of modernity within a public sphere of open, democratic discourse. Their supporters and librarians promoted them as sources of both useful knowledge and rational recreation. Information in the form of books, newspapers, periodicals and reference sources were provided for both serious study and training for good citizenship. The aim was to help meet the educational and technical needs of an increasingly complex, industrial, democratic society, yet one in which diversionary, imaginative literature played a role in countering the tensions and dehumanisation associated with abrupt social and economic change.

On the other hand, a less positive picture can be drawn of public library provision, in terms of both purpose and methods. Interest shown by reformers in the public library idea quickened during times of social crisis, pointing therefore to the institution's function as an institution of social control and cultural conservatism. Its recreational role, although given a rational direction, was not accepted by librarians without a great deal of soul searching and debate. The political orientation of the pre-1914 public library, although rooted in liberalism, was often hostile to truly radical perspectives. Suspicion of working-class political aims was a recurring feature of public library history, while little attention was paid to groups at the margins of society, namely the 'undeserving' poor, what we might today collectively term the 'underclass'. Additionally, the methods and intellectual rationale which librarians developed to further their institutions' aims might also be viewed critically. In parallel with the emergence and growth of public libraries, librarians developed professional practices which, although constituting the development of a modern profession with a (just about) defendable knowledge base and a strong public service orientation, none the less generated an image of officiousness, largely due to the bureaucratized nature of library administration. Alongside the desire to realise citizen emancipation and empowerment, it is possible to bestow upon Victorian and Edwardian librarians a controlling dynamic, their aim being to help bring order to society and to impose order also on the burgeoning book collections of the modern age.

The New Library History

Belying its 'everyday' status, the public library thus demands and deserves considered analysis as a 'meaningful' social and cultural institution. In recent years the variety of perspectives employed by historians of the public library, of libraries generally in fact, has widened. Despite the almost complete disappearance of library history from education for librarianship, and the resultant thinning of the subject's seed-bed, a good deal of imaginative work is still being undertaken in the field.[15] In many respects these are also new times for library history.[16] There are even grounds for suggesting the arrival of a *new* library history.[17]

Although not necessarily sure of their footing, historians are able to peer into the past partly because they are able to stand on the shoulders of other historians. A debt of gratitude is thus owed to those who have previously written general histories of the public library movement, most obviously Thomas Kelly;[18] or who have explored specific themes of public library provision.[19] This said, one of the main motives underpinning this book is the presentation of an alternative to the descriptive, technique-centred and progress-centred methodology *mostly* (meaning certainly not wholly) employed in the field. Much interesting and innovative work has been undertaken in recent years, but, in the words of J.G. Ollé, 'it cannot be denied that much of the literature of library history is dull', a statement not quite as true today as when he wrote it in 1979, but still relevant all the same.[20]

Consequently, I am seeking to continue here the approach I adopted in the prequel to this study. In *A New History of the English Public Library: Social and Intellectual Contexts 1850-1914* I attempted to locate the history of the public library in a relatively generous historical frame. Mobilising knowledge and debates in contiguous historical disciplines enabled me to counter the notion of the public library as an 'innocent', uncontroversial institution, whose story has been one of largely unproblematic, linear progress since its inception in the middle of the nineteenth century. The methodology of standing outside the library world and casting a critical eye over its activities is hopefully repeated here. In particular, the danger of producing a history dominated by purely technical, professional or administrative issues – the subjective, insider's view – is hopefully avoided. Thus the reader will not find this book replete with acronyms – such as SINTO, MARC or the incomparable and exhaustive LADSIRLAC[21] – of technological, professional and organisational developments. Such developments are important and are woven into the discussion at appropriate points, but the book is intended to be more a social than a techno-bureaucratic history of the public library.

Community, Modernity and the Self

Further, the intention in this book is not to give the reader a detailed, blow-by-blow account of the twentieth-century public library; but to offer an *interpretation* constructed to a large degree from previously unexplored themes and sources. A core theme of the book is the interface between the public library and the self. It is striking how in recent years considerable emphasis has been placed on the public library as a 'community' institution, lying at the heart of neighbourhood networks: the cultural equivalent of the village pump, the epicentre of local cultural life. Moreover, on inspection of the historical record it is clear that the 'community mentality' commands a long tradition, the public library at various times being presented by its supporters as the 'jewel in the crown' of civic culture. To be sure, local libraries have historically exhibited a community dimension, utilitarian in the way they provide a shared resource, idealist in the common cultural experience they afford and in the civilising effect they have on the 'social whole'. The public library has always sought to satisfy community *and* individual needs. 'The necessities of both individual and communal life make the public library an essential part of the equipment of modern society', declared the Library Association in 1943.[22] More recently, in the context of the social potential of special library projects and initiatives, stress has been laid on the way public libraries contribute not only to social cohesion and community development, but to personal development also.[23] Another commentator is of the opinion that, as local 'information junctions', the value of public libraries to 'community life and individual well-being is far reaching, distinctive and irreplacable'.[24]

However, as with appeals to such sentiments as national pride or nostalgia, where there is always a danger that rhetoric can cloud reality, invoking the community function of the public library has in the past almost certainly served purposes other than the mere desire to state the institution's true potency as a social harmoniser. The word 'community' tends to stimulate uncritically positive reactions: feelings of well-being, participation and common ownership ('stakeholding' in modern jargon) flow readily from it. Laying stress on the community ideal is thus good for 'authority', public library policy-makers and professionals included. It can divert attention from the unsavoury reality of service provision. It can inflate professional self-image beyond its true worth by helping to internalise the exaggerated power of librarians to manufacture social solidarity. That public libraries 'remain at the heart of every community',[25] or that 'books build communities',[26] are propositions that surely appear trite in view of the massive under-use of libraries and the 'poor press' which public opinion often awards them.

Excessive resort to the public library's community dimension in professional discourses also obscures the enduring, principal purpose of public library use and provision: citizens' search for self-improvement and personal betterment, and the everyday satisfaction of individual needs. The public library and the self have always been intimately related. The same might be said of the self and modernity, the latter being the word which describes the fundamental change in Western thought and culture set in train by the Enlightenment. According to one commentator, modernity may be understood

as the very expression of individual and collective reason to bring about the achievement of some great social project. The emancipation of the individual, social progress, the development of harmonious social relations, the overthrow of fixed social institutions, from church to calendar ... became the victorious definition of the idea of modernity.[27]

Modernity is multi-faceted. One of modernity's most compelling facets – one which reflects all its aspects – is the notion of the autonomous, rational, self-directed person, or self. In the pre-modern world, the self was located in local structures; sources of socialisation were few – essentially church, estate and family – and before the age of print, means of communication with and from the outside world were for most people non-existent. The human person was believed to be under divine guidance, his or her spiritual core owned by God, inhabiting a temporal body ever open to sinful temptation. An individual's life path was preordained, but at the same time open to revision in the form of gifts of divine grace as rewards for good works. Knowledge and truth in the medieval world were arrived at through divine revelation: the human person employed reasoning merely to understand the complexity of that which had been revealed from above.

The advance of science transformed the role of reason. The rational person of the modern age came not to use reason passively, as a means of merely contemplating that which God as chosen to reveal, but actively, in terms of investigating and testing the world that he or she inhabits.[28] In the Enlightenment, reason replaced revelation as the arbiter or truth; and the notion of the self began to replace the earlier notion of the soul. Placing the individual mind at the centre of the epistemological stage has implications, of course, for the relationship between the human person and nature. Reason can be used to control the natural world, thereby investing the human self with considerable potential and power.

For the past three centuries, libraries – of all types – have served as fonts of reason and catalysts of progress. Libraries have been, if not central to the 'project of modernity', then certainly notable contributors to it.[29] In proposing the establishment of public libraries in Scotland, in the late seventeenth century, James Kirkwood justified the existence of such institutions by proclaiming evangelically that:

It is essential to the nature of Mankind to be desirous of Knowledge, as it is for them to be rational Creatures, for we see no other end or use for our Reason, but to seek out and search for the Knowledge of all these things of which we are ignorant ... That being born Naked, Indigent and Ignorant, we should be forced to enquire by the help of Reason, into the Nature and Knowledge of all such arts and Manufactories, as are necessary for the support of our Lives.[30]

As modernity matured in the twentieth century, Sir Frederick Kenyon (Director and Principal Librarian of the British Museum) noted, in 1930, that 'the recognition that progress comes by knowledge, and that a large part of knowledge comes from books, is becoming general'.[31]

But modernity has been characterised as much by individual, as by social, progress. In 1937 the American librarian Lowell Martin argued that the public library existed 'not only to control and repress the person but, even more basically, to provide him with freedom and opportunity for self expression and self-fulfilment'. Thus, although as 'a control agency' the public library conserved and transmitted the cultural heritage, and provided 'lanes of conduct for the individual' also, it equally performed a powerful 'individualising function', enhancing the individual's rationality, 'the arena of singularity and specialisation'. These 'socialisation' and 'individualisation' roles of the public library had been regarded by idealists, argued Martin, not as contradictory but symbiotic; the idealist consciousness being based on the idea that everybody, every self, had a role to play in, and a contribution to make to, the social world.[32]

The idealist tradition in library provision and use has also been evident in the way people have (mostly subconsciously) linked their own life projects with the historic accumulation of wisdom and the cultural record which library collections represent. Libraries have long been regarded, as the librarian W.C.B. Sayers once noted, 'as shrines where all the relics of the ancient saints, full of true virtue ... are preserved and reposed'.[33] Libraries have often been thought of as sacred places, sites of worship in the name of modernity and self.

Whether in the public library context or otherwise, celebrating the modern self has become a dangerous philosophical pastime in our so-called postmodern age. Deep within the Western cultural tradition lies the notion of the self-contained individual carrying a unique central core, one's 'true self'.[34] During the twentieth century this notion was critically examined on a number of fronts. Freud, for example, emphasised the existence of a sub-conscious darker side of personality (the 'Id'), which was in conflict with our conscious, rational side (the 'Ego'). Clearly also, the self cannot exist in isolation, but is worked upon by society. We are inevitably, 'social selves', our self-consciousness being formed through social relations.[35] In the 1930s, the interaction between self and society was theorised by G.H. Mead.[36] Mead divided the self into the 'I' and the 'me'. The 'I' was the active, unsocialised part of the self, that seeks innately to *inform* society independently of the reaction stimulated as a result. The 'me', on the other hand, is formed *by* society: we become a 'me' when we see ourselves through the eyes of others (the looking-glass self). Consequently the 'I' is not permanent but can be transformed by social relations and the development of the 'me'.

The idea of the 'social self' contains, however, the seeds of its own destruction. In the early-twentieth century, Saussurean structuralism heralded the death of the self; by emphasising the primacy of hidden social forces in moulding individuality, structuralists questioned the self's capacity for originality, the Enlightenment notion of the self as 'prime mover'. Later in the century, post-structuralists, took the demise of the self (subject or author) one step further by claiming that 'the person' had no power of self-direction not due to the operation of structural forces, over which he or she had little control, but essentially because the self, like any text, is open to multiple interpretations by others. We are not the authors of our identity; that is in the gift of others.[37]

All this tends to undermine the legitimacy of the modern self. However, other theorists emphasise continuity over change. Giddens has referred to the reflexivity of the self in the late modern age.[38] Far from abandoning the 'progress-improvement' core of the modern project, individuals, argues Giddens, constantly self-monitor their identities and life projects in an unremitting effort to re-make themselves. Further, Beck has raised the proposition of a 'risk society' in which progress and science give rise to problems for both self and society which in turn require further 'progress' in order to be solved.[39] Here again, the 'improving self' displaying critical reason is at a premium. Such re-assertions of faith in the continuing existence of the modern self are clearly to the benefit of an institution, like the public library, with such impeccably *modern* credentials.

Situating the self at the heart of public library philosophy is clearly a risky business, therefore. It would not have been so for Victorian librarians and library users, driven as many of them were – the respectable working class included[40] – by an evangelical, as well as a practical, belief in the benefits of self-endeavour. In the increasingly collectivist twentieth century, however, championing the self in a public library context appeared less 'safe' than cosy appeals to community spirit. Even in the Thatcher-dominated 1980s, against a backdrop of resurrected Victorian values, the 'public library self' could make little headway. This was not only because the culture of individualism 'as greed' and as 'social atomism', which infected huge swathes of British social and economic life at the time, bore little resemblance to the immensely strong idealist heritage of the public library, which set out the institution as a means of advancing the individual through collective provision. It was also because the library movement, broadly liberal in complexion historically, reacted against the attacks made on it, financial and otherwise, and could never have allowed itself to engage in the vocabulary of the self – even if this was deeply ingrained in its language and identity – for fear of being misunderstood as converts to the economisers' cause. Then, in the last decade of the twentieth century, community became the rage: initially under the Major government's rhetoric of

classlessness and a policy of 'back to basics', promoted by *English* cultural images of
warm beer, village green cricket and Sunday morning church; later, inspired by the
Blairite vision of a New Britain pursuing social inclusion and cultural pluralism and
tolerance.

What chance the 'public library self' in this cultural atmosphere of virulent
community? It would appear more important than ever, therefore, to redress the balance
and reassert the centrality of the individual in public library use. One of the ways of
achieving this is to extract evidence of a 'sense of self' from the public library's past,
thereby allowing those who have grown tired of the rhetoric of community to point to a
tradition as strong as, if not stronger than, that which fancifully places public libraries at
the heart of community life or in the vanguard of institutions which dissolve social
conflict. Hence, each chapter in the book will conclude with a reflective discussion of
how the self featured as an aspect of public library activity in the period concerned.

A Note on Sources

Whereas the theme of self-realisation in the context of the public library is hardly new –
this study merely seeks to resurrect its primary importance – some of the sources
employed to explore this and other themes are exploited *extensively* here for the first
time. Five documentary collections are to be noted in this respect. First, records of
government dealings with the library movement, held by the Public Record Office.
Second, evidence concerning a wide variety of subjects – including, unexpectedly, the
activities of a librarianship Masonic Lodge in the 1920s and 1930s – contained in
correspondence between the Carnegie United Kingdom Trust (CUKT) and
representatives of the library world, deposited by the Trust in the Scottish Record Office.
Third, the Library Association's collection of newspaper cuttings which, although
packaged and presented to the researcher in a highly edited form, none the less provide a
valuable and, to a degree, alternative view of public library events. Fourth, the papers of
the public librarian William Benson Thorne, whose professional 'life history' is reported
here in detail because of the way it typified both the ethos of public service and the desire
to promote self-improvement which many twentieth-century public librarians embraced.
Fifth, commentaries from individuals on aspects of public library use and provision
contained in the Mass-Observation Archive (University of Sussex). Two main sets of
documents are relevant here: directives on 'Regular Pastimes' (Autumn 1988) and 'The
Public Library' (Summer 1999). The reader will also find occasional references to other
archival sources, such as those relating to First World War library policy held by the
Library Association. Finally, mention must of course be made of the documentary
records of public libraries themselves, normally deposited in local history, or local
studies, libraries (institutions visited in the course of the research are noted in the Preface
and Acknowledgements above). Such records include annual and other reports,

newspaper cuttings, library committee minutes, photographs, in-house staff magazines and ephemera of various kinds.

Notes and References to Chapter One

[1] Library and Information Commission, *Building the new library network* (London, 1998).

[2] Library and Information Commission, *New library: the people's network* (London, 1997).

[3] Audit Commission, *Due for renewal* (London, 1997).

[4] R. Linley and B. Usherwood, *New measures for the new library: a social audit of public libraries*, British Library Research and Innovation Centre Report 89 (1998).

[5] L. England and J. Sumsion, *Perspectives of public library use: a compendium of survey information* (Loughborough and London, 1995), 8-9.

[6] J. Morphet, 'Libraries – community centres of the future', *Streetwise: Journal of Places for People* 8:4, Issue 32 (1997-8), 5.

[7] MOA, Public Libraries, 1999.

[8] Ibid., D2839, B2623, W2731, A883.

[9] Ibid., O2349, S2207, B2728, L1504.

[10] F. Matassaro, 'Unleashing the potential', *The Parliamentary Monitor, Supplement 2: 'L' is for learning* (March 1999), 16.

[11] J.W. Clark, *The care of books* (Cambridge, 1901)

[12] Quoted in 'Libraries call in computers to catch up on knowledge', *Times* (29 June 1966), deposited in PRO, ED 221/104.

[13] *Evening Despatch* (16 April 1930), LANC.

[14] A. Black, *A new history of the English public library: social and intellectual contexts 1850-1914* (London, 1996).

[15] E.g., E. Kerslake, *A history of women workers in English libraries, 1871-1974*, unpublished PhD, University of Loughborough (1999); P. Jenkinson, *Heritage and the public library*, unpublished PhD, Leeds Metropolitan University (1999); J. Everitt, *Co-operative society libraries and newsrooms of Lancashire and Yorkshire from 1844 to 1918*, unpublished PhD, University of Wales, Aberystwyth (1997).

[16] A. Black, 'New times for library history', *Librarians' World* 7:3 (1998).

[17] A. Black, 'New methodologies in library history: a manifesto for the 'new' library history', *Library History* 11 (1995).

[18] T. Kelly, *A history of public libraries in Great Britain 1845-1975* (London, 2nd edn., 1977); T. Kelly, *Books for the people: an illustrated history of the British public library* (London, 1977). See also a number of other general histories: J. Minto, *A history of the public library movement in Great Britain and Ireland* (London, 1932); W. Munford, *Penny rate: aspects of British public library history 1850-1950* (London, 1951); W.R. Aitken, *A history of the public library movement in Scotland to 1955* (Glasgow, 1971); W.J. Murison *The public library: its origins, purpose and significance* (London, 3rd edn., 1988); P.H. Jones, 'Welsh public libraries to 1914', and G. Evans, 'Welsh public libraries 1914-1994', both in P.H. Jones and E. Rees (eds.), *A nation and its books: a history of the book in Wales* (Aberystwyth, 1998).

[19] E.g., A. Ellis, *Library services for young people in England and Wales 1830-1970* (London, 1971); R.J.B. Morris, *Parliament and the public libraries: a survey of legislative activity promoting the municipal library service in England and Wales 1850-1976* (London, 1977); J.E. Pemberton, *Politics and public libraries in England and Wales 1850-1970* (London, 1977); P. Whiteman, *Public libraries since 1945: the impact of the McColvin Report* (London, 1986); R. Snape, *Leisure and the rise of the*

public library (London, 1995). For other thematic works see the journal *Library History*, and D.F. Keeling (ed.), *British Library History Bibliography* (London, 1972, 1975, 1979, 1983, 1987; Winchester, 1991).

[20] J.G. Ollé, *Library History* (London, 1979), 22. This comment might be balanced by P.A. Hoare, 'Library history', in L.J. Taylor (ed.), *British Librarianship and Information Science 1976-1980. Vol. 1* (London: 1982), 241, who wrote that 'it is very encouraging that the subject is in such good health, its fundamental basis is still developing from antiquarianism to a wider social and professional awareness'. K.A. Manley, 'Sunshine in the gloom: the study of British library history', *Libraries and Culture* 25:1 (Winter, 1990), similarly offers a positive view. For critical views of library history methodology, see Black, 'New methodologies', op. cit., and A. Black, 'Lost worlds of culture: Victorian libraries, library history and prospects for a history of information', *Journal of Victorian Culture* 2:1 (Spring 1997).

[21] The roots of Sheffield Interchange Organisation (SINTO) can be traced back to the early 1930s. MARC (machine-readable catalogue) technology was introduced in Britain in the late 1960s. Liverpool and District Scientific, Industrial and Research Library Advisory Council (LADSIRLAC) was created in the mid-1950s.

[22] Library Association, *Proposals for the post-war reorganisation of the public library service* (London, 1943), p. 3.

[23] F. Matarasso, *Beyond book issues* (London, 1998).

[24] R. Proctor, 'People, politics and hard decisions', *Public Library Journal* 14:1 (Spring 1999), 4.

[25] Morphet, op. cit., 5.

[26] M. Phillips, 'Books build communities', *New Times* (July 1999), 12.

[27] P.N. Cooke, *Back to the future: modernity, postmodernity and locality* (London, 1990), 5.

[28] S.J. Grenz, *A primer on postmodernism* (Grand Rapids, MI and Cambridge, 1996), 61-3; J.R. Gibbins and B. Reimer, *The politics of postmodernity: an introduction to contemporary politics and culture* (London, 1999), 54-6.

[29] P. Hoare, 'The development of a European information society', *Library Review* 47:7&8 (1998). See also, P. Sturges, 'The place of libraries in the English urban renaissance of the eighteenth century', *Libraries and Culture* 24:1 (Winter 1989).

[30] J. Kirkwood, *An overture for founding and maintaining of bibliothecks in every paroch throughout this kingdom* (1699), reproduced in W. Blades (ed.), *Proposals made by Rev. James Kirkwood in 1699 to found public libraries in Scotland: reprinted ... from the rare copy in the Free Public Library, Wigan.* (London, 1889).

[31] F. Kenyon, *Libraries and museums* (London, 1930), 31.

[32] Lowell Martin, 'The American public library as a social institution', *Library Quarterly* 7:4 (October 1937), 552-3.

[33] W.C.B. Sayers, 'Presidential address: in the spirit of their profession', *LAR* (June 1938), 292.

[34] R. Billington, J. Hockey and S. Strawbridge, *Exploring self and society* (London, 1998), 37-40.

[35] I. Burkitt, *Social selves: theories of the social formation of personality* (London, 1991).

[36] G.H. Mead, *Mind, self and society* (Chicago, 1962, 1st published 1934).

[37] P.A. Rosenau, *Post-modernism and the social sciences: insights, inroads and intrusions* (Princeton, NJ, 1992), especially chapters 2&3. Ferdinand de Saussure (1857-1913) questioned the traditional view that language developed according to discoverable rational laws, arguing that it was formed socially, determined by social convention and not by the structure of thought: Grenz, op. cit., 114-5.

[38] A. Giddens, *Modernity and self-identity: self and society in the late modern age* (Cambridge, 1991).

[39] U. Beck, *Risk society: towards a new modernity* (London, 1992).

[40] A. Robson, 'The intellectual background of the public library movement in Britain', *Journal of Library History* 11:3 (July 1976).

CHAPTER TWO

Science and Citizenship

1914-1919

During the First World War the public library continued to contribute, as it had in the Victorian and Edwardian periods, to the on-going search for social stability. Moreover, it saw its role in this regard sharpened in response to the escalating socio-political problems of the day which its supporters hoped it could help solve. The period threw up serious – if not entirely new – problems of social order. These problems were primarily the concern of the state, which inserted public libraries, albeit late in the war, into its plans for reconstruction. Equally sensitive to the instability of the time, the library world sensed the prospect of radical social and political change, if not upheaval, and evolved policies accordingly. Some in the world of business, expressing anxiety over the possible detrimental effects on production caused by the war and the accompanying transformation in economic and political expectations, added their voice to the call for public library renewal. A number of ideas on how the public library could help ensure social stability were shared during the war and its immediate aftermath by library establishment, government and business. These ideas focused on the fundamental link between reduced social tension on the one hand, and the public library's efforts to help deliver social calm and economic confidence on the other.

The role of the public library between 1914 and 1918 was defined by two central aims. The first was to construct a durable, stabilising civic consciousness through the promotion of education, in particular non-vocational adult education. Idealist influences were crucial in this regard. However, at the very moment when idealist notions of 'education for citizenship' were receiving unprecedented attention, they began to be undermined by their Germanic-Hegelian heritage.[1] Before the war, philosophical idealism had stressed the virtue of state action, including the provision of public libraries, in assisting the moral action of individuals. In the short run, increased state control was deemed necessary: it was the natural corollary to 'total war'. In the long run, however, idealist arguments favouring an increased role for the state became tarnished by the philosophy's association with the centralised, authoritarian Prussian system which was believed to have provoked the war.[2] A contributor to the *Library Association Record* in 1915 wrote of 'unmoral economic ideas made in [pre-war] Germany', and castigated 'persons who placed their faith in German economics, and in the schools of educational and economic thought that have done so much to imperil the very existence of human society'.[3]

The second concern of the public library was to help reconstruct the national economy, partly through the support it could give to education but more importantly by disseminating technical and commercial information. Of this aim relatively little has been said, historians concentrating instead on the public library's role as a cultural and socialising institution. Yet in the First World War the economic role of the public library, fuelled by an explosion of interest in matters scientific and technological, achieved a profile if not surpassing, then broadly matching, its cultural concerns.

Reconstruction, Education and the Revolutionary Threat

The main context of the development of the public library during the war was the debate on reconstruction. War – especially 'total war' – has been a potent catalyst for change. Marwick[4] discusses various schools of interpretation in this regard: for example, the 'conservative' positing of war as 'the great auditor of institutions', compared with the 'liberal' emphasis on the likelihood of war as a prompt to authoritarianism, moral degeneracy and anti-intellectualism. Adopting a 'liberal' perspective on the effects of the First World War would be to point to a slowing of social improvement and reform;[5] or, indeed, to a complete failure of social policy.[6] Some developments experienced by the public library as a result of the war – especially its new legislative framework and its commercial and technical libraries – would appear to deny the 'liberal' school and support the 'conservative' position. Other activities – such as its propagandist and anti-labour roles – would appear to endorse the 'liberal' perspective.

The conflict of 1914-1918 brought about a new commitment on the part of the state to the management of the nation's social and economic condition. This amounted to the most extensive state direction of society that Britain had known. As the war progressed, the spirit, if not the reality, of reform strengthened. Lloyd George recalled that: 'The Great War was not an end in itself. We waged it in hopes of winning through to peace and a new and better age.'[7] B. Seebohm Rowntree spelt out what Lloyd George's 'new and better age' entailed:

The war has torn the scales from our eyes, and forced us to see things as they really are, and by the light of this clearer vision we have come to regard many conditions as intolerable which before had only seemed inevitable .... We have completely revised our notions as to what is possible or impossible. We have seen accomplished within a few brief months or years reforms to which we should have assigned, not decades, but generations. I do not believe for a moment that in the future we shall allow millions of our fellow-countrymen, through no fault of their own, to pass through life ill-housed, ill-clothed, ill-fed and ill-educated.[8]

That a committed reformer such as Rowntree should have been optimistic about the prospects of social reform is hardly surprising. Nonetheless, his words echoed a desire for change issuing from a variety of social groups and political factions. However, motives behind the promotion of reform differed, and can be categorised in three ways. First, there was a sincere radical and liberal-reformist concern over the inadequacy of existing social provision. Second, all mainstream political groupings recognised the need to espouse social reform for fear of the electoral consequences of not doing so. Third, faced with the prospect of serious unrest, the state aimed at a 'containment of labour' to meet the structural needs of British capitalism. Of these motives the last was perhaps the most crucial: that is to say, the need to construct an assured social stability out of the potentially destructive and socially divisive effects of war. As Lloyd George pleaded: 'We want neither reaction nor revolution, but a sane, well-advised steadiness of bold reconstruction.'[9]

Serious disaffection confronted the state in the second half of the war and its immediate aftermath.[10] Its causes were seen at the time as multifarious: rising prices (especially food and rents);[11] poor housing; restrictions on trade union practices and labour mobility; narrowing of differentials between the skilled and unskilled; strict licensing laws; industrial fatigue; resentment against supervisory grades required to manage increased semi-skilled labour; the growth of militancy amongst the semi-skilled worn down by monotonous work processes; inequality of sacrifice in the war; lack of faith in government to keep pledges and in the parliamentary process; uncertainty as to the industrial future; and anger at the handling of the military effort, summed up in the belief that 'lions' were being led by 'donkeys'.[12]

In surveying this evidence, some historians have readily agreed on the existence of a semi-revolutionary situation precipitated by the war. The view that at the end of the war Britain stood on the edge of revolution is in the tradition of Alan Hutt who in the 1930s assessed that:

During the first few months of 1919 British capitalism was skating on thin ice. The revolutionary outburst that was threatening in 1914 now seemed likely to materialise in a far more acute form and in circumstances vastly more menacing to the existing social order.[13]

Retrospectively it can be judged that the chances of a revolutionary upheaval along Bolshevik lines were in fact negligible. The working class generally, and its leaders in particular, remained attached to pragmatic and conservative traditions. It is true that, on the one hand, many trade unions found themselves for the first time negotiating with the state over wages and conditions, thereby dragging political issues into the economic sphere. On the other hand, it is likely that most workers undertook industrial action for economic rather than political ends, in an attempt to take advantage of favourable collective bargaining opportunities delivered by full employment.[14] This is not to say, however, that some in authority did not mistake economically derived working-class volatility for revolutionary intent. For example, in the months following the Armistice a fear of a Bolshevik-style uprising at home was expressed by several leading figures in the government;[15] anxieties encapsulated in J.A. Hobson's remark that: 'Property is seriously afraid.'[16]

Yet such fears of revolution require refinement. Public utterances on the prospect of revolutionary insurgency should not be taken at face value. Lloyd George, for example, skillfully used the bogey of Bolshevism to rally Conservative support for the social polices in which he genuinely believed.[17] The image of impending social collapse was thus used to justify piecemeal social reform and lessen the chances of serious social unrest. This tactic manifested itself most clearly in the work of reconstruction, comprising an extension of social policy and measures for economic recovery. Government noted that two of the main reasons for disaffection were the psychological feelings of 'inequality of sacrifice' and a 'woeful uncertainty as to the industrial future'.[18] Hence, policies were developed and promises were made concerning improved living standards and quality of life. Notwithstanding practical needs to plan for post-war renewal, reconstruction was initiated in the middle of the war as a means of boosting morale in helping to prosecute the war more effectively: workers would be more productive and soldiers more inclined to fight if convinced of the prospect of a better post-war world.[19] By the end of the war, reconstruction had also become an insurance policy against social unrest. For example, a vast housing programme was inaugurated, aimed at delivering 'homes fit for heroes' who sought repayment for sacrifices made. Duly rewarded with improved living conditions a potentially disruptive working class would, it was hoped, assume the responsibilities of participatory citizenship so crucial to the maintenance of social stability.[20] Other defensive reforms were made in areas such as rent control, unemployment relief and education, the latter being an important context for public library renewal.

Education (alongside housing) became the most prominent means of promoting social stability through social reform. The Education Act (1918) – which raised the school-leaving age to fourteen and offered part-time 'day continuation' classes up to the age of eighteen – demonstrated a determination to make use of a better educated population to solve the problems the war had revealed. The importance which government attached to the education of those beyond school age was demonstrated by the Ministry of Reconstruction's inauguration of an Adult Education Committee, which produced four reports over the course of 1918 and 1919, including one on libraries and museums.[21] Non-vocational continuing and adult education was promoted in the First World War with considerable enthusiasm, partly for conservative reasons. In 1917 the chairman of the Adult Education Committee, the idealist A.L. Smith, wrote that continuation classes for 14-18 year olds were essential:

to carry on the moral and disciplinary influence of the elementary schools .... If industrial harmony is to take the place of social unrest ... education on the moral and social side must be taken up in a way that had hardly been experimented upon as yet .... Unless we educated our democracy there will be the greatest social and political trouble.[22]

Education was viewed by H.A.L. Fisher, President of the Board of Education, as crucial to a reinforcement of the civic consciousness which helped safeguard existing social arrangements. It would make individuals more 'reasoned' and therefore more 'reasonable' in their attitudes to the state and to employers, thereby enabling otherwise alienated individuals to become true citizens of a participatory, pluralistic, capitalist society. Education, said Fisher, had the power to affect, for better or worse, whether a child be 'imprudent or profligate, cultured or ignorant, brutal or refined, social or anti-social, a citizen or an anarchist'.[23] He also stressed the effects of education on economic activity: 'I venture to assert', he told the House of Commons, 'that no country in the long run suffers economic injury from an improvement in the general education of its people'; for education had the effect of 'strengthening physique, shaping character, and enlarging the intelligence of the community', which inexorably resulted in 'benefits to all engaged in the economic life of the country, whether as producers, distributors, employers or employed.[24]

Increased expenditure on education was considered appropriate because of perceived improvements in wartime economic efficiency. Industrial productivity would in turn be boosted by educational investment made affordable by a more prosperous economy.[25] This theory – of an upward spiral of favourable cumulative causation – was attractive to economic planners due to the pervasive fear of depression. Although high levels of demand continued into the post-war period, politicians, as well as business leaders, often expected the worst. Despite displaying a rousing public commitment to reconstruction, government never felt completely at ease with the high taxation it required. Politicians of the Right, urged on by business, were particularly vocal in urging a return to financial normalcy. The attitude of the well-off to the high public expenditure which social reform demanded was relatively hostile. The Ministry of Reconstruction did not fully grasp the extent of the transfer of resources from rich to poor which social reform demanded and was thus unable to anticipate the strength of opposition to reform. Social reform was barely tolerated by the rich. Consequently, after an economic downturn commenced in the autumn of 1920, plans for social legislation were quickly dropped. Rising unemployment seriously weakened the challenge of the Left, the state believing it no longer needed to pay the premium on the insurance policy against unrest which social reform represented. Yet before the "Geddes Axe' was taken to social planning in 1922, it would be true to say that some reforms had attracted less criticism than others. Money for education was perhaps the form of public spending viewed with least suspicion: this by virtue of its apparently 'productive' and, consequently, self-funding nature. This perhaps explains why education attained such a high priority in reconstruction.

How, broadly, does public library development during the First World War interact with the events and circumstances outlined above? Drawing on the wartime spirit of reform, especially in the field of education, the public library was advanced by the war in three broad ways. First, the war did much to precipitate the legislation which the library establishment had for so long sought. By any measure the Public Libraries Act (1919) represented an extensive overhaul of previous levels of provision. It not only allowed county councils in England and Wales to become library authorities, thereby bringing library services to rural areas, but also encouraged increased spending by abolishing the 'penny in the pound' rate limitation which had existed since 1855.[26] It is possible that abolition would have been achieved irrespective of the war. Standards of provision in 1914 had not been seen by the library establishment as seriously deficient,[27] but pre-war inflation had begun to have disadvantageous effects which, if continued, would have placed pressure on government to legislate. The war added impetus to pre-existing inflationary pressures and brought services to a point of crisis, opening the way for legislative action probably earlier than would have been the case without the sense of urgency which the wartime crisis engendered. The extremity of the crisis meant that government for the first time began to take more than a passing interest in the public library. Previously, parliamentary action had been confined to individual initiative (for example , the work of William Ewart and Lord Avebury). In 1919, however, it was a government department (Education) which promoted the new bill, an indication perhaps of the acceptance generally of increased state intervention necessitated by war.

Secondly, just as reconstruction encompassed a psychological, spiritual dimension denoting a sense of rapid social change, public libraries also were considered to be on the threshold of something new. This 'watershed' mentality manifested itself most clearly in the excitement surrounding the new public commercial and technical, or business, libraries which emerged during the war (more about these later). Such developments were thought to be in step with the strategy for delivering Lloyd George's 'new and better age', noted above.

Thirdly, use of public libraries was regarded as a simple but effective means of helping to maintain morale, of keeping citizens sane, on the home front. The National Home Reading Union, which had a long standing association with public libraries, noted that the war had brought a strain:

on our outward circumstances in being cut off from luxuries and comforts and familiar habits; but, more vitally still, a strain on our inward temper ... In loss, in discomfort, in anxiety, we can keep our heads clear and our thoughts high. This is one of the things in which reading helps us.[28]

Fourthly, public libraries benefited from the fresh interest in education which reconstruction promoted. News that readers were switching to more serious, reading – though the extent of this was probably exaggerated – was welcomed.[29] Serious issues raised by the war, and the desire of people to read about them, gave greater recognition to the public library as an educational agency. In Sunderland in 1915, to exploit growing interest in the war, a glazed screen (illuminated after dark) was erected outside the library to exhibit a variety of information about the conflict, including maps, news reports and books dealing with the belligerent nations.[30] That same year a similar exhibition was mounted in Croydon.[31] In Leeds shortly after the war it was enthusiastically reported that issues of fiction had fallen to 52 per cent, in contrast to the 70 or 80 per cent registered in earlier years.[32]

This invigorated education role included a greater awareness of the public library's economic and civic education potential. The notion of education's 'productive' characteristic influenced conceptions of the public library's function. The idea that education supported by the public library had a materialist dynamic, that it aided individuals – such as technical education students – in their personal economic ambitions and contributed to national economic regeneration, grew significantly. When, for example, the Minister for Reconstruction, Christopher Addison, addressed the Library Association in 1917 he expressed the hope that public libraries would become 'infinitely more useful than they have been in time past' if, amongst other things, they forged 'a proper working relationship between our higher educational system and the businessmen and industries of the country'.[33] The public library was also seen as 'useful' in relation to the perceived increased demand for non-vocational adult education. The institution was presented in idealistic terms as the natural haven for the civic-minded individual thirsting for knowledge about a rapidly changing world. The fact that the war more clearly presented the institution's image as 'useful', politically for the 'citizen' and economically for the 'producer', enabled the librarian G.A. Stephen to speak after the war of the public library as 'the fountain of mental health for the whole community, providing pure education, which is the foundation of citizenship' as well as 'material for technical and vocational instruction and generally ... information useful to those engaged in commerce and industry, whether as employers or manual or non-manual workers'.[34]

But the war's effect on public libraries should not be viewed as entirely positive. The library establishment issued loud warnings about the crumbling fabric – buildings and services – of public libraries. A depressing picture was painted of the abandonment or curtailment of book acquisition (partly due to the high cost of paper); premises and departments not maintained, or closed, or handed over to war work; the postponement of building programmes; reduced opening hours (despite a slight upturn in demand in 1917-18); withdrawal of staff on active service; and pressure on income due to inflation.[35]

More important than tangible deterioration, however, was the ideological blow which the war dealt to the public library's 'liberalising' tendency; this by virtue of the war's reinforcement of the institution's conservative characteristics. The history of the public library in the First World War lends weight to that school of thought which views war as inherently productive of anti-liberal tendencies. Like the strategy of reconstruction generally, the public library was seen by some as a bulwark against social disaffection. The aim was not exactly to 'buy off' discontent: for it could not be said that either a disaffected working class at home, or soldiers in the trenches or awaiting demobilisation, clamoured for better library provision in preference to improved housing, higher pay, the dole or rent control. The public library has never mapped perfectly onto the Marxist explanation of social reform, according to which the ruling class is forced to pay a 'social' ransom to avoid proletarian wrath. Quite simply, the working class has never taken enough interest in the public library to justify calling its provision and improvement a 'ransom'. Rather, a propagandist role was envisaged for the public library; it was the library's 'educative' power which attracted the interest of those seeking social stability at a time of increasing working class demands. Further, education (and information) of a 'material' nature, disseminated through the public library could help eradicate, it was said, the chances of national economic dislocation upon which social confrontation fed. This strengthening of the public library's social stability objective, via education for both social conservatism and material progress, places the public library in line with the forces of reaction which emerged during the war; although the historic liberating role of the institution did not, of course, disappear.

The Role of Government

For central government the fate of public libraries was for much of the war a relatively unimportant issue. It is easy to take the initiative of Christopher Addison, Minister of Reconstruction, in addressing the annual conference of Library Association in 1917 as evidence of a new commitment on the part of government to support the institution.[36] A close reading of Addison's address, however, reveals an ambivalent attitude. On the one hand he acknowledged the value of the public library, particularly in the economic sphere. On the other hand, he questioned the efficacy of extensive public provision by appearing to prioritise the development of private collections of higher technical and commercial information in businesses and by doubting the existence of any significant demand for increased public library funding: 'We know ... that the powers of public authorities are limited by statute in various directions, although it is evident, looking through your records, that there are a large number who do not even exercise them.'

Although it is true that legislative action was eventually taken – in the form of the Public Libraries Act (1919) – the decision to include the crucial clause abolishing the rate restriction was taken late in the day as a result of persistent lobbying by the library establishment, and from John Ballinger in particular.[37] As late as March 1919, in answer to a question in the House of Commons, the government perceived no widespread demand among local authorities for altering the rate limit. To an extent the government was correct in this assessment. The town clerk of Loughborough was of the opinion that 'the produce of a rate of one penny in the pound has been sufficient to meet the expenditure on the public library and that up to the present no difficulties have been experienced in maintaining the institution.'[38] This position was supported by the

Whitchurch Public Library Committee which considered that 'the burdens on local rates are too great already, and that if the present statutory limitation were removed the effect would be that private individuals who now contribute voluntarily to library funds would be discouraged from continuing to do so'.[39] Other local authorities opposed to the abolition of the rate limitation included Bromley, Portsmouth and Lambeth.[40] In Torquay the resistance to the increased expenditure which abolition would bring was particularly strong. The chairman of the public library committee believed that the library rate was being used to subsidise general council expenditure.[41] The fight over the library rate, widely reported in the press, boiled down to an interpretation of patriotism. The economists, adhering to requests from central government to cut expenditure, saw prudence as supportive of the nation's cause; whereas those in favour of maintaining and increasing expenditure on libraries argued that 'keeping up the mental spirits' was the truly patriotic thing to do.[42] However, most public library authorities supported the view expressed by A.L. Hetherington, Secretary of the Carnegie United Kingdom Trust, who asserted that:

The growth which the library movement has made, despite the financial disabilities under which it has laboured, has been noteworthy, but evidently a position has now arisen which is indicative of an approaching crisis ... Serious though the financial strain has been in the past, the position of public libraries today is precarious. Unless early and effective steps are taken to allow each town to decide for itself what annual sum is necessary to conduct efficiently one of its most popular institutions, it appears highly probable that many public libraries will have to close their doors or be administered unsatisfactorily.[43]

Only in June 1919, by which time responsibility for public libraries had passed from the Local Government Board to the Board of Education, was there any indication that government was aware of the rating problem.[44] The public library cause was taken up in 1919 by H.A.L. Fisher, who later claimed that he 'in a humble way, had been instrumental in improving the position of public libraries'.[45] Both the Act and the Board of Education's sponsoring of it were widely viewed as a natural corollary of the Education Act (1918), and the plans for continuing education in particular. This was certainly the view of the Leamington Spa Public Library Committee which praised the Board of Education's involvement: 'This recognition by a great Department of State of the place of public libraries in our national life is a cause for satisfaction to those who have so long felt that the library movement in this country was 'nobody's child'.[46]

However praiseworthy the involvement of Fisher and his department was considered at the time, government support for public libraries was not unqualified. When discussing the issue in cabinet committee, Fisher said that one of the reasons he supported the Bill was that 'no charge upon the exchequer was involved'.[47] The Act was clearly based on the prospect that no government expenditure was entailed, and at no time was any form of central funding seriously considered. Public libraries were to remain essentially 'voluntary' bodies, whereby local users chose to tax themselves to fund services. The idea lingered – even if the reality in many places was a strong middle-class presence – that public libraries were established under 'class legislation', that they were provided primarily for the working class. As such, it was believed that compulsion should be avoided and expenditure limited because the service was not in the first instance for the entire community.[48] The continuing strength of these sentiments were revealed in the debate at the Bill's committee stage when objections centred on the rates issue, one Member exclaiming: 'Go where you like in this country you hear bitter complaints of the continually increasing rates. They are a tremendous burden especially upon the middle class, the people with fixed incomes and diminishing incomes.'[49]

Relative to other areas of social policy public libraries attracted little government interest. Yet such indifference is at first sight belied by the preparation during the war of a report on libraries by the Ministry of Reconstruction's Adult Education Committee, the first government appointed committee since 1850 with terms of reference specifically relating to public libraries. The importance of the proposed report was not lost on Stanley Jast: 'For the first time, I fancy, we have been included in a far-reaching scheme of education reconstruction, bearing the imprimatur of a responsible body of educational reformers.'[50]

The report's recommendations, published in 1919, were indeed not inconsequential. It advised that: power be given to county councils to adopt the Public Library Acts; the penny rate limitation be abolished; greater prominence be given to government publications in libraries; local education authorities should control public libraries; responsibility for libraries be transferred from the local Government Board to the Board of Education.[51] These proposals underlined the report's description of the public library as 'a valuable national asset'.[52] But for many the report did not go far enough. The idea of financial assistance from central government, for example, had been put to the Committee during its deliberations but was eventually rejected. Those unhappy with the report's limitations would have been doubly disappointed by the legislative proposals arising from it. The initial library bill of 1919 made no mention of the 'penny rate' abolition, merely envisaging an extension of provision to rural areas, where county councils – the only real bodies with the resources to provide costly services to dispersed communities – had heretofore not been permitted to charge a library rate.[53]

Clearly, government's prime consideration was for library provision in rural areas. The paucity of non-urban provision was highlighted by the Adams Report in 1915.[54] The viability of providing a service to rural communities was demonstrated by the Carnegie United Kingdom Trust's wartime experiment of distributing bookboxes to villages (the Staffordshire scheme).[55] The aim of bringing public library services to the counties was intertwined with the policy of revitalising rural communities. Agriculture in Britain had long been in decline. Whereas in 1870 Britain imported about one-fifth of total food requirements, by 1913 this fraction had risen to about a half.[56] The inadvisability of such external dependence was highlighted by the German wartime submarine campaign which served to amplify existing anxieties over the state of agriculture. Pressure to restore agriculture also came from those who saw the extension of urban life as a social threat. It was widely felt that towns, notwithstanding their capacity in many respects to provide a richer and fuller life, created physical and moral degeneration. Re-establishing rural life was an attractive alternative. Government thus urged a post-war re-settlement of the land, believing that: 'The stability and physical strength of our nation depends largely on those classes who have either been born and brought up in the country or have had the advantages of the country life.'[57] In its report on the way adult education was affected by industrial and social conditions, the Adult Education Committee drew a picture of a demoralised rural labour force exposed to low pay, poor housing, isolation and seasonal unemployment. This social existence resulted in 'alienation', class deference, feelings of inferiority and exclusion from any 'higher' village social life.

Rural regeneration meant attracting workers and ex-servicemen back to the land, something which could be achieved by improving rural housing, increasing the number of smallholdings and ensuring 'a general provision for increased amenities of village life'.[58] The public library was patently one such amenity. In 1916 a government report on re-settlement recognised the public library's attractiveness as an educational and recreational agency in any re-settlement programme.[59] In 1918 the Ministry of Reconstruction reported that good village libraries would aid social and educational development, a increased demand for education coming from men returning from the war having tasted a wider world.[60] It was also believed that adult education, supported by institutions like public libraries, could encourage social cohesion.[61] Government perceived the public library as a factor in re-stabilising declining rural communities. Rural regeneration would generate a 'corporate life', which would also be encouraged by the furtherance of adult education, in which the public library played a full part. It was a policy which derived its existence to a significant degree from the class antagonisms of the day, which affected countryside as well as town.

In respect of economic activity, the librarian George Shaw had stressed the practical potential of public libraries for agriculture, arguing that it could dispense technical literature on the latest methods in agriculture and husbandry, as well as Board of Trade commercial information relative to markets.[62] But government considered financial assistance only at the highest level, for research and educational activities undertaken by local councils, universities, agricultural colleges and research institutes.[63] The Ministry of Reconstruction did consider the idea of establishing Rural Information Offices 'to centralise at suitable places in each locality the provision of any information available from official sources that might be of interest or value to the local agricultural community'.[64] However, it is not clear whether the public library was viewed as the natural home for these offices, although public commercial and technical libraries were seen (by librarians) as highly relevant to agriculture.

The fact that government had to be coaxed to extend its legislation in 1919 to do something for libraries in urban areas (namely relieving them of the rate restriction) does not imply that it did not recognise the urban library as a promoter of social stability. The problem of rural degeneration was considered acute, and had attracted attention before 1914. It is not surprising that the rural dimension took priority in 1919, not least because a revitalised and stable rural society might channel away tensions from the urban scene. Further, existing urban library provision might have been seen as adequate in terms of the social stability function it had to fulfil. This argument is especially relevant to adult education, to which government attached considerable importance as a social pacifier. Public libraries were a mainstay of adult education. W.C.B. Sayers wrote that the public library was 'the most active influence in general adult education'.[65] Further, one of the reasons why government had proposed local education authority control of public libraries was that adult education and libraries were seen as natural partners. If, therefore, it can be shown that adult education was to be given a social stability role, then a similar function can be ascribed to the public library.

Government certainly realised during the war the part which libraries could play in complementing various of its objectives. They contributed to the war effort in a number of ways. They were liable to be requisitioned as offices of food control or for recruitment with the librarian acting as director. Departments or whole buildings were commandeered as hospitals, as in the case of the Islington North branch library which served as an annexe to the nearby Great Northern Central Hospital between 1916 and 1919.[66] The Ministry of Food, via the Library Association, urged a provision of books on food economy.[67] Posters were displayed and leaflets made available. Bookmarks advocated war loans. Overtly propagandist material was also purveyed at the government's behest. At Bolton public library government pamphlets entitled *The Great War and How it Began* (300 copies) and *If the Kaiser Governed England* (4,000 copies) were distributed.[68] But the post-war propagandist role which government planned for the public library was more sophisticated, with adult education supported by the institution being employed as a subtle instrument of attempted control.

Viewing the four reports produced by the Adult Education Committee, it is evident that government identified two main impulses behind adult education. Firstly, that it provided a means of self-expression and individual fulfilment. Secondly, that it contributed to the attainment of 'new standards of citizenship and a better social order'.[69] Expanding on this last motive H.A.L. Fisher captured the mood of the day when speaking in favour of the Education Bill:

We have been asking them to fight and work for their country; we have been asking them, not only to appreciate the forces of great political arguments and the significance of grave political emergencies, but to translate their appreciation of those arguments and emergencies into acts of renunciation and sacrifice .... I ask them whether the education which is given to the great mass of our citizens is adequate to the new, serious, and enduring liabilities which the development of this great world-war creates for our Empire, or to the new civic burdens which we are imposing upon millions of new voters? I say it is not adequate.[70]

Education, including post-school provision, would serve as the enemy of socially disruptive tendencies arising out of the 'liabilities' of war; it would imbue the masses with reason and reasonableness, thus awakening a sense of citizenship and social responsibility conducive to the existing social order and the demands of a rapidly changing world.

Yet motives went deeper than a mere desire to 'educate our masters'. Government believed strongly the prospect of social unrest was heightened by unfettered Marxist rhetoric: a demagogic insurgency of 'false' politics and, in particular, economics. This belief was expressed on numerous occasions by the Home Office's Directorate of Intelligence, which briefed the Cabinet virtually weekly during the post-war crisis. It reported in July 1919, for example, that 'the crying need for the moment appears to be education in elementary economics, for the judgement of the British working man may always be trusted when he knows the facts'.[71]

The kind of adult education which the government feared was that which emerged spontaneously amongst labour organisations. The Commission of Enquiry into Industrial Unrest reported that through their educational work some trade unions had become 'centres of social and political activity more potent perhaps than any other of the social movements in the community'.[72] It noted that in some cases education 'tends, though intensive, to be partial .... [The worker] studies along restricted lines .... Economics is often degraded into a gross materialistic conception of cause and effect, and the essential spirituality of education is neglected or forgotten.[73] Government duly set out to nullify harmful, revolutionary teaching. The aim was to oust the 'direct action' propagandists from labour organisations and bolster the traditional, 'reformist' leadership. It was perceived that workers were demanding more education than ever before and it was assumed that they would readily assimilate 'correct' arguments if only the 'right' message were shouted loudly enough. This was especially true with regard to the more intelligent and skilled workers who on the one hand might provide leadership in a revolutionary direction, but who on the other could aid stability if won over to the 'establishment' cause. In government circles the idea emerged that more power had to be given to those at the hub of the labour organisation wheel than to those at the rim: 'trade union organisation', said Bonar Law in 1919, 'is the only thing between us and anarchy'.[74]

Adult education was important to the scheme for containing social disaffection: it could act as a 'valuable corrective to all methods of study of a purely partisan character undertaken for propagandist objects'.[75] This was very much the objective of the Adult Education Committee which was almost entirely populated by adult education specialists who, moreover, displayed a close affinity to the reformist, liberal, Balliol tradition in adult education.[76] The chairman of the Committee was the idealist A.L. Smith, master of Balliol from 1916 until his death in 1924. The Committee represented a continuation of the ideological mainstream of adult education which had close links with the labour movement and which 'occupied a position in the political spectrum which ranged between the social-democratic reformist centre and the non-Marxist ethical socialism of the labour left'.[77] That is to say, the Committee espoused adult education as a means of liberation via reform, not revolution.

The Committee's final report was very much an advocacy of general-liberal studies as opposed to industrial-technical training. The form of education considered appropriate to the social crisis of the day was through the teaching of 'social' subjects – such as civics, economics, politics, history and economics – which enhanced 'good citizenship'. These were subjects which armed individuals with the power to 'understand' and 'accept' the problems of a rapidly changing post-war world and which, moreover, were easily supported by collections of books and periodicals in public libraries.

Nowhere was this strategy needed more than in the workplace. The Adult Education Committee believed the existence of a recent trend towards industrial concentration, mechanisation, division of labour, semi-skilled work and monotonous processes had rendered the worker 'a mere cog in the machine'. This, allied to the treatment of labour as a commodity to be bought and sold, had created 'a revolt in the minds of a large section of the community'.[78] Lip-service was thus paid to ideas of greater industrial participation. More realistically, adult education was proposed as a preventative remedy for unrest: as a means of developing intelligence, character and the perspective of the citizen. As a by-product material wealth would be enhanced, thereby further aiding social stability.

Liberal, reformist adult education was epitomised by the Workers Educational Association (WEA). It stood for the belief that social differences could be resolved by impartial study and discussion. It rejected the notion of class struggle and called for a 'fellowship of men and women drawn from every class'.[79] The WEA contributed much to the work of the Adult Education Committee whose final report mirrored the organisation's ethos.[80] The type of education promoted by the WEA, despite the latter's progressive objectives, fitted neatly with the government's prescription for social stability; even though at one point in the war the cabinet discussed the danger of the WEA spreading revolutionary ideas, requiring the WEA's secretary to assure the King of the organisation's loyalty.[81]

The function of the public library in respect of the support it might be expected to give to post-school education coalesced with the adult education ideologies and objectives outlined above. The ethos of independent learning promulgated by organisations like the WEA, the National Home Reading Union and the university extension movement was shared by the public library and, indeed, the Central Library for Students for which public libraries around the country acted as lending agents.[82] A large part of the public library's clientele was the type of skilled, intelligent worker who had the potential to assimilate knowledge for either 'establishment' or 'revolutionary' political activity. The public library was seen as an agency which could help refute dangerous and radical demagogy, and promote participation in conventional politics. The Adult Education Committee considered the importance of reading, stimulated by agencies like the public library, in preventing revolution.[83] It also advised that greater prominence be given to official publications – a 'natural' information source for the public library to dispense – in view of the 'growing interest in political studies, and the extension of the franchise'.[84] Further, commercial and technical libraries were opened partly with the intention of reinforcing traditional attitudes to the efficacy of the existing commercial system. This echoed motives displayed a generation earlier, when in 1898 the wider dissemination of commercial information, partly through public libraries, had been advocated by the Board of Trade in the hope of educating trade unions and workers out of their tendency towards disruptive industrial relations.[85]

A similar strategy was advised in 1919, with the public commercial and technical library serving as a weapon for indoctrination in conventional political economy. They were seen as effective agencies for countering 'false' politics and economics. At the opening of Manchester's commercial library, for example, Admiral Frederick Sturdee was reported to have said that: 'The British people did not know enough about economics which, after all, were fairly simple. He thought if the people were told in a simple form the principles of finance they would back the country up in every possible way.'[86] A similar line was taken by Arthur Steel-Maitland, Parliamentary Secretary at the Department of Overseas Trade, at the opening of Wolverhampton's commercial library, when he called for a greater understanding of trade and commercial matters, both national and international:

Here we had friction of one kind and another in the industrial world - friction which, during the enthusiasm for war, we did not think would occur. This occurred ... through the two parties in industry not understanding the other man's point of view. In the next place there was no real understanding of the real economic conditions which ruled the situation. Owing to the war we had practically to give up our foreign trade, and now we had not only to recover it but to get more of it.[87]

The message here is clear: if only people were better educated in commercial matters they would come to understand the unavoidable problems of capitalism and create less 'friction' as a result. This function of the commercial library is an example of the control role which government hoped the public library might fulfill.

The Work of the Public Library Movement

Although during the war government recognised the public library as an appropriate instrument of propaganda and channel of information, and was eventually persuaded to include the institution in its legislative programme, librarians believed they had too little support from government at a time when the future of the public library was in the balance: 'Either government was indifferent to them [public libraries] or it was hostile,' said Stanley Jast.[88] Librarians generally considered that it was their responsibility to lead the fight for public library renewal. As we have seen, it was the work of committed individuals, like John Ballinger, who pushed forward the public library cause towards the

end of the war. However, organisational backing was also evident, in the form of the
Carnegie United Kingdom Trust, often working in tandem with the Library
Association.[89] Regarding the contribution of the latter, it was J.Y.W. MacAlister's view
in early 1918 that the Association's 'ambitious programme ... made me believe that it
was getting out of its old groove and was going to do some really useful work', although
he added that he feared the 'flourish of trumpets' was now fading.[90] The Association was
active in the war in establishing a range of committees investigating post-war library
policy, in areas like training, provision for business and outreach. In the specific case of
public libraries, the Association hoped its strategy would:

> embrace and extend all the present spheres of its activities, educational and recreative, and in addition,
> making it [the public library] the centre of commercial and technical activities; of scientific and industial
> research, public-information, public records, local antiquarian and other like interests of the district in
> which it is placed.[91]

Librarians were included in the work of the Ministry of Reconstruction's Adult
Education Committee,[92] and pushed for issue of library reconstruction to be given a
separate report.[93] Finally, any accusations of library establishment apathy and inactivity
during the war would need to contend with the fact that librarians fought strongly against
control of libraries being awarded to education authorities, something which challenged
their professional authority but which they were not able to prevent in the counties after
1919.

   Librarians chose to launch the battle for public library renewal in relatively unfamiliar
territory: that of economic regeneration. Traditionally a cultural institution, the public
library had nonetheless always to a degree been viewed and used to stimulate economic
activity. Many librarians had long been aware of the argument that economic progress
could be accelerated by the diffusion of knowledge via the public library. This belief was
entrenched by the war which created the need for advances in industry and science. War
had revealed underlying weaknesses in Britain's commercial position, particularly
regarding the more modern branches of production such as electrical, chemical and
chemico-metallurgical industries. At the start of the war Germany was found to have a
virtual monopoly in products like tungsten, synthetic dyes and drugs, magnetos, and
optical and chemical glass.[94]

   As scientists and technicians began to recognise the value of libraries and
bibliography to research, librarians responded. In 1915 Ernest Savage initiated a
programme of commercial and technical book acquisition in Coventry Public Library,
and by 1917 was able to tell his committee that a number of industrial bibliographies of
interest to local firms had been produced and distributed, whilst 'no journal of
importance in motoring engineering and works' chemistry' was not supplied.[95] In 1916
the Library Association appointed a special committee to oversee the strengthening of
scientific and technical departments in public libraries.[96] Librarians engaged
enthusiastically in the commercial language of economic survival, acknowledging the

coming battle for post-war international commercial expansion. The librarian W.E. Doubleday wrote that:

Currently with this commercial expansion, one may look for progress in home manufactures; new ideas, new inventions will be brought forward and it will require an alert and mentally well-fed people to take advantage of these fleeting opportunities. What better than a public library can facilitate this work, and feed commercial and general institutes?[97]

Librarians endeavoured to satisfy the wartime demands of science, industry and commerce by establishing discrete technical and commercial libraries within their institutions. The *Library Association Record* was unequivocal in its assessment of the importance of such ventures: 'Arsenals of scientific and technical information will become, nay have become, as necessary as arsenals of war-like materials, and if steps are not taken promptly we shall be as little prepared for peace as we were for war.'[98]

Technical and commercial library provision was the most significant wartime public library achievement. 'Commercial and technical' libraries were formed in Sheffield (1916; initially a collection, a separate library being formed 1920), Lincoln (1917), Leeds (1918), Leicester (1919), Middlesborough (1919) and Bath (1920). 'Commercial' libraries were set up in Coventry (1915; initially a collection, technical library status awarded 1917), Northampton (1916) Richmond-on-Thames (1916), Glasgow (1916), Liverpool (1917), Bradford (1918), Derby (1918), Wolverhampton (1919), Birmingham (1919), Manchester (1919), Dundee (1919), Bristol (1920), Newcastle (1920). 'Technical' libraries' emerged in Birmingham (1915), Darlington (1918) and Nottingham (1920).

It appears, therefore, that the advice of the Library Association was being taken: that 'public libraries must probably devote a larger proportion of their resources to work more directly useful to industry and commerce'.[99] Librarians developed ambitious plans in this regard.[100] A plea was made for government assistance in establishing a large central repository of technical literature into which public libraries could tap.[101] The plan was for a central technical library to be developed along the lines of the Central Library for Students, established in 1916 as a national repository lending books to educational organisations and students. It was also envisaged that public commercial libraries in the major industrial centres would act as agencies of the Board of Trades' Commercial Intelligence Department. Bradford initiated its commercial library partly on the basis that this would be the case, the corporation's library committee pledging its 'active support in carrying out the scheme'.[102] In reflecting on the prospect of a system comprising government, large town and branch commercial and technical libraries, Stanley Jast employed a biological metaphor: 'the relation of the Board of Trade library to the provincial libraries would be that of the brain to the great nervous plexuses, and the smaller collections would be the knots or ganglia, the whole forming the Commercial Intelligence Department of the British nation'; and added that for such a system to work, public commercial and technical libraries required government grants.[103] But neither the system nor grants were forthcoming. Librarians had to be satisfied instead with making a contribution to technical and commercial knowledge dissemination from the library system's own resources.

Librarians became caught up in the euphoria of reconstruction, not least in terms of its economic dimensions. They were genuinely concerned about the economic problems of the day and devised ways in which they thought libraries could help solve them. Moreover, they believed an economically active public library could make a contribution to social development. It could help give a much-needed psychological boost to a national self-confidence buffeted by pre-war European (particularly German) material and military progress. Time and again librarians proclaimed that their technical and commercial libraries had evolved primarily from patriotic motives. As the Patent Office librarian, E. Wyndham Hulme, stated: 'I claim for our programme of technical libraries that it forms part and parcel of a series of measures which are essential to the security of the state in time of war, and to its prosperity as an industrial nation in those of peace.'[104] The deputy chairman of the Manchester Public Library Committee displayed equal national pride in his support of technical education:

The day has gone by when this country can afford to rely upon its traditional reputation for supremacy in the markets of the world The full resources of science must be utilised, the inventive genius of our practical craftsmen encouraged and fostered, and the mechanical improvements adopted without delay.[105]

It was believed that the public library could act as a 'social healer' by working for economic progress advantageous to all. Communal material gain, it was felt, would lessen the social tensions which economic uncertainty had fostered. In the words of one supporter of commercial and technical libraries:

We are in a stage of affairs, both national and commercial, as well as political and industrial, which may be called practically a revolution, a revolution of all our preconceived notions. The great thing we have to face is not the development of individual character as displayed in connection with our commercial enterprises, but the problem of relations between employer and employed .... The fact is you cannot benefit any section of a community [i.e. through commercial library provision] without benefiting the whole of it .... We must get rid of industrial disputes.[106]

Commercial and technical libraries were not used by corporate bodies alone. They were intended as much for students engaged in commercial and technical education. Nottingham Public Library advertised that it provided: 'Text-books for commercial students dealing with practical auditing, accounting, and banking; commercial arithmetic, dictionary of book-keeping, book-keeping simplified, balance sheets, costs, and percentage reckoner.'[107] The town clerk of Macclesfield told the Carnegie United Kingdom Trust that extra funding was required to buy 'books suitable for students who are taking courses in the various trades';[108] while J.Y.W. MacAlister found it 'difficult to see how some of the reconstruction proposals can be adequately dealt with unless in the great commercial and manufacturing centres there is placed at the disposal of the workers the literature, technical and other, a knowledge of which is essential to success.'[109]

In Leeds a determined appeal was made to non-corporate users: 'Why spend your life gaining experience?', asked a promotional flyer, when 'the experience of centuries is available at the commercial and technical department of the Leeds Public Libraries.'[110] A special effort appears to have been made in Leeds to attract women to the technical and commercial collections. It was recognised that certain opportunities for women had arisen during the war, but peace threatened to erode them, thereby placing a premium on education for women to maintain or win back the advances (particularly in terms of employment) they had secured. A local newspaper, no doubt carefully briefed by the city's public librarians, explained that:

Women have to go out into the great world of human affairs and encounter the various aspects of human experience ... Education is going to play an important part in the rebuilding of the nation after the scourge of war, and in the coming days women will have to possess the same qualifications as the men folk if the wish to secure responsible positions and establish themselves in the world of business affairs ... The war is responsible for a much more serious appreciation by business people of the value of women's service in industry, and with the beginning of the various processes of reconstruction women are endeavouring to establish themselves in certain definite lines. For those who have embraced a business career, or who wish to embrace it, the commercial and Technical Library offers facilities for study which no one should ignore.'[111]

Although librarians believed economic regeneration could aid social stability they were more convinced of the public library's broader cultural function in this respect. Despite being assigned a material, tangible role by librarians, the public library's 'spiritual' nature was not diminished. On the contrary, war helped promote it. In contrasting Britain's moral position with the aggressive materialism and expansionism of Germany, Sir Frederick Kenyon, Director and Principal Librarian of the British Museum, wrote to the librarian of Norwich that:

The cause for which we are fighting is the cause of civilisation, of the liberty and moral well-being of the people of Europe; and our confidence in our ultimate victory arises out of our belief that spiritual things must eventually triumph over material. Every influence that reinforces our spiritual nature makes us stronger for the struggle in which we are engaged, and the Public Library, whether as the source of knowledge or as a reservoir of mental refreshment and stimulus, is a spiritual influence of the first order.[112]

Furthermore, the gravity of war was believed to be having a beneficial effect on the nature of public library reading. Demands for 'reflective' literature on the causes, course and consequences of the conflict flooded into libraries, leading the *Times Literary Supplement* to declare that there is 'no department of activity or thought that has not been stirred by the upheaval'.[113] It was hoped that the war would enrich the library's literature and have 'a purifying effect on fiction'.[114]

Ultimately the war did produce a slight shift towards more serious reading via the public library, but any claimed achievement in this regard should be set against the retrogressive propagandist role which the library assumed. Leamington Spa's committee, for example, congratulated itself for providing suitable works exposing and denouncing German aims and methods, and stimulating British ideals and patriotism'.[115] German intellectual development, praised before the war, was now attacked as lacking 'the essential elements of freedom and morality'.[116] Articles appeared in local newspapers proudly advertising the acquisition of new titles like *The Germans in Africa*, which was said to trace the efforts of Germany to secure an African Empire through intrigue and trickery.[117] Newspapers critical of the war's prosecution were occasionally withdrawn.[118] In addition, literary propaganda and censorship was backed by lectures often of a vehement anti-German nature.[119]

But it was not simply by a crude castigation of the enemy that the public library sought to intensify the war effort. In keeping with the optimism of reconstruction the public library aimed to boost morale. As food for the mind its literature was presented as a 'source of strength' and a 'spring of energy'.[120] F.G. Kenyon summarised this optimistic spirit:

We shall fight better and endure hardships better if our minds are trained and our spirits refreshed; and both for knowledge and for imaginative literature we must come to the library. Therefore, in cherishing our libraries we are increasing the fighting strength of our nation and making it worthy of victory in this, its hour of trial.[121]

Librarians shared the view that the war was a fight for democracy and liberty against autocracy and authoritarianism. As an avowedly democratic institution, the public library symbolised this cause. Its traditional function of offering a free and open assessment of differing political creeds was frequently invoked. It was Stanley Jast's belief that in Germany public libraries indoctrinated the citizenry, whereas in Britain they served to 'sanitise' the people intellectually:

If the public library serves out what some regard as intellectual poison with one hand, it serves its antidote with the other and when all sides obtain a hearing the natural predilections and cleavages in the minds of the hearers prevents any overmastering ascendancy of any one exponent or school.[122]

However, the war was being fought not just for democracy but for a better, greater democracy. It was accepted that the war had thrown up new social problems. Thus, in soliciting support for the public library, Winchester's librarian spoke of the duty:

to prepare for the task of reconstruction that would be necessary after the war by reading about such important social questions as unemployment and wages, woman suffrage, the relations between capital and labour, technical education, and many other similar subjects; whilst a general study of history would be an excellent topic now.[123]

Librarians hoped that the public library could help mould an educated and wise electorate which 'must be called upon to pronounce on so many subjects of difficulty, and whose decisions must affect not only this nation but the world'.[124] It is not surprising, therefore, to see the Adult Education Committee's report on libraries calling for the free distribution of government publications to public libraries to complement a widening franchise.[125] It was hoped the library's efforts in the area of expanding democracy would promote a feeling of participation – an 'enlightened sense of a real stake in the country'.[126]

But the public library's contribution to stability went beyond an 'education for democracy' dynamic. A more positive policy was identified: one which directly confronted socially disruptive influences. As a speaker at a Library Association meeting was reported to have explained:

There never was a time ... when the thoughts of their people needed more to be directed in the right course. In regard to their social, industrial, and political matters he did not know that they had the books in their own hands, but he believed there was a great amount of influence which they could use if their libraries were furnished with such literature, and the thoughts of their people could be directed in the right course.[127]

Purveying the 'right' reading would devalue the arguments of those seeking radical change and secure British democracy in its traditional, conservative pattern. This the public library tried to do through, amongst other means, its alliance with the National Home Reading Union which told librarians that:

The courses of reading pursued at the suggestion, and with the help of the Union, which offer a large choice to readers of all ages, tastes, and acquirements, have been found, in time of war, a steadying, refreshing, and heightening influence. Systematic reading has proved itself a powerful antidote to the spirit of unrest, and an aid towards carrying on national service cheerfully, steadily and effectively .... It claims to be helping in no small measure to maintain in the present, and secure for the future, a standard of high thought, intelligent interest, and true patriotism.[128]

A greater emphasis on serious reading became evident as the war progressed. This led librarians to believe that they were now much closer to the forefront of education, particularly for adults. It was proclaimed that: 'The precise educational value of public libraries has immensely developed of recent years, and their scope should be greater than ever in this direction in the reconstruction after the war.'[129] Shortly after the war the Mitchell report on public libraries stressed the external and adult education roles which, it was believed, the institution should fulfil.[130]

Librarians felt that the war helped boost the image of the public library. They recognised the opportunity which the war brought to advance their professional status.

At the start of the war the public notion persisted that the librarian was a mere handler of books. Even in 1917 it was said that: 'The term 'librarian' is lightly used, and often is applied to an official who is placed in charge of a collection of books, with very meagre knowledge of their contents and still less knowledge of the profession to which he purports to belong.'[131] Arguably, it was the premium on knowledge for scientific and industrial development which gave a boost to the morale of wartime librarianship. 'It is hard to exaggerate', wrote F.G. Kenyon:

the extent to which the welfare of the nation depends on the prosperity and development of our Public Libraries. The great need of the country is knowledge and respect for knowledge. Knowledge, in any scientific sense of the term, is impossible without books.[132]

Librarians, as indicated above, set out to increase the supply of 'practical' literature. In opening technical and commercial libraries they hoped to forge stronger links with business. This would result in greater prominence and prestige, as explained by Jast after his retirement: 'the fact that he [the businessman] can find the information quickly makes him a friend of the library, and adds to the strength of that public opinion on which the success of the library in other and more vital directions depends'.[133] Business libraries were expensive. It has been suggested that they were established as a lever to win an abolition of the penny rate restriction, thereby releasing funds for increased salaries.[134] It is also evident that services to business, as well as to other 'serious' readers, would require better trained and, hence, higher status staff.[135] At a time of downward pressure on salaries and severe cuts in services, the hope of future promotion to the status of 'expert', with the material rewards that entailed, must have been sensed widely in the profession. However, given the lamentable standards of professional librarianship, it is difficult, retrospectively, to speak seriously about the notion of 'expert' status, despite the plans laid for a full-time library school attached to London's University College, which began in 1919.[136]

Support from Business

The business community gave measured support the economic objectives which the public library movement set itself during the war. Ideas linking improved production and higher profits with inputs of information were not widely acknowledged by British industry and commerce, unlike in the United States where enterprises were more likely to view information and library (or bureau) provision as 'a wonderful medium for the promotion of increased efficiency' and 'the great essential to discovery', on a par with the laboratory.[137] In Britain, although some in business and a few librarians were aware of advances made across the Atlantic, pre-First World War enterprises largely eschewed the assembly of information and research collections. These were to be is found in only a few large firms.[138] In small firms the absence was virtually complete. Collections were uncommon for reasons of either cost, or ignorance of potential benefits, or both. The factor of cost, particularly in regard to expensive items like directories and periodicals, was a main reason why firms did not create their own specialist reference libraries or information bureaux. But lack of recognition of potential benefit, an important factor before the war, became less so after 1914 when increased emphasis was placed on research into industrial processes and marketing.

The First World War has been seen as a period of disadvantage for the long-term performance of the British economy, exacerbating as it did longer-term problems such as overcommitment to technically backward staple industries exporting to low income countries; an overcommitment which was to the detriment of investment in production for newer, higher-yield, science-based goods. This unfavourable assessment has tended to obscure the fact that a wartime profit bonanza was experienced across a wide range of industries, by firms large and small. Many overseas markets were lost, but were compensated for by buoyant wartime demand. Notwithstanding anxieties over the prospect of increased post-war foreign competition, British businessmen prepared for peace 'in a decidedly bullish mood'.[139] It is argued that the period should be seen, commercially at any rate, less as one of shock and despair than as one marked by an optimistic assessment of future demand resulting in steady investment. In financial terms, therefore, the war provided an ideal opportunity for firms to innovate.

This did not happen, for although investment was high it was directed towards boosting production along existing lines: via amalgamation and mere expansion of capacity. Although confident about the immediate post-war future – with the economic impetus of war spilling over into peacetime production – industry and commerce feared the cold international economic climate which might eventually materialise. Some expressed a pessimistic view of economic prospects in the long-term. As one industrial commentator asserted in 1915: 'With regard to industry as a whole, it is apprehended by some people that the resumption of the normal will only be affected after a terrible depression and much unemployment'.[140] There existed a real fear of an aggressive campaign of state-assisted trade warfare conducted by Germany once peace had arrived. At a meeting of the Leamington Philosophical Society at the town's public library in 1916 one speaker reminded the audience that: 'England would not cease to be the centre of international exchange, and would always have a financial standing above Germany's. The latter country would not cease to be a great trading nation, nor was it desirable to cripple her activities too much.'[141]

Faced by the prospect of stiff post-war international competition, some (although a small minority) in the business community began to realise that they could no longer conduct their affairs 'flying by the seat of their pants', but had instead to invest in, and give support, to the effective gathering, organisation and dissemination of commercial and technical intelligence. This growing awareness lent weight to the idea of rate-supported commercial and technical libraries. The *Manchester Guardian* reported that public business libraries had arisen: 'in response to the demand now prevalent in the commercial world, that the business of the future can be more carefully conducted than formerly. Gone are the old rule-of-thumb systems with their risky characteristics'.[142]

Public commercial and technical libraries were seen as aiding 'all who wish to build up, strengthen and excel in our efforts for future supremacy'.[143] Stress was laid on the need to win back lost trade by boosting exports to those who had obtained new suppliers, perhaps indigenous, as a result of European trade dislocation. Although it was recognised that a large firm engaged in regular exporting might afford its own intelligence department or library, this would not be the case regarding firms engaged in exporting in a small way.[144] Thus, public provision of technical and commercial literature was seen as beneficial to middle- and small-sized enterprises. Moreover, this provision - which had always existed to a greater or lesser extent - had to be organised in departments separate from the general reference library, partly because of the poor reputation of business people for retrieving items dispersed through the collection.[145]

The exact extent to which business sought the establishment of public commercial and technical libraries is not known. Interest could certainly not be described as widespread or strong. In some areas, however, support was very visible. In Leeds, for example, business interest was relatively described as relatively enthusiastic. The Leeds Chamber of Commerce praised the town's new commercial and technical library as a great municipal development: 'one of the most complete collections of its kind in the country'.[146] Given the structure of business in Leeds this is perhaps not surprising. A significant proportion of the workforce was located in manufacturing, in 1911 some 43 per cent in the four industries of textiles, clothing, engineering and footwear alone.[147] Moreover, the town was well equipped with amenities for the trading (wholesale and retail) and marketing of local products. Clearly, technical and commercial literature would have been of some value. Certainly there was an appreciation of the importance of technical knowledge in Leeds, businessmen having supported the establishment of the Yorkshire College in the 1880s (which became an independent university in 1904) with the threat of mounting foreign competition in mind.[148] On the other hand, reasons for supporting the library could have been based less on practical value than municipal rivalry. Leeds had seen commercial and technical libraries set up as praiseworthy civic institutions elsewhere and so support for its own institution might be put down to the 'continuing alertness of the business community and the council to what was happening elsewhere, and their willingness to take action when serious competition appeared'.[149]

With regard to *commercial* information, specifically, business helped set up public commercial libraries in many areas and supported them once established. In Croydon the public library's Commercial Information Department was said to have been formed with the active support of the local Chamber of Commerce.[150] The Chamber of Commerce in Coventry gave financial assistance to their local public commercial library.[151] In Liverpool, when business managers met representatives of the public library to plan a commercial library for the city, they expressed surprise at 'the wealth of current mercantile facts and statistics' already in the public library, and looked forward to it being made more accessible in a separate department.[152] In 1918 representatives from Glasgow's public commercial library were invited to occupy a stand at the British Industries Fair held in the city that year; the stand was well used, with 'a considerable amount of commercial intelligence ... provided for enquirers'.[153] When a commercial library was proposed in Bradford representatives of commercial organisations in the city estimated it 'would prove of first assistance to the whole business and commercial community'.[154] The long list of organisations invited to the opening of the Bradford Commercial Library in May 1918 (Chamber of Commerce, Chamber of Trades, Technical College, Textile Society, Dyers and Colourists Society, Engineering Society, Wool Combers Federation, Dyers Federation, Manufacturers Federation, Spinners Federation, Yorkshire Managers and Overlookers Association, Weaving Overlookers Association and the Accountants Society)[155] demonstrates that business interest had not waned in the meantime. Once opened the Bradford Commercial Library proved extremely popular, users no doubt being wooed by such stories as information on trade in South America dispensed to one firm resulting in £4,000 worth of business.[156] People were said to use commercial libraries like the one in Bradford to answer basic questions on trade such as: Who makes it? Where can I get it? What are the industries in any town or district?[157] In other words, information was sought in keeping with age-old adages concerning traders selling in the most favourable markets and not being prepared 'to buy a nag till he has examined it at all points'.[158]

From the evidence given above it is possible to agree with Alec Ellis that the business community's enthusiasm for commercial libraries was at least moderate.[159] Regarding the public library's provision of technical information (although the distinction between commercial and technical libraries was in reality minimal, labelling being simply a matter of local preference), the evidence of business interest appears less frequently. However, interest *is* visible in the literature of the professional and scientific societies and in the trade press. Fears were expressed that workers did not have sufficient access to technical literature. The *Practical Engineer* lamented in 1918 that very few of our free libraries cater as they might do for the technical reader, and they were not usually adjacent to large works. Hence, it was said, 'workers were losing their grip of fundamental principles, and their value as producers is lessened'.[160] The *Electrical Review* urged better provision by private means: 'business firms and manufacturers should provide well-stocked technical libraries for the use of their employees', it argued in 1918; though at the same time it welcomed the establishment of public technical libraries like that in Leeds where 'a careful selection has been made of literature likely to prove useful to the electrical and allied trades'.[161] In Nottingham in 1918 local scientific and technical societies deposited their collections with the public library (a separate technical section opened in 1920) for loan to members and for public reference.[162]

The movement to establish of a technical library in Manchester demonstrates that in one large industrial centre at least there existed significant enthusiasm for the public provision of technical literature in separately planned accommodation. A technical library had first been proposed there in 1907 when local businessmen and industrialists had formed a deputation to interview the Free Libraries Committee. The issue was formally resurrected in March 1918 when a meeting at the Engineers' Club called for a separate technical library, a call subsequently supported by nine other scientific societies in the city. The meeting affirmed 'the necessity, in view of the future of the industries of Manchester and District, of an adequately equipped Technical Department of the Municipal Libraries'. A deputation subsequently visited the Libraries Committee and presented it with a detailed memorial. After pointing to the efficacy of local public technical libraries in America, it went on to stress the long tradition in Manchester of 'technical education to train students to the highest form of research', and hence the need for study collections in this respect. Manchester central library was by no means bereft of technical literature. For example, of the 370 periodicals in the reference library, 98 dealt with technical and commercial subjects. However, many of these were British publications and so were already taken by local firms. What was needed were foreign journals which were not generally available. Foreign patents were also required. These could only be viewed in London, with the exception of American patents which Manchester did take. It was believed that funding by local firms would not provide sufficient support, nor would it be appropriate for Manchester's ratepayers alone to foot the bill. Hence, a provincially based library was advised; one which drew funds from surrounding districts. Assistance from central government, moreover, was called for.[163]

The knowledge of German state aid for technical libraries was not lost on the scientific societies. Stanley Jast reminded the Society of Chemical Industry: 'The German Government, by the almost lavish equipment of libraries of technological works, has immensely facilitated the studies of their own scientists and students'. In fact, no sooner had Manchester's public technical library opened in 1919 then representatives of the engineering, chemical and other industries in the city, along with the library committee, met the Minister of Education, H.A.L. Fisher, to urge that some of the £1 million parliament had voted for scientific and industrial research should go to their local technical library. But in keeping with government policy – that money for research be channelled by the Department of Scientific and Industrial Research into the new industrial research associations and their own libraries – the plea for central funding was rejected.[164]

The emphasis placed on the need to acquire foreign literature and the awareness of government assistance in library provision abroad shows that anxiety over international trade competition was a leading motive for the advocacy of a local technical library by Manchester's scientific societies. In Sheffield, also, the international trade dimension was to the fore. It was seen by some as particularly important to make headway, as Germany had done in the newer industries like electrical engineering and metallurgy. The Vice-Chancellor of Sheffield University, in a newspaper interview of 1918, recognized that Sheffield, unlike say Manchester, was dominated by one great class of industry – iron, steel and metallurgy – and to survive had to invest in metallurgical research, as opposed to pure engineering which had a longer history. In support of a public technical library he said that: 'New ideas were beginning to flow, and hence the literature of the great societies connected with these trades had to be made available.' The public library, he added, 'would need to be more closely associated with the national life and industries than ever before'.[165]

Amongst professionals and technicians, therefore, there was no absence of support for public technical library provision. This is not surprising in that, as E.A. Savage wrote: 'The needs of the war have brought home to technical men the desirability of obtaining information rapidly.'[166] However, support for public initiative competed with enthusiasm for private business libraries. There was also considerable enthusiasm for the establishment of a central technical information and indexing service.[167] The idea of a Technical Information Office with material indexed for speedy bibliographic retrieval commanded fairly wide support, partly because it was a formula tried and tested elsewhere. As the Assistant Secretary of the Institute of Civil Engineers reported in 1917: 'In other countries, the importance of this service is fully recognised. Belgium before the War, had organised, under the auspices of the International Institute of Bibliography, an index-library covering the whole field of scientific knowledge.' Such an index to the location and content of material was considered an essential corollary to the great reservoir of technical knowledge in technical societies, universities, government departments, the Patent Office, etc.

In the final analysis, therefore, it is clear that business gave some support to the idea of public business libraries, though its extent should not be exaggerated. The limited nature of the support is demonstrated by the move in 1918 to obtain more representatives of science and industry on the Library Associations Technical and Commercial Libraries Committee in the hope of reversing the 'inadequate appreciation of the work public libraries (state and municipal) now do'.[168] But any attempt to enliven business interest had first to overcome the traditional obstacle to improved public library provision, namely the distaste for public expenditure. When, for example, a resolution was proposed at the 1915 annual meeting of the Society of Chemical Industry 'that technical libraries should be established at the public expense in all great centres of industry' some delegates objected to public money being spent in an area where industry could provide for itself.[169]

On the basis of evidence surveyed there appears to have been more business support for the public provision of commercial rather than technical information. This probably had less to do with any wild enthusiasm for commercial literature than with long-standing prejudices against technical education and information. Compared with commercial information sources, technical literature was costly to both buy and track down. Its value to the accumulation of technical knowledge was also questioned. Finally, there remained the historic distrust of public technical education which, because workers from different plants meeting and exchanging ideas, threatened to disclose the secrets which gave a firm an advantage over its rivals. This said, it is important not to distinguish too closely between technical and commercial information when assessing the strength of support by business for providing such information in public libraries.

Citizenship, Science and the Self

Historians appear divided on the question of whether war has been a promoter or destroyer of citizenship. The First World War might be seen, on the one hand, to have expanded citizenship through three distinct, yet inter-related, processes.[170] Firstly, an attempt was made to 'buy off' working-class radicalism with promises and policies of social inclusion. Secondly, a genuine collectivism emerged from a sense of shared responsibility, experience and sacrifice (although feelings of social solidarity and national purpose, being perhaps more pronounced among the better off,[171] was not as strong or widespread as in the Second World War). Thirdly, the economic vitality and high employment brought about by the war represented tangible gains for the vast majority of citizens, the increased power and confidence of labour reflected in the doubling of trade union membership to 8 million by the end of the war. Together, it might be argued, these informers of citizenship contributed to a spirit of reform and reconstruction which delivered real social advances: the massive extension of unemployment insurance; new educational legislation; an expanded housing programme; an extension of the franchise; and, for public libraries, a new legislative framework and sense of national purpose. One of the unintended consequences of war and militarism, therefore, is the development of citizenship rights (social, political and economic) to complement the duties of citizenship which the circumstances called upon individuals to discharge.[172]

Adopting the perspective of the 'liberal' school would be to underplay progress in areas like education and housing, as well as library provision, and to view them as merely a restoration of the pre-war situation, a retrieval of losses incurred during the war.[173] Similarly, the perceived expansion of opportunities for women, mostly in terms of their entry into the labour market, needs to be set alongside the narrowing of opportunities which occurred in peacetime. The 'liberal' view would also point to the war's promotion of cultural authoritarianism and intolerance: the celebration of British culture at the expense of foreign, especially German, traditions; the use of propaganda; and a distinct climate of anti-intellectualism. Certainly the idealism which had informed so much intellectual thought and social reform (including progress made by the public library) in the late-Victorian and Edwardian eras was strongly challenged by the war. This was not simply due to idealism's Germanic roots and its presentation as a philosophy of regimentation more suited to Prussian despotism than to British democracy. The carnage on the battlefields questioned idealist notions of the innate goodness of human nature and made it difficult, moreover, 'to take seriously the idea that reality was a harmonious whole tending towards perfection';[174] ideas about the *intrinsically* cohesive nature of society having infused the public library movement with life and purpose for decades.

In assessing the effect of war on public libraries both liberal and conservative positions can be drawn upon. According to Wiegand,[175] the public library in America during the First World War encouraged intellectual intolerance and social narrowness. Plagued before the war by the interminable question of what constituted the 'right' reading leading to 'good' behaviour, librarians in the United States were relieved, particularly after 1917, to leave controversy and division behind them and fall in behind a bullish, patriotic program of propaganda, Americanisation, nativism, and censorship; the latter resulting in some cases in the burning of classic works of German philosophy, books advocating American pacifism and even simple German-language texts. In short, during the war American public librarians 'willingly took their place in the service of the state', prioritising service to the state above service to society and engaging in practices which Wiegand classes as 'reprehensible'.[176]

As far as the British public library scene is concerned, conservatism and intolerance of nonconformity was certainly visible during the war. Like their American counterparts, British public librarians became instruments for propaganda – whether in terms of distributing anti-German pamphlets or displaying government posters – and tended to side with the patriotism rather than the protest which the war engendered, as the evidence from Leamington Spa, presented above, shows. Many librarians at the time would have agreed with American Henry Legler who considered public libraries a means of containing the menace of the city and averting threatened disruption by 'the restless and turbulent elements which now make up so large a portion of the dwellers in cities.'[177] Indeed, one of the prominent discourses underpinning the public library during the war was the belief that the education and knowledge it purveyed would reduce the likelihood of irrational insurrection, or merely labour extremism. Although it would be ridiculous to place it alongside the propaganda machines of anti-labour organisations like the National alliance of Employers and Employees and the Economic Study Club, the public library played a role, albeit at a low level, in the campaign to neutralise the labour threat.[178] Public librarians in Britain also took the anti-radical opportunities which the war offered to strengthen their institution's cultural conservatism by promoting what they saw as the 'right' reading, challenging the rising popularity of light fiction which had characterised pre-war public library reading.

The extent to which British librarians' adopted a reactionary role appears to have been less marked, however, than the adoption of such a role across the Atlantic. Moreover, to note only the illiberal aspects of provision and practice would be to tell only half the story. Positive aspects of British public library activity during the war can clealy be emphasised. These include the way in which librarians embraced growing interest in serious reading and in science and technology, translating this into the provision of new technical and commercial collections and into the marketing of 'weightier' literature. In addition, the part they played in securing a new Public Libraries Act – promising increased expenditure on libraries and an extension of services to rural areas – might be regarded as a worthy attempt to promote an expanded citizenship through social inclusion. Consequently, it might be argued that there is absolutely no justification for the claim made by one commentator that librarians in Britain displayed few positive attitudes during the war; that, in short, the British library profession did not 'go to war' between 1914 and 1918.[179]

The war's celebration of science and technology (albeit mostly for destructive ends) enabled the public library to play down its recent idealist, anti-materialist past – not least in terms of its function within post-war economic reconstruction – and attach itself more securely to the utilitarianism which had informed its mid-Victorian genesis. The war may have called into question the efficacy of classical British liberalism, which had envisioned the growth in the population of sound moral action conducive to the common good, but the scientific and technological progress the war had promoted dovetailed with the personal intellectual enlightenment and moral edification which stands at the heart of modernity and forms the basis of the liberal, modern self. Public libraries engaged enthusiastically with the wartime promise of self-realisation and -development, or as the Adult Education Committee termed it, the desire for self-expression and individual fulfilment. These were to be encouraged less by the heavy hand of state intervention (of which there remained considerable suspicion) than by meaningful social participation by individuals who chose to take advantage of the educational opportunities on offer and to contribute to the new climate of educational seriousness being created. To the extent that the First World War 'intensified the search for citizenship',[180] the public library equally sought to further social inclusion through the support it gave to education (especially post-school learning); its promotion of 'serious' reading; and its provision of commercial and technical collections aimed not only at the business fraternity but also at self-motivated individuals, including women, seeking personal material and mental, or spiritual, betterment. The public library during the First World War invested heavily in the notion of the modern self. In this respect, it continued to fulfil that part of its traditional mission which was liberal and enlightenening. This is not to say, however, that it managed to to avoid – for it patently did not – being contaminated by the war's anti-noncompliant, anti-radical tendencies, resurrecting, as a result, images of that part of its heritage which was censorious and controlling.

Notes and References to Chapter Two

[1] See A. Black, *A new history of the English public library* (London, 1996), 142-67, for a discussion of the public library's idealist-Hegelian roots.

[2] P. Gordon and J. White, *Philosophers as educational reformers* (London, 1979), Chapter 11.

[3] J.E.G. de Montmorency, 'Literature of the war: economics and international law', *LAR* 17 (1915), 462.

[4] A. Marwick, *War and social change in the twentieth century* (Basingstoke, 1974), 6-8.

[5] As noted by P. Thane (ed.), *The origins of British social policy* (London, 1978), 18.

[6] As argued by P. Abrams, 'The failure of social reform 1918-1920', *Past and Present* 24 (April 1963).

[7] D. Lloyd George, *War memoirs* (London, 1938), 1994.

[8] B.S. Rowntree, *The human needs of labour* (London, 1919), 9-10.

[9] Speaking on 12 September 1918, quoted in P. Rowlands, *Lloyd George* (London, 1975), 451.

[10] J.E. Cronin, 'Coping with labour 1918-1926', in J.E. Cronin and J. Schneer (eds.), *Social conflict and the political_order in modern Britain* (London, 1982).

[11] Due to shortages, the annual inflation rate jumped from a pre-war level of around 2% to 25% in the first two years of the war.

[12] Commission of Enquiry into Industrial Unrest, *Summary of the reports of the Commission*, Cmnd. 8696 (1918).

[13] A. Hutt, *The post-war history of the British working class* (Wakefield, 1972, first published 1937), 15.

[14] A. Marwick, *Britain in a century of total war* (London, 1968), 143.

[15] C. Wrigley, '1919: the critical year', in C. Wrigley (ed.), *The British labour movement in the decade after the First World War* (Loughborough, 1979), 1.

[16] Quoted in S. White, 'Ideological hegemony and political control: the sociology of anti-Bolshevism in Britain 1918-1920', *Scottish Labour History Society Journal* 9 (June 1975), 3.

[17] G.C. Peden, *British economic and social policy* (Oxford, 1985), 49-50.

[18] Commision of Enquiry into Industrial Unrest, *Summary of the reports*, op. cit., 7.

[19] S. Andrzejewski [or Andreski], *Military organisation and society* (1954), wrote of a 'military participation ratio', which linked high levels of social welfare (and the promise of it) to the proportion of citizens called upon to fight a war or work for its prosecution. 'The greater the demands of war ... the more the pyramid of social structure would be flattened': R. Pope, *War and society in Britain: 1899-1948* (Harlow, 1991), 9.

[20] M. Swenarton, *Homes fit for heroes* (London, 1981).

[21] The Ministry of Reconstruction, Adult Education Committee produced the following: *First interim report on industrial and social conditions in relation to adult education*, Cmnd. 9107 (1918); *Second interim report on education in the army*, Cmnd. 9229 (1918); *Third interim report on libraries and museums*, Cmnd. 9237 (1919); *Final report*, Cmnd. 321 (1919). The Adult Education Committee was one of several sub-committees formed by the Ministry of Reconstruction in March 1917. Other sub-committees covered agricultural policy, demobilization of the army, women's employment and local government. For a description of the Ministry's brief, see Ministry of Reconstruction, *Report on the work of the Ministry for the period ending 31 Dec. 1918*, Cmnd. 9231 (1919).

[22] Quoted in B. Simon, *Studies in the history of education: education and the labour movement 1870-1920* (London, 1965), 333-4.

[23] H.A.L. Fisher, *Educational reform: speeches* (Oxford, 1918), ix.

[24] Hansard, *Parliamentary Debates*, 104 (1918), col. 394.

[25] PRO, CAB 24/19, GT 1304, Reconstruction Committee, Memo on the Education Bill to Lloyd George (June 1917).

[26] In Scotland the counties were already permitted to provide a library service without financial restriction under the terms of the Education (Scotland) Act (1918). Regarding non-county authorities in Scotland, the Public Libraries (Scotland) Act (1920) raised the rate restriction from a penny to three pence in the pound, this restriction not being removed by statute until 1955.

[27] A. Ellis, *Public libraries at the time of the Adams Report* (Stevenage, 1979), 72.

[28] The National Home Reading Union, *To keep sane* (October 1916).

[29] Even before the war some believed they were seeing an increase in serious reading. 'There has been a remarkable decline in the reading of fiction from public libraries in the United Kingdom during the year that has closed', reported the *Readers' Index: the bi-monthly magazine of the Croydon Public Libraries* (1913), 5.

[30] Sunderland Public Libraries, Library circular (c. January 1915).

[31] *The Readers' Index: the bi-monthly magazine of the Croydon Public Libraries* (1915), 1.

[32] *Yorkshire Evening Post* (29 May 1922).

[33] *LAR* 19 (1917), 434.

[34] *Publisher's Circular* (17 June 1922).

[35] A. Ellis, *The development of public libraries in England during the First World War*, unpublished PhD thesis, Council for National Academic Awards (1974), 34.

[36] *LAR* 19 (1917), 431.

[37] J.G. Ollé, *Ernest Savage* (1977), 92, highlights Ballinger's strong representations to Herbert Lewis, Parliamentary Secretary to the Board of Education, asking that the abolition clause be included. Hansard, *Parliamentary Debates*, 122 (1919), col. 369, relates Lewis' statement at the Bill's second reading that he had received 'most urgent representations, by deputations and otherwise, from all parts of the country, from Library Authorities'. E.A. Savage, 'George Roebuck and the rate limit', *Library World*, 55 (1954), 167-171, describes how agitation for the Act had been fronted by London librarians led by George Roebuck.

[38] SRO, GD 281/8/82, H. Perkins to A.L. Hetherington (3 June 1919).

[39] SRO, GD 281/8/82, W.H. Owen to A.L. Hetherington (3 June 1919).

[40] SRO, GD 281/8/81-82.

[41] SRO, GD 281/8/82, Rev. J.C. Johnston to A.L. Hetherington (18 February 1916).

[42] 'Robbing Peter to pay Paul' (c. March 1916) and 'Torquay Public Library', *Torquay Directory* (10 May 1916), newscuttings deposited in SRO, GD 281/8/82.

[43] SRO, GD 281/8/82, A.L. Hetherington to all public library authorities (10 May 1919).

[44] A. Ellis, *Public libraries during the First World War* (London, 1975), 14.

[45] *Yorkshire Post* (9 October 1920).

[46] Leamington Spa Public Library, *Annual Report* (covering 1918-1920).

[47] PRO, CAB 26/2, Cabinet Home Affairs Committee, Minutes (25 November 1919).

[48] PRO, RECO 1/677, Ministry of Reconstruction, Adult Education Committee, Libraries Sub-Committee, Memo from Local Government Board (28 September 1916).

[49] Hansard, *Parliamentary Debates*, 122 (1919), col. 1782. See also cols. 1771-1772, 1775 and 1778-1779.

[50] Address to the Library Association annual meeting in 1917, quoted in L.S. Jast, *Libraries and living* (London, 1932), 3.

[51] Ministry of Reconstruction, Adult Education Committee, *Third interim report*, op. cit.

[52] Ibid., 3.

[53] E.J. Carnell, *County libraries* (London, 1938), 31.

[54] W.G.S. Adams, *A report on library provision and policy to the Carnegie United Kingdom Trust* (Dunfermline, 1915).

[55] The 'Staffordshire scheme' derived its name from the fact that this county was the first to run the experiment; in fact nine other counties, from England and Wales, also participated.

[56] British consumers spent £669 million on food in 1913, £216 million of this on imported products: P.E. Dewey, *British agriculture in the First World War* (London, 1989), 15.

[57] Board of Agriculture and Fisheries, *Final Report on the settlement or employment on the land ... of discharged soldiers and sailors*, Cmnd. 8182 (1916), 6.

[58] Ministry of Reconstruction, *Report ... ending 31 December 1918*, op. cit., 25.

[59] Board of Agriculture and Fisheries, *Final report on the settlement or employment on the land*, 20. See also, G.T. Shaw, 'The place of the public library in the government scheme of state settlements', *LAR* 19 (1917), 93.

[60] Ministry of Reconstruction, Adult Education Committee, *First interim report*, op. cit. 26.

[61] Ministry of Reconstruction Adult Education Committee, *First interim report*, op. cit., 22-4.

[62] Shaw, 'The place of the public library ...', 94. The Carnegie United Kingdom Trust's Libraries Sub-Committee hoped rural libraries would similarly 'furnish more suitable means of distributing books on agriculture, horticulture, arboriculture and the like': Minutes (20 March 1919).

[63] PRO, CAB 24/71, GT 6453, Memo from President of the Board of Agriculture and Fisheries on financial requirements for agricultural education (10 December 1918).

[64] Ministry of Reconstruction, *Report ... ending 31 December 1918*, 25.

[65] PRO, RECO 1/677, W.C.B. Sayers to Arthur Greenwood, Ministry of Reconstruction, Adult Education Committee, Libraries Sub-committee, Minutes (7 September 1918),.

[66] E.A. Willats, *A History of Islington public libraries*, unpublished essay, North West London Polytechnic (c. 1970), deposited in Islington Public Libraries.

[67] Library Association Council, Minutes (14 December 1917).

[68] Ellis, *The development of public libraries*, op. cit., 127.

[69] Ministry of Reconstruction, Adult Education Committee, *Final report*, 168.

[70] A similar motive was attributed to education in the army. Colonel Lord Gorrel (R.G. Barnes), *Education in the army* (Oxford, 1921), 46, wrote that education in the armed forces would give men 'a wider realisation of their duties as citizens of the British Empire'.

[71] PRO, CAB 24/84, GT 7790, Home Office, Directorate of Intelligence, Report on revolutionary organisations in the UK (24 July 1919). This belief was repeated in many more of the Directorate's reports.

[72] Commission of Enquiry into Industrial Unrest, *Report of the Commissioners for Wales*, Cmnd. 8668 (1917), 17.

[73] Ibid., 18.

[74] Quoted in C. Rosenberg, *Britain on the brink of revolution: 1919* (London, 1987), 68.

[75] Commission of Enquiry into Industrial Unrest, *Summary of the reports*, op. cit., 20.

[76] F.J. Taylor, 'The making of the 1919 Report', *Studies in Adult Education* 8:2 (1976).

[77] R. Fieldhouse, 'Conformity and contradiction in English responsible body education 1925-1950', *Studies in the Education of Adults* 17:2 (1985), 121.

[78] Ministry of Reconstruction, Adult Education Committee, *First interim report*, op. cit., 13-14, 19-20.

[79] W. Temple, *Tradition, policy and economy in English education* (London, 1915), 9.

[80] Taylor, 'The making of the 1919 Report', op. cit., 140.

[81] M. Cole (ed.), *Beatrice Webb diaries, 1912-1924* (1952), 97.

[82] J. Allred, 'The library as an educational resource', *Public Library Journal* 5:1 (January/February 1990).

[83] This argument was contained in a pamphlet by G. Radford, *The faculty of reading*, (1910), 17, viewed by the Committee; pamphlet deposited in PRO, RECO 1/901, item AE48.

[84] Ministry of Reconstruction, Adult Education Committee, *Third interim report*, op. cit., 15.

[85] Black, *A new history of the English public library*, op. cit., 134.

[86] *Manchester Evening Chronicle* (23 October 1919).

[87] *Wolverhampton Express and Star* (28 June 1919).

[88] *Yorkshire Post* (29 May 1919), speaking at the annual meeting of the Library Association's North Central Branch.

[89] For evidence relating to the Trust's library reconstruction grant issued to the Association, see SRO, GD 281/13/40.

[90] SRO, GD 281/13/40, J.Y.W. MacAlister to A.L. Hetherington (2 April 1918). Frank Pacey wrote to the Trust's J.M. Mitchell (10 November 1920), describing the Association's 'apparent inactivity' in

respect of the reconstruction grant.

[91] Draft statement on library policy, Library Association Library Policy Sub-Committee, Minutes (14 September 1917).

[92] PRO, RECO 1/901, item AE49.

[93] PRO, RECO 1/677, W.C.B. Sayers to Arthur Greenwood (7 September 1918). Greenwood served as secretary of the Committee's Libraries Sub-Committee.

[94] Committee on Commercial and Industrial Policy after the War, *Final report*, Cmnd. 9035 (1918), 21.

[95] J. Ollé, *Ernest A. Savage* (London, 1977).

[96] A grant from the Carnegie United Kingdom Trust helped fund a questionnaire to public libraries and the production of a report issued by the Library Association: *Interim report of the Council on the provision of commercial and technical libraries* (1917), see SRO, GD 281/13/41.

[97] W.E. Doubleday, 'Symposium on public libraries after the war', *LAR* 19 (1917), 115.

[98] *LAR* 20 (1918), 110.

[99] Library Association, *Interim report of the Council on the provision of technical and commercial libraries* (Aberdeen, 1917), 3.

[100] It is interesting to note, however, that questions on science and technical literature do not appear in Library Association exam papers until the 1950s .

[101] Library Association, *Interim report ... technical and commercial libraries*, op. cit., 4.

[102] Bradford Libraries, Art Gallery and Museums Committee, Minutes (21 May 1917).

[103] L.S. Jast, *The organisation of British trade* (Manchester, 1917), 8.

[104] E.W. Hulme, 'Technical libraries', *LAR* 19 (1917), 487.

[105] T.C. Abbot, 'Commercial libraries', *LAR* 19 (1917), 475.

[106] *LAR* 19 (1917), 475.

[107] *The Trader* (16 February 1918).

[108] SRO GD 281/8/82, F.R. Oldfield to A.L. Hetherington (13 May 1919).

[109] SRO, GD 281/13/40, J.Y.W. MacAlister to A.L. Hetherington (24 April 1918).

[110] (c. 1919), Leeds Public Libraries, Local Studies Department, Ref. LP/022.15/L517.

[111] *Leeds Mercury* (6 February 1919).

[112] Norwich Public Library, Local Studies Department, F.G. Kenyon to G.A. Stephen (11 March 1917).

[113] *Times Literary Supplement* (29 July 1915).

[114] 'After the war' (c. 1916), Leamington Spa Public Library News Cuttings.

[115] *Leamington [Spa] Courier* (24 September 1915).

[116] *Pall Mall Gazette* (4 October 1917).

[117] *Borough of Woolwich Pioneer* (23 July 1915).

[118] This occurred in Bermondsey: Southwark Public Library News Cuttings (July 1915), PC021/BER. Attacks on Lord Kitchener in the *Times* and the *Daily Mail* led the Bradford Public Library Committee to consider withdrawing the papers: Bradford Public Library Committee Notes 1913-1946 (31 May 1915), 6.

[119] One example being an Oldham Public Library Lecture, 'The Great War', which argued that the war was being fought in honour of the British Empire, an institution that was synonymous with civilisation and opposed to the enslavement of smaller nations by German militarism: *Oldham Chronicle* (19 October 1914).

[120] *Bournemeouth Guardian* (20 May 1916)

[121] Norwich Public Library, Kenyon to Stephen (11 March 1917), op. cit.

[122] *Croydon Guardian* (3 April 1915)

[123] *Hampshire Chronicle* (11 December 1915)

[124] D. MacLeod, 'A wartime celebration: Mr Jast at Norwich', *Library World* 19 (April 1917), 258.

[125] Ministry of Reconstruction, Adult Education Committee, *Third interim report*, op. cit., 15.

[126] A.H. Jenn, 'Public libraries after the war: the need for immediate preparation', *Library World* 19 (March 1917), 228.

[127] *Harrogate Advertiser* (15 May 1920). Words of the Mayor of Harrogate.

[128] *LAR* 19 (1917), 424.

[129] 'Current view: cinema and libraries', *LAR* 18 (1917), 41.

[130] J.M. Mitchell, *The public library system of Great Britain and Ireland, 1921-23* (Dunfermline, 1924), 47.

[131] *Leamington [Spa] Courier* (9 March 1917).

[132] Norwich Public Library, Kenyon to Stephen (11 March 1917), op. cit. This plea was echoed in the Library Association's *Interim report ... technical and commercial libraries*, op. cit. See SRO, GD 281/13/41, for contextual details regarding this report.

[133] Although a representative of the automobile industry, A.F. Evans, complained that: 'My experience of public libraries has been very unhappy; I have never been able to get hold of a librarian who could help me. I have always found that the books put before me contained everything except the one item I wanted': quoted in E.A. Savage, 'The utilization of the data of the automobile industry through bureaux of information', *Institute of Automobile Proceedings* (February 1918), deposited in SRO, GD 281/13/41.

[134] Ellis, *Public libraries during the First World War*, op. cit., 15.

[135] Revised report on training in librarianship, Library Association Council, Minutes (21 March 1919). H.V. Hopwood, The educational standards of librarianship in relation to technology, Library Association Special Committee on Techniical and Commercial Libraries, Minutes (26 April 1917).

[136] Director's report on the School of Librarianship, 1919-20, in University College London, *Annual Report 1920-21*. Only 38 full-time students (compared with 61 part-time) enrolled in the School when it commenced lectures in October 1919

[137] O.P.R. Ogilvie, 'Libraries in science and industry', *Special Libraries* (16 June 1925), 10-11.

[138] Hulme, 'Technical libraries', op. cit., 494.

[139] B.W.E. Alford, 'Lost opportunities: British business and businessmen during the First World War', in N. McKendrick and R.B. Outhwaite (eds.), *Business life and public policy* (Cambridge, 1986), 209.

[140] S.J. Chapman, *The war and the cotton trade* (Oxford, 1915), 22.

[141] 'After the war', op. cit.

[142] *Manchester Guardian* (18 November 1920).

[143] *Leeds Mercury* (4 November 1916), letter to the editor.

[144] Mayor of Leeds addressing librarians, *Yorkshire Post* (13 January 1917).

[145] Library Association, *Interim report ... technical and commercial libraries*, op. cit., 4.

[146] Leeds Chamber of Commerce, *Commercial yearbook* (Leeds, 1920), 47.

[147] E.J. Connell and M. Ward, 'Industrial development 1780-1914', in D. Fraser (ed.), *A history of modern Leeds* (Manchester 1980), 173.

[148] R.J. Morris, 'Middle-class culture 1700-1914', in Fraser (ed.), *A history of modern Leeds*, op. cit., 219.

[149] K. Grady, 'Commercial, marketing and retailing amenities 1700-1914', in Fraser (ed.), *A history of modern Leeds*, op. cit.

[150] *Electrical Review* (11 August 1922).

[151] Ellis, *The development of public libraries*, op. cit., 167.

[152] *LAR* 19 (1921), 34.

[153] Glasgow Corporation, Minutes (17 September 1918).

[154] Bradford Public Libraries Committee, Minutes (28 June 1917).

[155] Bradford City Archives, *Opening of the Bradford Commercial Library ... 1 May 1918*.

[156] *Yorkshire Observer* (19 November 1918).

[157] Bradford City Archives, *Opening of the Bradford Commercial Library, op. cit.*

[158] F. Crunden, 'The public library as a factor in industrial progress', *The Library* 7 (1906), 388.

[159] A. Ellis, *Public libraries and the First World War*, op. cit., 40.

[160] *Practical Engineer* (6 May 1918)

[161] *Electrical Review* (19 July 1918).

[162] Ellis, *The development of public libraries*, op. cit., 167.

[163] 'Technical libraries: support by influential societies', *LAR* 20 (1918), 105-9. Supporting societies included the Society of Chemical Industry, the Institution of Electrical Engineers and the Textile Institute.

[164] *Manchester City News* (5 July 1919). A vehement campaign was mounted by librarians against the idea of research association libraries sponsored by the Department of Scientific and Industrial Research, a proposal which implied that public libraries were not appropriate repositories for high-grade technical and scientific information.

[165] *Sheffield Independent* (18 January 1918)

[166] E.A. Savage, 'Memorandum on the future work of the [Library Association's] Technical and Commercial Libraries Committee', *LAR* 20 (1918), 219.

[167] Ibid., 219-22.

[168] Ibid., 222.

[169] *Society of Chemical Industry Journal* 34 (1915), 764.

[170] J.M. Barbalet, *Citizenship* (Milton Keynes, 1988), 37.

[171] As suggested by Marwick, *War and social change*, op. cit., 81.

[172] B.S. Turner, *Citizenship and capitalism* (London, 1986), 70.

[173] Thane, *The origins of British social policy*, 18.

[174] S. Wallace, *War and the image of Germany* (1988), 53..

[175] W.A. Wiegand, *'An active instrument for propaganda': the American public library during the First World War* (New York, 1989).

[176] Ibid., 5, 135.

[177] H.E. Legler, *Library ideals* (Chicago, 1918), 1.

[178] For coverage of the propaganda campaigns of anti-radical organisations, see P. Maguire, 'Co-operation and crisis: government, co-operation and politics 1917-1922', in S. Yeo (ed.), *New views of co-operation* (London, 1988), and White, 'Ideological hegemony and political control ...', op. cit.

[179] D.F. Ring, 'Some speculations on why the British library profession didn't go to war', *Journal of Library History*, 22:3 (1987); and in this same issue the reply by Paul Sturges. The fact that a great many librarians literally *did* go to war is emphasised by G. Jefcoate, 'Roll of honour: the librarians' war memorial and professional identity', in K. Manley (ed.), *Careering along with books* (London, 1996), a special issue of *Library History* 12.

[180] K. Faulks, *Citizenship in modern Britain* (Edinburgh, 1998), 105.

CHAPTER THREE

Grids and Masons

1919 – 1939

The post-war years witnessed a notable strengthening of national identity, in contrast to the 'intense and variegated local and provincial culture' which characterised British social life before 1914.[1] The deepening sense of nationhood expressed itself, and was fostered by, a range of developments in communications and technology – such as radio and the reading of national daily newspapers.[2] A system of public (red) telephone boxes and a 'national grid' for electricity were put in place. Librarians, too, developed a 'grid' mentality. Sensing the growth in a national culture, some librarians responded radically, proposing the full nationalisation of public libraries: Archibald Sparke, Chief Librarian of Bolton, believed that libraries had done good work in the past, 'yet it is nothing to what can be done with a national Service, each Library forming a link in a great educational system, and its policy a national policy instead of a purely local one'.[3] However, the desire to view the public library project on a grander scale was matched, paradoxically, by the continuing cultural conservatism of some librarians, as seen in attitudes to an emergent mass media and the social problem of unemployment. An inward-looking conservatism was also evident in the involvement of a small but influential band of librarians in Freemasonry.

Class and Community

Despite the fact that Britain in this period was a country of classes into which people 'freely categorised themselves',[4] in the inter-war years librarians and library promotors redoubled their efforts to emphasise the classlessness of public libraries, investing heavily in the language of community to achieve this end. A report by a committee of the Board of Education in 1927 (the Kenyon Report) spelt out hopes for a new inclusiveness, universalism and dynamism:

The public libraries in the great cities, and in many urban areas of medium size, have developed notably during the last generation, and have established themselves as an indispensible element in the life of the community. They provide information essential for the progress of commerce and industry; they make research possible in every department of intellectual life; they aid solitary students in their investigations; they provide relaxation and refreshment for every class of the population.[5]

Librarians such as Stanley Jast were keen to increase the popularity of the term *'public* library' in preference to the competing term *'free* library'. The latter was said to smack of Victorian soup-kitchens[6] and services to ghetto populations, whereas the former was better suited to the new and meaningful – although as yet limited – developments in public policy.[7] In addition Jast was enthusiastic about the term 'community library' as an 'unambiguous name for all local government [public] libraries – in boroughs, districts, villages and counties'; libraries which, as he saw them, were 'owned by, supported by, managed by and used by the community at large'.[8] Strenuous attempts were made to dampen the reformist, 'social engineering' image of the pre-war public library by presenting the institution as a cultural service whose purpose lay outside the social amelioration concerns of previous generations. It was said to be the aim of Leicester City Council, for example, 'to see the branch libraries become cultural centres of the communities they serve'.[9] This new cultural momentum was based, it was believed, on an improvement in education since 1870. This had increased the number of readers and the incidence of reading, as well as having widened and deepened reading interests.[10] It was also said to be linked to a new interest shown in public libraries by the middle classes. 'There is no doubt', wrote Jast in 1933:

that the main idea behind the early promotion of the public libraries ... was the enlightenment of the working class. The middle class, especially the upper middle class, largely held aloof and, though heaven knows they needed enlightenment badly enough, there is this to be said, that a decent and often quite good collection of books was a common adornment of the [middle class] home ... Fortunately [now] we have the public library and the old prejudice and snobbery which kept the better – I mean the better-off – classes away has completely disappeared. Indeed it is difficult to think of any meeting ground so common to the whole of a town on which every type of citizen may be seen.[11]

Jast does not specify when middle-class prejudice, snobbery and aloofness in respect of the public library – typified by continuing concerns about disease-ridden books[12] – gave way to enthusiasm and increased use. Kelly, on the other hand, writing in 1977, was convinced that it was the inter-war years which had marked a break with the first 75 years of public library development. It was his opinion that by 1914 'although many libraries kept before themselves the ideal of serving the whole community, the service was still in practice directed mainly towards the needs of the urban working class.'[13] But at some time between the wars, he continued, 'the concept of libraries for the working classes gave way to the concept of libraries for all.'[14] In 1938 it was said that reading in the public library context was regarded 'still as the common denominator of fellowship, because it is possible to make the university professor engaged in advanced research the companion of the general reader'.[15] In Glasgow public libraries were advertised as a service for 'the business man, the student and the general reader'.[16] In connection with a Library Association meeting in 1937, a local newspaper in Leeds reported that: 'Library policy should serve the whole community.'[17] Yet being attractive to the whole community was still a long way off: Austin Hinton, City Librarian of Coventry, stated in 1934 that '15% of the population registered as borrowers suggests that we cannot feel too contented yet awhile'.[18]

Although Kelly believed it was not possible to pin-point the precise moment at which the working class barrier was broken, by the time of the Kenyon Report in 1927, he argues, it was officially recognised as having occurred. The problem with Kelly's interpretation of the contemporary discourses on class use is that it flies in the face of compelling evidence pointing to a strong middle-class presence in public libraries even before the First World War.[19] Of course 'middle class' is an umbrella term for many social groupings and, naturally, not all of these found equal interest in an institution like the public library; not even in the more highbrow intellectual reference department which in the big cities had always attracted a healthy working class clientele.[20] Even in the inter-war period, after decades of development, a large number of services offered by the public library fell far short of relatively sophisticated middle-class expectations. Moreover, in many areas the middle classes had only a distant access to a public library at all – for example, in the counties, as well as in some of the new outer suburbs which grew so rapidly during the period yet often without a commensurate increase in services, including public libraries.[21] This said, even though subscription libraries continued to attract middle-class readers in large numbers,[22] a strong middle-class dimension to public library provision and use between the wars is undeniable. The librarian B.T.W. Stephenson, speaking of his own Southport public library in 1937, said that it catered essentially for four classes: '*the well-to-do and better educated* [my emphasis], the artisan, visitors and children.'[23]

Given this tradition of middle-class use, therefore, what explains the enthusiasm of not only library historians like Kelly but also contemporary librarians like Jast for depicting a middle class revolution in public libraries? One possible answer is a deep-rooted desire to 'believe' the language of community and inclusiveness – or in Jast's case to actually help construct that language – because such vocabulary helped articulate a deeply felt, linear sense of progress. Librarians like Jast, continually fighting the public library cause, took every opportunity to talk up the achievements of, and prospects for, their institutions. Reinventing history to announce the arrival of new – in this case middle-class – groups on the library scene and to underscore this arrival, moreover, by investing in the discourse of community – to resurrect the principle of *town libraries* for use by all, as stated by the Victorian librarian and public library promoter Edward Edwards[24] – was something which librarians, eager to break with a Victorian past and to pursue a fresh start after the horrors of the First World War, could easily be tempted to do. That later library historians, surveying evidence from contemporary discourses, also came to believe in the period as one of 'social class progress' (in library terms) is not surprising, particularly if they are intent on writing history as a saga of improvement; in this case the evolution of the public library from lowly, parochial beginnings to the status of a respected and accepted national institution.

This is not to say that no progress was made in public library provision between the wars. Indeed a great many improvements and innovations are evident in the period. For example, the shift towards open-access lending libraries, barely underway before 1914, gathered considerable pace between the wars, to the great benefit of readers and librarians alike: when Bradford Public Library became open-access in 1932 fiction issues increased by over 40% and non-fiction issues more than doubled.[25] However, in some places open-access led to overcrowding. In Sunderland Public Library it was found that: 'Borrowers are frequently congested, and books on the bottom shelves are practically lost to view. Almost daily it is necessary to request borrowers, in certain gangways, to hasten their selections in order to make room for others.'[26] Such experiences led to accusations that libraries, although popular and therefore at times overcrowded, were none the less dull and depressing.[27] Many libraries retained a strong whiff of Victorianism, but others it must be stressed, such as Sheffield Public Library, were able to boast splendid new premises. But the most obvious improvement in service came in the counties, as a result of the Public Libraries Act (1919) and financial aid from the Carnegie United Kingdom Trust (CUKT). The public library service was extended not just to the countryside and villages but to small rural towns also. The economies of scale which the operation of services county-wide delivered were widely recognised. For example, Aberdeenshire reminded the Scottish Education Department, in 1937, that: 'In this county no Public Library, with the exception of Fraserburgh, has sufficient funds to be able to stand alone, and the present arrangements result in a more uniform library service over the whole area than was possible in the past.'[28] In some places it was children who appeared to be the major beneficiaries of the county service. In Lanarkshire, in 1934, juvenile literature formed a massive 35% of the county's book issues.[29] County provision was often on a very modest scale, however. Nottinghamshire's first county branch library was opened in a church hall in Warsop in 1930, with a stock of just 1400 volumes, under the direction of a local teacher. Another Nottinghamshire branch opened in Eastwood in 1935 in a wooden hut.[30] Also, even after a generation of expansion, the number of users of county libraries relative to population still lagged behind levels recorded in urban areas.[31]

Libraries were seen as contributing to the regeneration of rural industries and culture and, along with motor transport and the radio, to the breaking down of rural isolation. Some bestowed a 'national efficiency' function on rural libraries. Addressing the Library Association in 1920, Herbert Lewis MP stated that: 'A vigorous and numerous rural population was essential in the interests of national stamina and a sturdy national stock.'[32] Public libraries were said by the end of the 1930s to be 'making country life more attractive', partly because of their recreational function but also because they enabled citizens to 'verify facts' and question 'blushing mis-statement'.[33] Libraries were very much part of the North Ridings Rural Development Scheme which was publicised in the following way:

One of the most gratifying manifestations in the communal life of the present day is the provision of social amenities for those who live in villages and other sparsely populated areas of the countryside. While the towns have long enjoyed the privilege of social, intellectual, recreative and religious advantage which organised effort can provide, the villages have in many cases been largely or wholly neglected in all these directions, with, perhaps, the single exception of the strictly religious.[34]

In Cheshire by 1931 some 279 village branch libraries (often set up in the local school or village hall) were co-operating in the distribution of books.[35] County provision was enhanced by the introduction of mobile libraries (not to be confused with travelling libraries which were stocks of books changed periodically and transferred to other distribution centres).[36] It was said that library motor-vans in Norfolk were 'seeking to correct the disadvantage of county-dwellers in being cut off from the use of municipal libraries'.[37]

In urban areas, too, mobile libraries began to make an impact. The first urban mobile service, named the 'Bibliobus', was introduced in Manchester in 1931 to serve the city's new outlying estates.[38] Far from being a second class service, Manchester's mobile provision was viewed as an opportunity for readers to improve their social status through their 'public' borrowing of highbrow texts:

The few moments during which the library stops at the corner to take back the finished books and hand out fresh ones will provide an unrivalled opportunity for oblique boasting. People who want their wide culture properly respected will be able to cap their neighbours requests for light tales ... with short superior demands for the latest and gloomiest Scandinavian or Russian [novel].[39]

Even the less well-off, those in streets 'which do not put forward pretentions to garages and small cars', would be able to show that they were people of some account by borrowing heavyweight literature in public view of their neighbours.[40]

Not only did the public library extend itself spacially, it also sought to develop the quality and range of its services. 'Library extension' – activities and materials beyond the provision of basic lending and reference services[41] – became a popular phrase in the vocabulary of inter-war librarians seeking to display a new dynamism. External activities ranged from books for the blind and hospital services to exhibitions, talks to children and support for adult education classes.[42] Regarding the latter, the Mitchell Report in 1923 announced that the public librarian 'is the friend of every serious body of students', and the library itself 'in many cases the centre of organisation for University extension lectures, the Workers Educational Association, the National Home Reading Union and for a very large number of local learned societies'.[43] Jewish children in London's East End were said to make extensive use of both the general collection and books in Hebrew in the Whitechapel Public Library where, in the summer holidays, 'a queue awaits the opening of the door at mid-day'.[44] The 1930s also saw the beginning of local authority library services to prisons.[45]

Despite financial restrictions (although these eased in the late 1930s),[46] public libraries, by 1939, can thus be said to have experienced notable progress over the previous two decades. Contemporary librarians were right to point to the ground they were gaining and, as suited the language of progress, the great amount that was still to be covered. But by investing in the discourses of class cohesion and community as key facets of progress, public library supporters were in effect playing down their institutions' 'social safety' dimension, even if they truly believed that the public library could contribute much in this regard. In Manchester in 1931, at the height of the depression, the reading of public library books was advocated as a means of keeping people indoors at night and away from trouble, thereby reducing expenditure on the police, the courts and other services.[47] The social pacification role of the inter-war public library, especially in the unemployment years of the 1930s, *is* visible, but it is clouded to a degree by the florid language of communal solidarity engaged in by public library protagonists at the time – one facet of this language being the appeal to national solidarity into which the library community enthusiastically tapped.

The Library Grid

The library movement's enthusiasm for the language of community said much about contemporary anxieties over social problems. But it was also derived from an earlier close relationship between civic pride and library provision. The building of a new central library in Manchester in the 1930s showed that expressions of community, voiced the medium of through civic feeling and pride, remained strong and were not confined to the Victorian age. After the ceremony for the laying of the foundation stone, conducted in the presence of the Prime Minister, Ramsay MacDonald, it was reported that:

Cultured inhabitants of Manchester have long been burdened by the indignity of having to admit that one of the great cities of the world, a community professing to value wisdom above rubies, still valued it [the library] so far below gray cloth, tram cars, or frozen meat, that what they had of it stored up in reference books was housed in a group of the huts left over from the tea-or-coffee-catering side of the war.[48]

Stanley Jast, referring to the new structure as 'the finest public building in the country', added that: 'there need be no pretence about the pride of the citizen in the knowledge of what this implies. The finest is good enough for Manchester, and Manchester is worthy of the finest'.[49]

The sense of community which the public library world promoted, although irrevocably linked to localism and civicness, was amplified by appeals to national pride and projects. Just as in the inter-war years a national grid for electricity was constructed, plans were similarly laid in the library world for a national library grid.[50] Librarians began to speak more convincingly of a national library service and a coordinated public library policy.[51] The Kenyon Report asserted that there had been 'a growth of late in the public appreciation of the important place which the library service holds in the life of the *nation* [my emphasis]'.[52] It is true that the report rejected the idea of central funding (and, it follows, the inspection that would have gone with it), expressing the fear that government would 'impair the local independence which is a healthy instinct in English public life',[53] and arguing that 'persuasion and example are the stimuli on which we should rely'.[54] However, the document as a whole is peppered with calls for integration, coordination and co-operation – on both a national and regional scale. The report advocated the establishment of a central government bureau to which application could be made for information and advice, as well as a system of cooperation between libraries.[55]

The report's advocacy of co-operation reflected the belief held by some, even before work on the report had begun, that the defects of public libraries were less due to a deficiency of funds than to lack of co-ordination.[56] It would be wrong to assume, however, that central government made no allowance for increased funding of libraries during the inter-war years, although amounts that were allocated directly were small.[57] Full-blown central funding (accompanied by a state department with responsibility for libraries)[58] may not have appeared, but the long-standing debate about its value, as well as its implications in terms of inspection, continued. Basil Anderton told the Carnegie United Kingdom Trust in 1935 that:

It seems to me that in many places there is a good deal to be said for keeping local autonomy, and for letting towns shoulder their responsibility ... On the other hand a broad-minded Government supervision might do some Library Committees a wholesome amount of good, and perhaps might lead to the provision of more adequate funds in many places.[59]

Some librarians embraced the prospect of central funding because they thought it would improve the status of their profession.[60] But in general, librarians appeared to be suspicious of proposals for increased government involvement. J.M. Mitchell, of the Carnegie United Kingdom Trust, wrote of the fear he detected of overbearing government control, the 'nationalisation' of the library system and 'grant-aid-plus-inspection'[61] – a fear intensified by librarians' unequivocal rejection of escalating control of libraries by local authority education committees, which many saw as the real meaning of proposals for a central government direction of library services.[62]

What librarians and planners envisaged in the absence of a heavy, centralised authority was a giant grid – a network of library institutions and mini-grids – designed to improve public accessibility. At the lowest level would be found the network of branch, or satellite, libraries within library authorities – the existence of which the mid-nineteenth-century public library pioneers had not envisaged. These would combine to provide, in effect, a single, integrated library system for each library authority. As Stanley Jast was reported to have explained at the opening of a new branch library in Croydon:

The libraries were really all one, for they were all connected by private telephone and a motor service ran between them daily to convey books quickly to the library where they were needed. Books drawn from one library could be returned to another.[63]

By the early 1930s public libraries in Glasgow were networked into a book exchange service linking 26 sites, books and periodicals in request collected and delivered twice a day.[64] In some places the local network incorporated non-public libraries. In Sheffield, for example, the public library initiated a city-wide interchange of technical books and periodicals, combining the resources of the public library system and the libraries of other institutions and firms.[65] Regarding co-ordination in areas controlled by the county library service, a suitable metaphor mixing horticulture and landscape painting was employed by one observer: 'The organisation of a county library system may well be compared with the painting of a tree, the library area being the canvas. When it is finished, there must be no gaps in the work, no branches missing, no break in the continuity from trunk to fruit.'[66]

Library authorities also co-operated between themselves. Readers in Poplar in 1937 were told that their library tickets were valid when they travelled on holiday to resorts like Eastbourne and Worthing.[67] On a grander scale regional schemes, building on earlier voluntary co-operative schemes, began to appear from 1931 onwards. This system mirrored that organised on a country-wide basis by the National Central Library (partly funded by the CUKT and known between 1916 and 1930 as the Central Library for Students).[68] The regional system was designed to serve as a clearing house for requests from individual public library readers for loans from 'outlier' libraries, including the libraries of professional associations, research associations, scholarly societies and universities.[69] The network was conceptualised as an 'over-library' which had 'a roughly similar relation to the country as a whole that the central library of a town had to its branches'.[70] It was stated that the objectives of the North Regional Library Bureau, for example, were to relieve pressure on the National Central Library and to 'promote the inter-availability and inter-loan of books so that less money may be spent upon books which are in small demand and consequently more will be available to spend upon books that are in great demand'.[71] Finally, beyond the national scene, an international interchange of resources was foreseen.[72]

These co-operative arrangements – assisted by technological improvements like the telephone and the photostat[73] – were not of course aimed at the frivolous library user. They were designed to accommodate the needs of the serious reader: the self-improver, the student, the researcher and those from the business world. The idea of the library grid was founded on the long-standing desire to see the public library achieve what many believed to be its true destiny: an institution providing information and education for tangible, material advance. The Kenyon Report stated that:

there is now a far healthier belief in the value of knowledge, and in the importance of intellectual life, in all the busy centres of national activity, than in any previous period of our history. In such centres the public library is no longer regarded as a means of providing casual recreation of an innocent but somewhat unimportant character; it is recognised as an engine of great potentialities for national welfare.[74]

The Report also acknowledged that:

Commerce and industry have learned ... that study and research are essential, not merely for progress but for survival in the struggle for existence. The war of 1914-18 brought home this necessity with irresistible force, and few would now deny it that if a crowded industrial population, such as that of Great Britain, is to continue to hold its own, it can only [do so] by the utilisation of its best brains and by the application of all the resources of knowledge and intellectual culture.[75]

Librarians were keen to celebrate the work of the public commercial and technical libraries which had begun to appear during the First World War:

Wherever these libraries had been established they have become a vital factor in the business life of their communities, which have been wise enough to see that the old methods of trade are no longer applicable to the modern world, and that organised information is an essential element of twentieth-century business.[76]

In Keighley, in 1932, it was reported that there had been a steady demand for works on engineering and textiles: for instance, 'an abstruse work on the diesel engine has been issued 20 times, a highly technical work on high speed internal combustion engines 14 times, practical tuning of power looms 18 times'.[77] Many large public libraries continued to develop special collections relevant to the local economy: for example, in Kidderminster (carpet design), Preston (agriculture) and Wakefield (coal mining). In Sheffield, in 1930, the public library was deemed to have been 'instrumental in securing large orders for Sheffield firms by the information which staff had been able to supply.'[78] The benefit of public libraries to public administrators seeking out facts, statistics and statutes was stressed.[79] Public libraries began to be promoted as important sources of hard, wealth creating facts and data. Folkestone Public Library, it was proudly announced, 'supplied not only books but also information'.[80] The 'enquiry bureau' in Croydon Public Library was described as providing 'facts for all'.[81] By 1930 it was receiving over 1,000 telephone enquiries per year, subjects ranging from 'the name of the inventor of glass to the definition of an inferiority complex'.[82]

It is in the 1920s and 1930s that the word information becomes an established aspect of public library provision and self-image. The term 'information bureau' becomes fairly common during this period, some London public libraries advertising themselves as such on posters.[83] The librarian J.H. Shaw described the public library in 1930 as 'a storehouse of knowledge *and* [my emphasis] a bureau of information'.[84] Manchester Public Library's commercial department was described as a 'vehicle of information';[85] while the public library's role generally in this respect was believed to represent a sophisticated 'information complex'.[86] In 1920 the Library Association confidently declared that 'the new ideal of the public libraries as bureaux of information has become a commonplace'.[87]

The Unemployment Threat

Riding two horses at the same time, librarians boasted of a shift towards serious use, yet many were equally happy to open their doors to the army of poor and unemployed who periodically, during the severe economic downturns which marked the inter-war period, but most notably in the early-1920s and early-1930s, resorted to the public library for job-seeking, as a place for rest and shelter, or as a means of escape. Bad times were said to be good for books.[88] Loans, as well as use of reference departments and reading rooms, soared in line with rising levels of unemployment.[89] It was not just the working classes moreover, who accounted for this increase. In 1921, for example, it was reported that in London: 'Middle-class people who can no longer afford books are also making increasing use of the public libraries.'[90] As the post-war recession deepened, the number of books issued by Sheffield public libraries jumped by 50% in February 1922 compared to the same month a year earlier;[91] similarly, in Bradford, as unemployment began to *fall* in the mid-1930s, loans reduced accordingly.[92]

The reading room in Liverpool's central library in the depression of the early-1920s was said to be 'so crowded that many men had to sit on the floor, shoulder to shoulder', and proposals were consequently made to open an extra room in the Labour Exchange so that readers, in addition to consulting newspapers, books and periodicals, could speedily receive information about job vacancies.[93] Such was the demand that 'large crowds of men gathered outside the reading room every morning waiting patiently for admission'.[94] Moreover, it was noted – although this was perhaps more wishful thinking than reality – that a great deal of serious reading was being done by the unemployed of Liverpool, 'who were finding public libraries better than the streets'.[95] During the depression of the early 1930s, Liverpool's public libraries once again offered shelter to the poor. The reading room in Christian Street was said to be attracting 10,000 visitors a week in 1933: 'Here', it was reported, 'the city has a reading room for the masses, a home away from home, which is visited by old age pensioners, unemployed by the hundreds, down-and-outs, and all classes.'[96]

Beyond serving as a means of passing the time and as sources of hard information pertinent to the predicament of the unemployed,[97] public libraries were in some cases also frequented for the purpose of begging. 'A pernicious custom', it was reported by a journalist in 1922:

is that of many unemployed men's practice of accosting others for the purpose of begging. Recently one such person came up to me asking whether I would read through a certain advertisement for him. I naturally did, whereupon he began dilating on his suffering ... eventually acknowledging quite frankly that he had no desire to see any advertisement, but simply wanted a few 'coppers.' Others, too, have informed of similar instances where 'reading' is merely a pretence for meeting people to beg from.[98]

Such behaviour presented ammunition to those who found mass, plebeian use distasteful and threatening.[99] The Librarian of Liverpool, George Shaw, commented disapprovingly in 1922 that: 'Providing shelter for the poor and unemployed was not library work, but social work';[100] while in Cambridge in 1931 one section of public opinion was adamant that scarce money would be better spent on slum clearance than on a new reading room for the unemployed of a working-class housing estate.[101] In 1922, in Middlesbrough, opinion among councillors was said to be evenly divided on the question of whether it was the job of the Public Library Committee or the Unemployment Committee 'to provide a rendez-vous for the legions of unemployed'.[102]

In Bideford, also in 1922, pro-library councillors fought hard to lessen the effects of post-war expenditure cuts.[103] In some areas of public spending, the economic downturn of the early 1920s meant that the premium on preventing social unrest, if not revolution, on the scale seen in Europe a few years earlier, could be lowered: expenditure on public services, welfare, education and housing could be reduced safely because rapidly rising unemployment effectively depoliticised workers. Although economizers in local authorities might have held this opinion, librarians and library supporters appear to have dismissed this strategy and endorsed a policy of control and social pacification through increased resources for libraries, something which they persistently requested but rarely received.

According to a librarian in Liverpool, the liking of the majority of those slum dwellers who used the public library for popular fiction was that such books:

transported the reader from the grim realities of life to realms of happiness. Just as opium was a drug for the smoker, so books were a drug for the slum dwellers, and would carry them into a state of forgetfulness.[104]

Providing a route to escape the grim realities of life was a long-standing motive of public library work. But beyond the dissolution of the effects of squalor, libraries had, since their inception, also sought to fulfill a political role in dampening social unrest. This role was very much apparent between the wars. Drawing on the rhetoric of 'the common good' and on feelings of anti-radicalism, the library community argued that no department of the local corporation was more justified in its existence in terms of producing 'good', passive citizens and contributing to the assets of the nation. 'At times such as the present', commented a pro-library newspaper report in 1932, 'when slackness of trade and labour disputes bring unsought leisure to so many, the institution is especially valuable in preventing, or minimising discontent.'[105] Or as J.H. Wellard put it, in pointing to the public library's political role, as opposed to its status as an innocuous, independent social institution:

Public libraries, in brief, are no longer self-explanatory and self-justificatory public services, independent of political parties and political theory. They may be judged one day as another example of democratic sentimentalism, no more justifiable than, and certainly not as colourful as, the Roman bread-and-circuses.[106]

At the opening of the new extension to Nottingham Central Library in 1932, J.M. Mitchell declared: 'Never was the value of a library greater than at a time when unemployment was rife', for the public library was 'an asset of the highest practical value and a safety valve of the greatest civic and social importance'.[107] It was Mitchell's view that libraries in districts of high unemployment 'safeguarded men from deterioration'; a belief echoed by another observer who claimed that: 'Libraries abound while prisons are diminishing in number ... It is not unreasonable to infer that the waxing and waning of these services are connected.'[108] Further, social tensions and problems could be reduced, it was believed, through the public library's role as an economic regenerator. Boasting of its utilitarian value, Harrogate Public Library explained how its purchase of an expensive text on the history of English furniture enabled a local firm which borrowed it to produce and sell replica furniture, thereby creating new jobs.[109] Here was the image of a dynamic, practical, class-free institution, in stark contrast to the impression held by some that the public library, although used by a wide range of classes and types of user, traditionally existed primarily as a magnet for the indolent, or 'undeserving' poor. The large and sudden increase in the numbers of unemployed after 1929 revealed the illegitimacy of the distinction made between the 'deserving' and the 'undeserving' poor. Clearly it was economic forces beyond the control of individuals, not an overnight mass deterioration in personal morality, which catapulted millions of workers into idleness. It was inconceivable that all the public libraries' new readers were career tramps, and the fact that more of the poor were now seen to be 'deserving' probably persuaded many librarians that mass use of their institutions by the unemployed was generally a good thing.

In looking back to the Victorian age, W.C.B. Sayers wrote, in 1938, that: 'The notion that the [public] library was for all and not only a charitable institution to the poor had scarcely then lifted its feeble head.'[110] In the 1930s the idea of the public library as a charity, which inevitably created the irritation of having to assess who was 'deserving' of such benevolence, began to fade fast. It was perhaps this, as much as any sudden influx of middle-class readers, which gave the public library the democratic, universal feel which intensified during and after the second World War.

Mass Media, Popular Culture and Englishness

The threat posed by the unemployed to society – and by association to the public library also – which many librarians and library supporters sensed, was compounded by the continuing debate on the appropriateness of the public library as a dispenser of popular literature, as well as by attitudes to the way it interfaced with the new mass media of film and radio. Writing in 1930, the librarian Ernest Baker declared that, rather than being 'dead and done with', the question of light literature supplied by public libraries, which had been a prominent feature of Victorian and Edwardian public library debate, was 'not really dead, but very much alive'. Armed with replies from a recent questionnaire he had issued to thirty of the country's largest library authorities, Baker was scathing in his condemnation of the policy of compromise he detected. Librarians, he found, were on the one hand proclaiming their duty to raise standards and reach the masses, yet on the other were 'purchasing thousands of copies of this deleterious literature'. Baker believed that supplying trashy literature corrupted the tastes of impressionable people who would otherwise have become intelligent readers. In 'muddling the brains of a large section of the community', the public library was contradicting the essence of what it stood for. 'By supplying facilities for mere mental dissipation', he went on:

the public library is not performing an act of kindness but doing something positively harmful, promoting the work of social corruption which it wants to counteract. If the worn-out charwoman and the jaded clerk, for whom our good-natured indulgence is asked, have not enough energy left to read anything but trash, we should be doing them a real service if we could prevent them from reading at all.[111]

This elitist position was shared by other librarians. Jast argued that if circulation became the acid test of a public library's success, then librarians were in effect abandoning their true selves: 'Are the figures we librarians ... quote so proudly in our annual reports of so much significance that we can afford to lose our souls for them?', he asked.[112] Among local taxpayers the old argument that those who wished to read light fiction should do so at their own expense continued to be rolled out: 'Ratepayers would soon complain', suggested one daily newspaper, 'if free cinema tickets or dances were provided out of their money, so why should they subsidise the reading of ephemeral literature.'[113] 'Coarseness and filth are put on the rates', declared the *Children's Newspaper*; the language in some of the popular literature purveyed by public libraries, it explained, was 'of the kind which, if used on a coach holiday with mixed company, would be stopped as intolerable and even beyond the bounds of the law'.[114]

It would be wrong to assume, however, that all public librarians rallied to the attack on the popular literature disseminated by the public library. Librarians in Sheffield defended the borrowing of light fiction as an appropriate introduction to both reading and the use of libraries.[115] There were calls for a scientific investigation into the possible beneficial effects of fiction reading.[116] Some objected to education authority control of public libraries because they thought there was a real danger that they would become 'an educational instrument in a very narrow sense and try ... to provide in the library the literature which they think people ought to read and not the literature they want to read.'[117]

Yet reading between the lines of what inter-war librarians were saying about the issue, one detects more often than not a grudging acceptance of the demand for light literature, as opposed to a sincere desire to endorse popular tastes. As Hertford's librarian explained:

Personally I would rather the people read a larger percentage of more serious books, but as they demand novels I have attempted to meet their demands. I should never dream of attempting to dictate to other people what they should read.[118]

In Leeds, while fiction reading was seen as inevitable and often valuable, the following plea for seriousness was made:

There is no desire to discourage fiction. It is realised that a vast amount of the best kind of recreation is derived from the reading of novels. But it is felt that a public library should be primarily an educator, a widener of the mind, a source of information to the enquirer, a handmaid to progress.[119]

In Norbury it was reported that: 'Every librarian would like to fill his shelves with only the best stuff, but his committee would quickly be smothered with complaints.'[120] Although forced out of necessity to stock light literature, many librarians appear to have done so with a heavy heart. Apart from the occasions when outright attacks on popular fiction were mounted – as in the case of Ernest Baker noted above – there is a great deal more evidence pointing to librarians and library supporters struggling with their conscience over the issue.

Firstly, even though the ratio of fiction to non-fiction reading changed little over the period,[121] rarely was a chance missed to 'talk up' the work which public libraries were doing to encourage serious reading. Bethnal Green's librarian was 'firmly of the opinion that people today are more ready to read serious literature than they were before the war'.[122]

Secondly, relief was often expressed concerning the phenomenal rise of the 'twopenny library' and the success of private circulating libraries generally.[123] Twopenny libraries – from which for tuppence per volume per week books could be borrowed without the payment of a membership fee or deposit – became very popular between the wars, especially as the economy improved in the mid-1930s. In his social survey of York in 1938, B.S. Rowntree found that loans by twopenny libraries amounted to about half those recorded by public libraries. Responding to this finding, York's librarian believed that although the literature peddled by twopenny libraries had a drugging effect if access were unrestricted, they did create some new readers who eventually graduated to the public library.[124] A more common view of the value of twopenny libraries, however, was the pressure they were believed to take off public libraries to supply light fiction. It was observed that:

The people who wanted the poorest of fiction – the most romantic of romances and the most adventurous of adventure stories – have turned their backs on the public library to be satiated at the twopenny library, thus giving public librarians the chance which the majority were only too anxious to seize upon of developing the more valuable side of their work.[125]

The same purpose was allotted to the more respectable circulating libraries which, far from being 'tract depots' feeding the middle classes with moralistic discourses, continued to provide the majority of their readers with 'books of a much lighter character for amusement'.[126] Thus the chair of the library committee in Leicestershire joyfully explained:

we are not afraid of the chain libraries or the libraries in the toffee shops ... They reduce the demand on the county libraries for certain kinds of fiction, and enable us to spend more on books of a lasting character.'[127]

Thirdly, it is true that attempts were made to present the public library in a more popular light. In 1937 Nottingham Public library held a 'holiday guide exhibition'.[128] That same year, the Gilstrap Public Library in Newark-on-Trent issued a questionnaire to its readers requesting suggestions as to how service could be improved.[129] However, services designed to bring the public library closer to its user communities at times merely served to reinforce high culture. Some public libraries embraced the prospect of lending gramophone recordings and providing gramophone facilities, but preferred classical music to jazz.[130] Storytelling for children, such as that delivered in Bradford in 1938, also grew in popularity.[131] It was reported in 1937 that on some evenings in the Gorbals Public Library in Glasgow around 250 children attended the story hour.[132] These were obviously ideal occasions for librarians to inculcate the benefits of 'good' literature to an impressionable young audience.

The same might be said of innovative activities linked to the radio. The use of public libraries for wireless study groups – run in association with broadcasts and handbooks by the BBC, designed to whet the appetite for serious discussion – might be construed as an imaginative exploitation of a modern, popular technology.[133] But, again, this initiative was a golden opportunity to promote the serious side of public library provision, the culture of the institution appearing to complement ideally that of the BBC under John Reith: formal, dignified, middlebrow-to-highbrow, even high-minded and puritanical.[134] Indeed, one of the main reasons why wireless discussion groups eventually failed was said to be the unattractive subjects broadcast: 'If Plato lived again' featured in one library's discussion group series.[135] The librarian M.C. Pottinger did not hesitate to contrast what he saw as the 'barbarism' of the 'mass habit of uncritical reading' of sensationalist light fiction and Sunday newspapers with his 'wholesome admiration for the broadcasting service in Britain'. Despite certain criticisms that could be levelled at the BBC, he asserted, 'nobody can say that listeners are degraded or exploited', because: 'Wisely it [the BBC] controls the quality of its programs within a liberal range.' Indeed what was required, he suggested, to prevent the reading habit 'from degenerating into a suicidal human weakness, is an analogous form of control'.[136]

Others were less convinced of the value of the radio in respect of cultural improvement. A member of the library committee in Cambridge, for example, defended the library's extensive purchase of daily newspapers because these enabled people to 'acquire something different from the half-baked knowledge one obtained on the radio'.[137] Similarly, the library world was far from united on the issue of the cinema and its contribution, or threat indeed, to culture. Some librarians were outright opponents of picture palaces. A.T. Hancock thought that because the lavish new cinemas were entertaining, comfortable, cheap and sometimes even instructive, they threatened to distract the attention of the public from reading.[138] In promoting his own library system, the chairman of Bradford's library committee declared that 'visiting cinemas and similar amusements does little to broaden one's outlook'.[139] Others believed that the cinema and the public library were mutually beneficial. It was proposed that 'films should be used to popularise books, and that film versions of books which a library desires to popularise should be shown'.[140] Far from being an enemy of the public library, luring people away from books, it was noted that 'enquiries for certain books greatly increased when they are made the subject of cinema presentation'.[141] Predictably, however, the type of film with which librarians wished to see their institutions linked were those that drew on the literary canon. For example, film versions of *As You Like It* and *Romeo and Juliet* caused a run on these titles in 1937, it was reported.[142] A film version of Dumas' *The Three Musketeers* was said to have led many to borrow the book, as well as other titles by the same author.[143]

The public library's determination to defend high culture and educational seriousness in the face of the threat posed by the social disruption of unemployment and the rise of the mass media was in keeping with its traditional role as censor of public culture. Whereas by 1938 some could say that 'the time has gone when a body such as a public library committee should act as a public censor',[144] others continued to take pride in the role of the institution as the guardian of both public morals and mainstream political ideology. Naturally political censorship by public libraries never approached the scale seen in Nazi Germany.[145] The public library in Britain continued to espouse liberal, tolerant values. In Sheepscar, Leeds, where a special collection of books for Jewish readers was housed, it was stressed that no distinction was made between race, colour or creed: 'The greatest of the German poets and Jewish authors are shelved side by side.'[146] However, censorship *did* occur. William Munford wrote that he was fully aware of 'libraries in which political censorship is a thing to be reckoned with'.[147] 'Bolshevik' and socialistic propaganda was frequently targeted for rejection by library committees.[148] In approving sensible, discrete censorship, Leeds' librarian, R.J. Gordon, said that there were 'too many novels more animal than intellectual'.[149] The practice of blacking-out the racing columns in newspapers to discourage betting continued (although it appears to have become less common than before the war).[150] Perhaps because of the adverse publicity generated by such blatant censorship, librarians and library committees tended to rely on indirect methods: the exclusion of what was 'bad' by the promotion of what was 'good'. Librarians were less interested in prohibition and repression than in persuasion and counter-attraction. Blyth's librarian was adamant that it was his duty to be the 'guide to the treasures'.[151] As in the Victorian age, librarians produced and promoted lists of recommended reading.[152] Such was the effectiveness of this strategy that even some members of the public internalised the idea that: 'The question as to which are the best books must be left to librarians, who give their whole time to the matter.'[153]

Die-hard attitudes in respect of popular culture conflicted with rhetoric boasting popular use and increasing readerships. Some librarians were uncomfortable with the new age of the mass media and with the prospect of popularisation. It was not just that mass use meant patronage by undesirable characters, which threatened a deterioration of conduct in libraries.[154] It was also that librarians viewed mass use as a symptom of an unhealthy mass culture which manipulated and degraded citizens. Stanley Jast, referring to modern journalism, characterised it as:

one of the menacing signs of the times. In the old days newspapers had ideals, but nowadays very few enterprises had ideals. They had a Press which was inaccurate, irresponsible, which played down in all kinds of ways to the ignorances, narrowness and prejudices of the masses of the people of this country.

As for cinema, he went on, there was no harm in it in itself, 'the harm was in cinema and nothing but cinema, [where] people were drugged by it'. The leisure of the people, Jast lamented, had 'swung almost entirely around amusements', the most popular being the most stupid.[155]

Thus, although lip-service was paid to the proposition that 'the age of jazz and "talkies" is the age also of a wide extension of the library services and an increase in the habit of home reading',[156] George Shaw was surely nearer the truth when he observed that 'the public library played such a quiet part in city life that in these advertising times there was a tendency to forget it existed'.[157] In response to economic instability and the arrival of the mass media and new leisure opportunities, the inter-war public library, if it did extend and popularise itself, did so only marginally, held back as it was by a distaste among many librarians and library committees for popular leisure and culture and mass use. As brightly decorated tea-houses and luxury cinemas exploded onto the urban landscape to satisfy 'the restlessness that made Tooting yearn for Piccadilly',[158] public libraries in many places remained tired, sleepy backwaters by comparison. This impression was convincingly conveyed by one user of the Minet Public Library in Brixton, of which he said:

few up-to-date books of reference are obtainable, the main object of its existence apparently being to supply antiquated pamphlets and works on Surrey which, no doubt, have a certain interest to a few, but are certainly of little use to the average seeker of information who is living in the present and not looking backward.[159]

Part of the public library community's suspicion of the emergent mass media, allied to a continuing propensity for censorship and preference for 'good' and classic literature, to a degree labels the public library in the inter-war period as culturally and politically conservative. In many ways the culture of the inter-war public library reflected developments in the world of conservative thought during the period: in particular, the construction and celebration of Englishness. According to Stanley Baldwin a major component of Englishness was: 'Ordered liberty – not disordered liberty ... but ordered liberty, at present one of the rare things of this topsy-turvy world.' The English, he continued, were well-equipped to face the challenges of an unstable world, due to 'our pertinacity, our love of freedom, our love of ordered freedom, our respect for law, our respect for the individual and our power of combining in service.'[160]

The great strength of the English, argued Baldwin, lay in their individuality: 'We are a people of individuals, and a people of character ... The preservation of the individuality of the Englishman is essential to the preservation of the type of the race ... Uniformity of type is a bad thing.'[161] Englishmen were 'honourable and upright and persevering, lovers of home, of their brethren, of justice and of humanity.'[162] But the real essence of England and Englishness was historic and pre-modern: 'To me', said Baldwin, 'England is the country, and the country is England ... The sounds of England, the tinkle of the hammer on the anvil in the country smithy, the corncrake on a dewy morning, the sound of the scythe against the whetstone, and the sight of a plough team coming over the brow of a hill ... The wild anemones in the woods in April, the last load at night of hay being drawn down a lane as the twilight comes on ... These are the things that make England.'[163]

This construction of Englishness was mirrored in aspects of public library discourse at the time. Stanley Jast pointed out that public libraries were run in a way which deliberately countered political, social and religious partisanship; hence he felt able to declare that the story of the public library was 'typical of the Anglo-Saxon genius for government.'[164] It was said that books of 'a demoralising and vulgarising influence' supplied by public libraries were undermining our national culture, for they were 'alien to the general standard of British life and thought,'[165] ('Britishness' being subsumed by the notion of 'Englishness'). Leading librarians spent a lot of time stressing the importance of defending the English literary heritage. For example, W.C.B. Sayers, lectured that 'it is the business of the library to provide classical literature in English, the desirable minimum being reached when every book mentioned in the ordinary literary histories of England has been acquired ... Such classical literature is the ballast of the library.'[166] Special collections of English literary classics were proudly publicised. In 1921 Northampton Public Library opened a 'Clare Corner', to commemorate the life and work of the English Romantic peasant poet John Clare whose work was inspired by the folk ballads passed down to him by his parents;[167] while Cambridge Public Library was keen to broadcast the existence of its Shakespeare collection which contained upwards of 2000 items. Finally, the extension of the public library service into villages complemented the *perceived* happiness and harmony of rural life. Although village libraries were seen as a means of broadening the minds of the intellectually and geographically isolated, thereby making country living more attractive, they were also presented, at times in a quasi-Baldwinesque style, as a force for preserving rural culture. Conjuring up romantic images of helpful school teachers providing 'out-of-hours' book loans, or of dutiful children trudging home from the village school laden with books for parents and neighbours, librarians invested a good deal of time promoting the rural library as an instrument of 'community' and social cohesion in the countryside.[168] In such ways, the inter-war public library, not only in respect of provision in the counties but also in discourses related to urban services, reflected the fears of authority over social unrest and its desire to avoid upheaval by *manufacturing* a social consensus which excluded radical solutions to the social problems of the day. The public library acted as an ideal instrument for conveying the socially calming messages that government and social elites wished to broadcast.

The Librarianship Masonic Circle

Librarians' cultural and social conservativism was also evident in the links some of them had with Freemasonry. In 1927 a Librarianship Masonic Circle was launched, and operated, as far as the records indicate, for a little under a decade. The idea originated at a Masonic dinner held at the Masonic Hall, Leeds on 7 September 1926. Freemasons attending the Library Association's annual conference in the city had been invited to the Hall by local Freemasons in the spirit of brotherhood which was deemed to characterise the movement, or 'Craft'. Although there is no evidence to confirm it, the possibility is that previous annual conferences had also contained a Masonic dimension. On this occasion, however, the library brethren expressed a wish to place their future meetings on a more formal footing; and the decision was taken to apply to the national Masonic authorities for official recognition of a Librarianship Lodge.

The distinction between 'lodge' and 'circle' is important. Lodge status was higher than that of a circle.[169] Under English and Scottish – but not Irish – Masonic Constitutions peripatetic Lodges were not permitted. Lodges had to have permanent accommodation and meet four times, or more, each year, at least one meeting being in the permanent home.[170] As the librarianship brotherhood revolved around the Library Association's annual conference, lodge status, not surprisingly, eluded them throughout.[171] One of the prime movers of the group wrote in 1926 that probably they had to be 'content to form ourselves as a Circle.'[172] However, Freemason librarians continued to aspire to lodge status, until in 1937 a decision by the Freemasons' deputy Grand Secretary finally dashed their hopes. This was a bitter blow to the Librarianship Circle which believed that leading Freemasons had always given the impression that annual informal meetings were 'a means to a regular and purposeful end'. The Circle's secretary appears to have been correct in his assessment that the decision 'affects the question of the continuance of the circle', for there is no evidence that the Circle met after 1937.[173]

Fifty-one brethren attended the Leeds dinner in 1926. By April of the following year, over sixty applications for membership to the planned Lodge had been received,[174] and by July 1928 over ninety members had been signed up.[175] Administration of the Circle in its early years was undertaken by Charles Sanderson, Librarian of the National Liberal Club (and a part-time lecturer in librarianship at University College, London and the University of Heidelberg). It was he who circulated Freemason librarians in January 1927 touting for members in advance of the formal launch of the Circle at the Library Association's annual conference in Edinburgh later that year. It appears that only practising or former Freemasons were considered for membership.[176] Both past and present librarians qualified, as did members of library committees.[177] The question of individuals outside, but close to, the library world being invited to join was also considered. Such 'tradesmen', as they were classed, might include publishers, booksellers, bookbinders, printers and others commercially connected to libraries. John Ballinger, Librarian of the National Library of Wales, thought that 'it might make things less comfortable if all our tradesmen were brought in', but it would be 'masonically difficult to announce definitely that they were excluded.'[178] The consensus appears to have been, in fact, that each application was to be treated on its merits.

Members were drawn from a variety of libraries, but the vast majority were from the *public* library sector, reflecting the dominant role public librarians played in the Library Association at the time. The members' lists[179] read like a 'Who's Who?'of early twentieth century public librarianship, and included names such as Albert Cawthorne (Stepney), Alfred Lancaster (St. Helen's), George Roebuck (Walthamstow) and John Singleton (Accrington). Other leading personalities included Ernest Baker (Director of the School of Librarianship, University College, London), Henry Guppy (Librarian of the John Rylands Library, Manchester) and J.M. Mitchell (Secretary of the Carnegie United Kingdom Trust and author of its important report on public libraries in 1924).[180] Mitchell appears to have played a major role in the foundation of the Circle. As Secretary of the 'Carnegie Trust' he had close links with the library movement generally, and with the public library movement in particular. The pivotal part he played in the Circle is illustrated by the fact that the only documentary evidence that has so far come to light of the Circle's existence is in the form of the letters sent to and from Mitchell in his official capacity at the Trust.

Each member of the Circle was listed with what appears to have been their individual Masonic identity code attached - this being a combination of their local Lodge's code name and the personal number issued to them by that Lodge. These codes make interesting reading in their own right. Exotic identities such as Edwina 4237, Charity 2651, Equality 1145 and Mendelssohn 2661, are not only intriguing but also underlined the clandestine nature of the circle. Indeed, the extent to which secrecy was cherished by the Brethren was illustrated in advance of the gathering in Blackpool in 1928 when news about the Circle was reported in the *Blackpool Times*, prompting Sanderson to state angrily that: 'I have twice emphasised to the Blackpool people that our Masonic gathering is an unofficial function and not only must not be allowed to come "into the picture" but should not be talked about except among ourselves.'[181] Yet knowledge of Freemasonry in librarianship had not always been entirely secret. In 1915, for example, one library journal carried the announcement that Albert Cawthorne of Stepney Public Library had been installed as Worshipful Master of the Borough of Stepney Lodge, following hard on the heels of the appointment of Wimbledon's librarian, Henry Bull, to a similar position in his borough.[182]

In the absence of first-hand testimony it isn't possible to obtain a clear picture of what Freemason librarians did at their exclusive, all-male 'Craft meals'. However, something of what occured can be gleaned from the programmes printed for the dinners. The programme for the 1928 'Craft meal' in Blackpool,[183] for example, included the

words to five songs (The Bonnie Banks O' Loch Lomond' [You take the high road ...];
Off to Philadelphia; Annie Laurie; I am a Roamer; and Auld Lang Syne). A guide to the
evening's entertainment listed the titles of these communal songs, as well as the titles of
contributions by several solo brethren vocalists. In addition, a number of humorous
pieces to be delivered by individual brothers was announced: 'Brother Percy Wilkinson
will dispense a little humour', read one item. The evening concluded with a long series
of 'male-bonding' toasts, to: The King and the Craft; The Grand Master; The President
of the Circle; The Vice-President of the Circle; The Blackpool Brethren; The
Committee of the Circle. At some later gatherings the list of toasts lengthened
considerably, glasses being raised to 'absent brethren' or 'past presidents'.

Meals were also an occasion for the speechmaking which librarians – rooted as
many of them were in the culture of books and of literary correctness – so much
relished. In 1931, J.M. Mitchell addressed the brethren in a particularly high-minded
fashion, attempting to spell out the ethos of the Circle, and linking this to the wider
social purpose of libraries and librarianship.[184] He spoke of members sharing duties as
both servants of the Craft and the library movement. His notes record the ideals of the
Craft, as he saw them: brotherhood, service, loyalty, sacrifice and constructiveness; the
clear inference being that these ideals were, in practice, transferred across into
professional library work. As members of both Craft and the library community, the aim
of 'library Masons' was to display 'a catholic attitude to all we serve', as well as a 'wide
knowledge of public interests, voluntary agencies ... the best books, and the best
periodicals'. A further duty of this wise, inner core of the library profession was to act,
said Mitchell, as a 'steadying influence in moments of stress.' The modern world had
arrived at such a moment, he implied. Contemporary social and economic ills, Mitchell
argued – he was speaking at the height of the depression – were caused by 'mass
production/distribution ... lack of foresight, and quick profits ... displacement of
individuality ... mass reliance replacing self-reliance [and] ... mass production of
thought'; and as for the remedies, he said, these were, firstly, 'the obvious ones' (which
he does not enlarge upon), and secondly, 'self education'. This perspective emphasises
the continuing endorsement of the public library as an institution founded on the ethos
of self-development rather than 'community', suspicion of which increased in the 1930s
as the spectre of mass, authoritarian, dystopian societies rapidly emerged.

The major implication of this evidence is the incongruity which it highlights
between the ethos of the public library and that of the Freemasonry which librarians
embraced. The public library was promoted by the profession as an open, rational and
democratic public sphere institution – at least this was the rhetoric. However, Mitchell's
belief, noted above, that the Craft similarly displayed a 'catholic attitude' is hardly
convincing in view of the exclusive, secretive nature of Masonry. Far from being a
democratic institution, it has been argued, Freemasonry has acted as a 'feudal pyramid',
whereby men of influence filter their values down through a layered social – or in this
case professional – structure.[185] Freemasonry has also been, pre-eminently, a means of
perpetuating male power. 'The real secrets of Freemasonry', reported J.S.M. Ward,

himself a Mason, in a fairly lengthy and detailed commentary on the practice in 1923:

do not have reference to physiological so much as to psychological differences which exist fundamentally between men and women – distinctions of inner qualities, which may be summed up and regarded as the foundations of true manliness in contrast to true womanliness ... The purpose of Freemasonry ... is to fit man, *as man*, to fulfill his duties in life.[186]

There is no reason to suggest that in embracing Masonry, librarians did not endorse this sexist outlook.

Certainly in the inter-war years, Freemasonry was a closed and prejudiced institution. Candidates for admission had to be professing Christians. Catholics, whose religion denounced the practice, were excluded. Exclusivity was further based on racist attitudes of the most virulent kind. Ward asked if Freemasonry was 'justified in refusing to admit coloured people?'[187] Answering this rhetorical question himself, he expressed the belief 'that there are certain races who are not yet sufficiently evolved intellectually, morally, and even spiritually, to be suitable for admission.'[188] Five reasons were given for justifying the exclusion of non-whites.[189] First, inadequate evolution to the same mental, moral or spiritual standard found among whites. Second, an inability, even among 'the far more evolved Hindoo', to work the ritualistic ceremonies properly and to run Lodges with appropriate self-restraint. Third, most non-whites were non-Christians. Fourth, 'the white races hold and must keep the mastery of the world' and admitting non-whites would damage this project. Fifth, other races held low opinions of women who, if they were admitted to a mixed-race Freemasonry, would not be treated as equals. Clearly, these beliefs did not coincide with the stated social ideals of Masonry at the time – good fellowship, charity and the search for truth[190] – and certainly not those of public librarianship; although it should be made clear that there is no direct evidence linking inter-war librarian Masons with virulent racism.

The existence of the Librarianship Circle gives impetus to the argument that the early development of public librarianship was to a large degree driven and overseen by a tight network of men forming a relatively exclusive inner core of the profession – similar to that seen in the United States.[191] The Circle both reflected and reinforced this exclusive network.[192] There is no direct evidence to suggest that the networking which the Circle undoubtedly assisted spawned nepotism or corruption. However, as one writer on Freemasonry notes, the practice is 'overwhelmingly concentrated in areas where there is strong competition for the available jobs, promotions and contracts'.[193] In public librarianship, although there existed a large number of library authorities, the tendency was for professionals to stay in post for many years, if not decades, thereby providing relatively few opportunities for promotion and personal career development – as the large number of candidates who came forward for vacant posts shows.[194] Further, the public librarianship network, like the Circle, was male dominated. Clearly, male networking in librarianship did not die a death when the Circle faded away in 1937. But the extent to which Masonry was linked with the network after this date is not known.

A more generous analysis of the 'networking' purpose of the Circle would be to consider the contribution it might have made to professional solidarity and collegiality, in particular the building of a shared ethical purpose. Masonry has always been to a large degree community-based, a local activity. But also, it has often been work that has brought brethren together.[195] This is obviously true in the case of the Circle, which offered an intimate forum for reinforcing purpose and principles in librarianship. However, to have engaged in such a sharing of aims and ideas, one would not, arguably, have had to engage in the rituals and secrecy of Masonic practices.

Civilisation and the Self

The language of community developed and spoken by the public library world in the 1920s and 1930s – even to an extent in the distorted form understood by library Masons – owed much to that part of the idealist tradition which stressed the importance of communal provision for individual self-development, which could in turn contribute to the social whole: empowered citizens being able to 'further enlarge the beauty of the common good.'[196] While utilitarian positivism came to influence intellectual life more and more in Britain between the wars, the idealist thought which had sustained the public library in the late Victorian and Edwardian periods was not extinguished. The classical frame of reference, in particular, remained omnipresent.[197] As the Fabian educator and political scientist Graham Wallas declared, as quoted in 1935 in a monograph celebrating a century of municipal progress in Britain, 'for the average English citizen ... the possibility of health, happiness, of progress towards the old Greek ideal of 'beautiful goodness', depends on his local government more than any other factor in his environment'.[198] The classical traditional was also invoked in respect of the new public library plan for Manchester, a scheme which was said to be renewing 'the age-old alliance between commerce and culture set forth as plainly in the history of modern Manchester as in the history of ancient Greece and Rome'.[199] And in Cambridge the chair of the library committee, in reverence to the Greek polis, believed citizens now had securely before them 'the vision of the ideal city', adding that: 'we who work in the Library have the same vision and the same high faith'.[200] In 1922 Harrogate Public Library announced its intention to adopt the slogan: 'The Public Library is for Public Service.'[201]

The Athenian vision found practical expression in the search for citizenship. In linking the notions of social and individual development, the Kenyon Report noted that: 'The principal underlying the library service is that it exists for the training of the good citizen. It must aim at providing all that printed literature can provide to develop his intellectual, moral and spiritual capabilities.'[202] In terms of the supply of newspapers in public libraries, and in keeping with the tradition of the classical public sphere, Kenyon further argued that there needed to be a variety of provision so that the *individual* did not become the slave of one stream of opinion and could make a worthwhile contribution to public affairs.[203] In Preston the public library was said to be helping to build the values of good citizenship and: 'The man or woman who achieves these things becomes a personality and a power in his or her sphere, and invariably a "leader" to a greater or lesser extent.'[204] Thus, through the medium of the public library, as with civic provision generally, community and individualism were neatly harmonised. Within this context it was possible to present each public library opened or improved as 'another spoke in the wheel of [social] progress';[205] but also as 'the great avenue, the great treasury, in which man may learn of *himself* [my emphasis]'.[206]

The discourse of public library promotion between the wars was redolent with appeals to the self. A guide to the use of the Blyth Public Library was entitled *On the Art of Pleasing Yourself.*[207] Public libraries in Glasgow were marketed with help from the prose of Arnold Bennett who wrote that in a public library one could take piecemeal the 'bricks of knowledge' and 'begin to build them into the edifice of your being'.[208] In the fight to open a library in Denbigh Town, the nineteenth-century mantra of self-culture was loudly chanted: learning achieved through the public library, it was argued:

must make for the moral and intellectual advancement of the citizen, for however excellent a school or college training may be, the best and most essential part of a man's education is often that which he gives himself, and it is this kind of education a Free Library service provides.[209]

The Scottish Library Association echoed this discourse of the self in 1933 when it stated: 'By the provision of full and authoritative information on all branches of knowledge, public libraries offer facilities of the utmost value in intellectual and vocational self-development.'[210]

A recurrent theme – no doubt stimulated by the technological and management innovations of the day – was the tension which librarians observed between the idealistic notion of inner self-realisation and the utilitarian impulse towards scientific, material progress. The Vice-Chancellor of Leeds University told a meeting of librarians in Leeds in 1921 that in 'an age of accurate and untiring specialism', people needed as an antidote 'an unremitting perseverance in self-culture', for this would 'make life happier and more full' – and it was up to librarians to help ensure this happened.[211] In Sheffield, one librarian warned against a preoccupation with 'the scientific achievements of modern man', for:

in following blindly the alluring path of scientific knowledge, man has completely forgotten, and neglected, the only subject worth considering at all, and that is – himself ... if civilised man is not to perish, he must turn from his boasted conquest of the world that surrounds him, and conquer his own body and soul. A public library can give the lead. It can turn from the provision of material fact, and concentrate on the awakening and stimulating of man's interest in himself.[212]

Further, anxieties in respect of the mass media were deeply felt by librarians. Hence library use was advocated as a means of reinforcing and protecting the self against attack from mass cultural corruption.

Regarding mass unemployment, sociologists between the wars produced a 'stages theory' of the psychology of the unemployed, believing that individuals who lost their jobs experienced a series of emotions, beginning with shock and anger and ending in resignation, waning of hope and social disengagement. Historians have questioned this process, pointing to a high degree of social participation by the unemployed in terms of leisure and political activism. Library use by the unemployed was also an expression of the desire to both socially engage and self-improve. Libraries and their books were at once means of escape and instruments of self-enlightenment. Thus, in Sheffield, between 1930 and 1932, the reading of library books on economics and politics increased threefold, reflecting people's desire to find out the reasons for the arrival of economic misery and increasing poverty, to situate their selves in the uncontrollable flow of human development.[213]

Although constantly warning of the dangers of over-indulgence in light fiction, librarians none the less defended stoutly the recreational role of the public library. Thus, Ernest Baker wrote:

We may adopt a utilitarian view of what the public library is for', wrote Ernest Baker, but 'we shall still retain recreation as one of the main objects, side by side with information and education.[214]

Libraries and their books continued to hold a non-material fascination for librarians: 'To me', wrote W.C.B. Sayers, 'a book is still a miracle of sorts, a collection of them is a modern Delphi, as much an oracular shrine as it is a laboratory'.[215] A similar perception of the role of the public library in hard times was evident in America where citizens flocking to borrow books in Cleveland were said to form 'a bread line of the spirit'.[216] The materialist-utilitarian notion of the library as laboratory, or workshop, was certainly encouraged in the 1920s and 1930s, but its idealist, poetic, individualist function was also very much to the fore in an era when for so many, especially the unemployed, the material rewards of life were proving elusive. In describing the public library as 'holy ground', Ramsay MacDonald echoed in 1930 the sentiments of most librarians at the time. The public library, he was reported to have told his audience on the site of Manchester's new central library building, was:

The dwelling-place of great spirits ... Without taking down a book we felt the presence of something that appealed to the noblest in us. When we had got the best out of that feeling, we could take down a book and find what we sought: knowledge or chaste imagination, wings to soar above sordid circumstance, stimulus to faith when the world was at its darkest.[217]

This mystical perception of the function of a public library bears witness to the enduring appeal of the institution as a vehicle for self-understanding and self-realisation. It also establishes the library as an institution sceptical of materialism,[218] and as a means of escape from the material world which, in the inter-war years, brought with it economic hardship, disquietening technological advance and, eventually, war.

Notes and References to Chapter Three

[1] J. Harris, *Private lives, public spirit: Britain 1870-1914* (Harmondsworth, 1994), 18.

[2] Sales of dailies increased from 3 million in 1918 to 10 million in 1939, the number of radio licenses from 125,000 in 1923 to 3 million in 1930: P. Clarke, *Hope and glory: Britain 1900-1990* (London, 1996), 116.

[3] A. Sparke, 'Nationalisation of public libraries', in R.G. Williams (ed.), *The librarians' guide 1923* (Liverpool, 1923), 9.

[4] R. McKibbin, *Classes and culture: England 1918-1951* (Oxford, 1998), v.

[5] Board of Education, Public Libraries Committee, *Report on public libraries in England and Wales* [Kenyon Report], Cmnd. 2868 (1927), 37.

[6] G.W. Byers, Harrogate's librarian, explained: 'A great deal is lost by the use of the word *Free*', because it encouraged people to look upon the public library as 'a mental soup kitchen where something can be obtained for nothing': 'Local opinions: Mr. G.W. Byers on the functions of a public library', *Knaresborough Post* (14 January 1922).

[7] L.S. Jast, 'Public libraries', in H.J. Laski, W.I. Jennings and W.A. Robson (eds.), *A century of municipal progress 1835-1935* (London, 1935), 245.

[8] L.S. Jast, *The library and the community* (London, 1939), 51.

[9] Centres of culture (25 November 1936), LANC.

[10] 'The reading habit', *John O'London's Weekly* (25 December 1936). In Bradford it was reported that: 'The tremendous strides which have been made in the education of the masses ... has created an ever-increasing desire for reading matter. The figures of subscribers to libraries are bigger each year': 'The value of books', *Bradford Telegraph and Argus* (3 July 1935). Blyth Public Library, *Report on the work of the year ending December 1936* (1937) noted the emergence of 'a body of readers more exacting in their requirements'.

[11] L.S. Jast, *Whom do ye serve? An address given at the jubllilee celebrations of the Gilstrap Public Library, Newark-on-Trent* (27 July 1933). Wigan's librarian, Arthur Hawkes, helped perpetuate the myth of the public library movement's working-class origins when he said that the 'idea in the minds of the early pioneers ... was the provision of a supply of literature for the unlettered masses': 'Training for library service', (22 August 1931), LANC.

[12] 'Infectious books', *Bradford Telegraph and Argus* (18 January 1934).

[13] T. Kelly, *Books for the people: an illustrated history of the British public library* (London, 1977), 145.

[14] Ibid., 167.

[15] 'The reading habit', *Bradford Telegraph and Argus* (21 July 1938).

[16] Glasgow Corporation Public Libraries, *What the Glasgow public library service offers the business man, the student, the general reader,* promotional leaflet (c. 1931).

[17] *Leeds Mercury* (4 June 1937).

[18] PWBT, A.E. Hinton to W.B. Thorne (10 November 1934).

[19] P. Sturges, 'The public library and its readers 1850-1900', in K. Manley (ed.), *Careering along with books* (London, 1996), a special issue of *Library History* 12. A.M. Black, *A new history of the English public library: social and intellectual contexts 1850-1914* (London, 1996), 170-179.

[20] Liverpool's librarian, George Shaw, said that people who used the city's reference libraries 'represented the best brains of the community': 'The use of a library', *Birkenhead News* (20 January 1922). On the other hand, in Manchester in 1930, it was reported that workers had been using reference facilities to research topics like medical history, infectious diseases, the Jacobite revolt of 1845 and 'Manchester in fiction': 'City library service', *Manchester City News* (2 August 1930).

[21] 'Libraries for the outer suburbs', *Manchester Guardian* (22 July 1937). Providing services to the suburbs also became a problem in country towns. In the mid-1930s the CUKT switched from funding county library work generally to assisting with library facilities on new housing estates in the counties: 'Libraries for new housing areas', *Times* (18 April 1936).

[22] Blyth Public Library, *Report*, op. cit., observed with regard to subscription libraries that there existed in the town 'an example of a book supply which *does* [my emphasis] always satisfy its patrons'.

[23] 'The new idea of public libraries', *Publishers' Circular* (6 March 1937).

[24] E. Edwards, *Free town libraries* (London, 1869).

[25] 'Appetite for books', *The Yorkshire Observer* (24 June 1932).

[26] County Borough of Sunderland, *Report on proposed scheme for the extension of the Central Library, Museum and Art Gallery building* (1934).

[27] 'Are public libraries dull?', *Harrogate Advertiser* (20 June 1936).

[28] SRO, ED 6/36/1, Questionnaire on Scottish County Libraries, reply from Aberdeenshire.

[29] SRO, ED 6/19, R.C.T. Mair to Scottish Education Department (3 July 1934). The order of popularity was found to be: adventure stories; school stories; fairy tales and mythology; historical tales; travel books; nature study books; books of a technical character, dealing with subjects like railways and stamp collecting.

[30] *Grapevine: Staff Magazine of the Nottinghamshire County Library Service* (June 1967).

[31] In the late-1930s a public library readership of 25-30% of the population was not uncommon in urban areas, but was rarely recorded in the counties: statistics reported in *LAR* 40 (October 1938), 538-539 and *LAR* 40 (November 1938), 583.

[32] 'Book lorries for villages', *Times* (8 September 1920).

[33] 'Great treasury of the public library', *Sussex Daily News* (8 July 1937).

[34] 'Development of rural life', *Yorkshire Post* (6 January 1922).

[35] 'Village library centres', *Manchester Guardian* (4 August 1931).

[36] In Kent each centre had its travelling library stock changed every 3 to 4 months: 'Travelling Library for East Kent', *Kentish Express* (18 March 1922).

[37] *Eastern Daily Express* (22 August 1930). For a fuller coverage of the development of the rural library service, see K.A. Stockham, *British County Libraries 1919-1969* (London, 1969).

[38] G. Orton, *An illustrated history of mobile library services in the UK* (London, 1980), 19-20.

[39] 'Travelling libraries', *Times* (5 March 1931).

[40] Ibid.

[41] Jast, *The library and the community*, op. cit., 145, described 'library extension' as 'a loose term employed in a loose way'; as originally employed 'it was meant to cover any and all activities which lay outside the work connected intimately with books – the essential service'.

[42] E.A. Baker, *The public library* (London, 1922), see Ch. 3: 'Library extension'. J. Minto, *A History of the public library movement in Great Britain and Ireland* (London, 1932), see Ch. 18: 'Libraries for the blind, children, hospitals and schools'. In Derby 188 braille books were circulated in one particular year: 'What Derby reads', *Derby Daily Express* (10 November 1930). Wigan Public Library subscribed to the National Library for the Blind, obtaining books for its blind readers through inter-library loan: 'Wigan public libraries', *Wigan Observer* (29 October 1921). In 1930 Bristol's children's library offered 12 half-hour talks on subjects ranging from 'Life in ancient Rome' to 'Explorers': 'Library talks', *Western Express* (4 August 1930). Gilstrap Public Library, in Newark-on-Trent, organised a book exhibition in the local gas showrooms: *Gilstrap Public Library Magazine* (October 1929).

[43] J.M. Mitchell, *The public library system of Great Britain and Ireland 1921-1923* [Mitchell Report] (Dunfermline, 1924), 49.

[44] 'Children of the East End on holiday', *The Star* (31 July 1930).

[45] Kelly, *Books for the people*, op. cit., 174.

[46] Kelly, *Books for the people*, op. cit., 159, notes that local government expenditure on libraries and museums increased by 45% between 1933 and 1939. The inter-war period as a whole saw a marked increase in government expenditure per se; in the years immediate to 1914 it averaged around 4% of GNP, whereas between the wars it never fell below 8%: G.C. Peden, *British economic and social policy: Lloyd George to Margaret Thatcher* (Oxford, 1985), 53-7.

[47] 'Travelling libraries', *Times* (5 March 1931).

[48] 'Books and men', *Empire News* (6 May 1930).

[49] Ibid.

[50] Jast, *The library and the community*, op. cit., see Ch. 10: The library grid.

[51] E.A. Baker, *The public library*, op. cit., see Ch. 5: 'A national library service'. J. Minto, A *history of the public library movement*, op. cit., see Ch. 11: 'Public library progress and policy'.

[52] Kenyon Report, op. cit., 148.

[53] Ibid., 149.

[54] Ibid., 38.

[55] Ibid. 150-151. For a contemporary assessment and description of co-operation, see L. Newcombe, *Library co-operation in the British Isles* (London, 1937). Newcombe was librarian of the National Central Library.

[56] PRO, ED 24/1197b, Memorandum on libraries in England and Wales to Board of Education (1 February 1924). The benefits of inter-library lending were stated by Sidney Webb, *LAR* 22 (1920), 118.

[57] Some public libraries received cash from the Special Areas Fund designed to stimulate business and demand in areas of high unemployment. In 1937 £15,000 was given to strengthen libraries in 'special areas', much of that year's allocation going to South Wales: PRO, ED 80/12.

[58] As discussed by J.M. Mitchell to Basil Anderton (15 October 1935), SRO, GD 281/13/84, and Ernest Savage to J.M. Mitchell (17 January 1935), SRO GD 281/13/84.

[59] SRO, GD 281/13/84, Basil Anderton to J.M. Mitchell (14 October 1935).

[60] SRO, GD 281/13/84, Ernest Savage to J.M. Mitchell (17 January 1935).

[61] SRO, GD 281/13/84, J.M. Mitchell to P.S.J. Welsford (27 October 1936). He gave a similar message to that year's Library Association's annual conference, held in Margate.

[62] SRO, GD 281/13/84, Basil Anderton to J.M. Mitchell (14 October 1935). PRO, ED 24/1197b, Board of Education memorandum (27 June 1924).

[63] 'New Norbury library', *Croydon Advertiser* (6 May 1931)

[64] Glasgow Corporation Public Libraries, *What the Glasgow public library service offers*, op. cit.

[65] 'Interchange of technical publications in Sheffield', *LAR* 40 (February 1938).

[66] B.O. Smith, 'Policy in the rural county', *LAR*, 40 (October 1938), 499.

[67] 'Books on holiday', *East End News* (22 June 1937).

[68] The Central Library supplied standard books (not text-books or fiction) to students who could not obtain them in any other way, borrowers merely paying the cost of postage: as explained in Skipton Public Library, *Catalogue of books* (December 1922).

[69] 'Outlier libraries' were generally in receipt of CUKT grants. See A.B. Hyslop, *The outlier policy of the Carnegie United Kingdom Trust* (1926), deposited in SRO, GD 281/10/54.

[70] Jast, 'Public libraries', op. cit., 250.

[71] 'All Yorkshire library plan', (9 January 1934), LANC. From 1931 onwards, in addition to the Northern Bureau, 7 other regional systems were established. A large part of the funding for the systems came from the CUKT.

[72] 'Libraries of the world: interchange of facilities', *Times* (4 August 1931). Evidence of international library co-operation can be found in SRO, GD 281/14/27.

[73] Use was being made of photostat technology by the 1930s: 'National library', *Cambrian News* (23 October 1931).

[74] Kenyon Report, op. cit., 37.

[75] Kenyon Report, op. cit., 39.

[76] Jast, 'Public libraries', op. cit., 254.

[77] Borough of Keighley Public Libraries, *Annual Report* (1931-1932), 5.

[78] 'Sheffield trade aided by library', *Sheffield Telegraph* (25 September 1930).

[79] 'How public libraries can help administrators', *Birmingham Post* (28 May 1931).

[80] 'The public library and business men', *Folkestone Express* (28 November 1936).

[81] 'Facts for all', *Daily News* (31 December 1921).

[82] 'Croydon public libraries', *Times* (15 August 1930). Examples given of enquiries to the commercial library in Glasgow included: import duties in South Africa, timetable of steamers to France, a telephone number in New York, the address of a manufacturer of wheels for toys: Glasgow Corporation Public Libraries, *What Glasgow public library service offers*, op. cit.

[83] 'Advisers in public libraries', *Daily Chronicle* (12 December 1921).

[84] 'The growth and usefulness of libraries', *Bury Guardian* (3 May 1930).

[85] 'A handmaid of commerce', *Manchester City News* (8 October 1921).

[86] 'The information complex', *Daily Express* (19 August 1930).

[87] 'The uses of advertisement', *LAR* 22 (July 1920), 220.

[88] 'Manchester reads more and more', *Manchester City News* (14 May 1931).

[89] 'Public libraries', *Yorkshire Post* (30 November 1921).

[90] 'Workless readers', *Westminster Gazette* (17 February 1921).

[91] 'Busy libraries', *Sheffield Independent* (18 March 1922).

[92] 'Books borrowed at Bradford', *Leeds Mercury* (22 August 1936). Although other reasons for falling issues were also given: cuts in book purchasing by libraries and competition from subscription libraries.

[93] 'Overcrowded reading room', *Liverpool Daily Courier* (3 December 1921).

[94] 'Shelter and reading matter', *Liverpool Daily Post* (3 December 1921).

[95] 'Overcrowding at the Brown Reading-room', *Liverpool Daily Post* (6 December 1921). Similarly, against the backdrop of the 1930s recession, some public libraries believed themselves to be gaining strength in areas like sociology and economics, as well as hobbies: 'New library service for Pannal', *Harrogate Advertiser* (1 October 1938).

[96] 'Our readers' views: unemployed's home from home', *Liverpool Evening Express* (9 May 1933).

[97] In Liverpool, between 1927 and 1933, over 4,000 people were sent to the Labour Exchange from the Labour Bureau in the Christian St. Reading Room: 'Our readers' views: unemployed's home from home', op. cit. In Glasgow the Council for Community Service in Unemployment was given permission to display its posters in libraries: Corporation of Glasgow Libraries Committee, Minutes (13 August 1934).

[98] 'Haunts of the workless', *Western Mail* (2 January 1922).

[99] Library supporters in Liverpool feared that good order would be threatened if cost-cutting proposals to withdraw the policeman who patrolled in front of the central library went ahead: 'Costly patrol', *Liverpool Daily Courier* (24 December 1921).

[100] 'The use of a library', *Birkenhead News* (20 January 1922).

[101] 'Free library problem', *Cambridge Daily News* (22 January 1931).

[102] 'Dome of silence', *North Eastern Daily Gazette* (18 January 1922).

[103] 'Let's have the axe', *Western Times* (14 February 1922).

[104] 'Books are drugs for slum dwellers', *Times* (2 July 1937). Also, 'Reading in the slums', *Liverpool Echo* (26 June 1937). Equating books with benign and beneficial addiction was a recurring theme, see 'Books taken as drugs', *Yorkshire Post* (11 September 1935).

[105] 'First public library', *Weekly Chronicle* (16 January 1932).

[106] J.H. Wellard, 'The significance to democracy of the public library', *LAR* 39 (January 1939), 10.

[107] 'Nottingham Central Library', *The [Nottingham] Journal* (26 October 1932).

[108] Words of the Vice-Chancellor of Liverpool University, reported in 'More books and fewer prisons', *Yorkshire Post* (20 September 1933).

[109] 'New library service for Pannal', op. cit.

[110] W.C.B. Sayers, Presidential address, *LAR* 40 (June 1938), 291.

[111] E.A. Baker, *The uses of libraries* (London, 1930), 308, preceding extracts 295, 302, 310. Baker listed examples of immoral literature he had noted at a railway station bookstall: *Eve and the Man*, *The Right to Motherhood*, *The Hour of Temptation*, *Mistress or Wife?*, *The Wife, the Husband and the Lover*, *Loose Love*, *One night*, *Three nights*, *Seven nights*, *Three weeks*, and *Cards, Women and Wine*.

[112] Jast, *Whom do ye serve?*, op. cit.

[113] 'Why should rates pay for cheap novels?', *Daily Sketch* (31 March 1937).

[114] 'The abuse of public libraries', *Children's Newspaper* (10 May 1930).

[115] 'Sheffield trade aided by library', *Sheffield Telegraph* (25 September 1930)

[116] H.S.A. Smith, 'Current views: wanted: facts about fiction', *LAR* 40 (April 1938).

[117] PRO, ED 24/1197b, Education Department memorandum.

[118] 'Hertford Public Library', *Hertford Mercury* (7 January 1922).

[119] *Yorkshire Evening Post* (29 May 1922).

[120] 'New library at Norbury', *Streatham News* (6 June 1931).

[121] In 1930 the public library in Welwyn Garden City issued 32,000 novels and 10,000 non-fiction books: 'Future of Garden City's library', *Welwyn Times* (20 August 1931).

[122] 'Book borrowers line up', *Hackney and Kingland Gazette* (4 January 1922). This trend was also noted in Wigan: 'Work of the Wigan libraries', *Wigan Observer* (27 September 1930).

[123] On Tyneside, it was said, 'there has been a considerable extension of private circulating libraries. These are supported not only by the employed section of the community but also by the unemployed. I have heard cases where six unemployed men have each paid the fee of twopence for a book from a private library, and during the week have each read the six books': SRO, GD 281/5/126, A.M. Struthers (Tyneside Council of Social Service) to J.M. Mitchell (11 July 1935).

[124] B.S. Rowntree, *Poverty and progress: a second social survey of York* (1938), 383-384.

[125] L. Montague Harrod, 'Is the literary taste of readers improving?', *Municipal Journal* (28 May 1937)

[126] C. Holland, 'Book borrowers and their habits', *Chamber's Journal* (April 1937).

[127] 'People reading more trash ... ' , *Leicester Evening Mail* (19 April 1937).

[128] *Nottingham Evening News* (5 June 1937).

[129] Gilstrap Public Library (Newark-on-Trent), *Good company* (August 1937); this publication being an example of the readers' magazines which many libraries issued.

[130] 'Public libraries and the gramophone', *Whitby Gazette* (17 July 1931).

[131] 'She tells stories seven days a week', *News Chronicle* (23 December 1938).

[132] 'Library has story hour for children', *Daily Express* (24 March 1937).

[133] 'Radio effects on reading', *Manchester Guardian* (6 April 1931). Groups met in a variety of public meeting-places, not just public libraries, and also in private houses.

[134] McKibbin, *Classes and culture*, op. cit., 459. Clarke, *Hope and glory*, op. cit., 117.

[135] Gilstrap Public Library (Newark-on-Trent), *Good company* (October 1935). Blyth Public Library, *Report*, op. cit., gave two reasons for the decline of the groups: poor subjects and equipment not equal to the task. Some talks, to be fair, were topical and relatively popular, such as the broadcast 'Time to spare', in which the unemployed were given the opportunity to speak about their hardships and anxieties: *BBC talks, April-June 1934*, 21.

[136] 'Reading – and radio', *Radio Times* (30 April 1937).

[137] 'Free library problem', *Cambridge Daily News* (22 January 1931).

[138] 'What libraries should be', *Walsall Advertiser* (2 March 1914).

[139] 'City's twelfth', *Bradford Telegraph and Argus* (4 March 1939).

[140] 'A Liverpool novelty', *Westminster Gazette* (15 February 1922).

[141] 'Cinema and reading', *Evening Standard* (13 January 1937).

[142] 'Novels losing favour: films', *Daily Telegraph* (6 July 1937).

[143] 'Cinema and reading', *Evening Standard* (13 January 1922).

[144] 'Sex, crime and mystery in literature', *Oswestry Advertiser* (16 June 1937). Indeed, in Sheffield a visible attempt was made to promote 'modern' literature by stocking 35 titles by D.H. Lawrence: J. Walker, 'Library censorship', *New Statesman and Nation* (5 December 1936)

[145] M.F. Stieg, *Public libraries in Nazi Germany* (Tuscaloosa, Alabama, 1992).

[146] 'No more eyesore', *Yorkshire Observer* (30 October 1936).

[147] W.A. Munford, 'Current views: the public library and the left', *LAR* 40 (February 1938), 74.

[148] 'Choosing their books', *Daily Mail* (4 January 1922). Wandsworth Public Libraries banned the Daily worker in 1937: 'Daily Worker not for Wandsworth', *Streatham News* (23 July 1937); as did Harogate Public Library in 1934: *Harrogate Advertiser* (16 February 1934). Glasgow's library committee accepted Guy Aldred's *Socialism and Parliament*, but rejected the *Blackshirt*, periodical of the British Union of Fascists: Glasgow Corporation Library Committee, Minutes (13 August 1934, 10 September 1934).

[149] 'Censorship of books', *The Leeds Mercury* (13 September 1935).

[150] In 1921 Lambeth Public Library found that of 26 libraries it surveyed only 2 practiced blacking-out: 'Betting news in borough libraries', South London Press (2 December 1922).

[151] Blyth Public Library, *Report*, op. cit.

[152] E.g. *Best books of 1929: selected and classified on the Dewey Decimal system of classification*, new series, volume 1 (London, 1929). Also, W.A. Munford, *Three thousand books for a public library: some significant and representative works for a basic stock* (London, 1939).

[153] 'Sneering at public libraries', *South London Press* (6 March 1931).

[154] Bad manners and behaviour in libraries was an enduring theme: 'Library manners', *Western Press* (25 September 1930). Complaints continued in some places about newspapers being monopolised by the racing fraternity: 'Public library hint', *Bradford Telegraph and Argus* (17 November 1932).

[155] 'Why boys read "bloods" ... Mr. Jast grieves over modern amusements', *Halifax Guardian* (7 March 1922).

[156] 'The library services', *Western Daily Press* (12 May 1930).

[157] 'The use of a library', *Birkenhead News* (20 January 1922).

[158] 'Lending libraries', *Manchester Guardian* (8 July 1930)

[159] 'The Minet Library', *Brixton Free Press* (9 December 1921).

[160] 'Our national character: a broadcast ... 1933', in S. Baldwin, *This torch of freedom* (London, 1935), 14.

[161] 'On England and the west', in S. Baldwin, *On England* (London, 1926), 5.

[162] Ibid., 9.

[163] Ibid., 6-7.

[164] Jast, 'Public libraries', op. cit., 259.

[165] 'Bad books on the rates', *My Magazine* (November 1930).

[166] W.C.B. Sayers, *The revision of the stock of a public library* (London, 1929), 12-13.

[167] 'Clare Corner at Northampton', *Peterborough Advertiser* (28 October 1921).

[168] A.S. Cooke, 'Village library services', *LAR* 40 (February 1938). B.O. Smith, 'Policy in the rural county', op. cit., 499. 'Great treasury of the public library', *Sussex Daily News* (8 July 1937).

[169] Two reasons in support of Lodge status were put forward. First, to cater for librarians who had been Freemasons in the past but on having moved to another part of the country had not been able to join a Lodge in their new locality. Second, it was believed that many librarians wanted to be Freemasons but wished to avoid making local connections for various reasons. Memorandum on the formation of a Lodge by the Librarianship Masonic Circle, by Richard Wright, November 1929. This and all other archive items noted here relating to the Librarianship Masonic Circle between 1926 and 1938 are to be found in SRO, GD 281/13/44.

[170] J.M. Mitchell to C.R. Sanderson (18 September 1926).

[171] There is evidence in the records of only one meeting additional to the annual conference having taken place – in London, in February 1929. Circular from C.R. Sanderson (31 January 1929).

[172] J.M. Mitchell to C.R. Sanderson (18 September 1926).

[173] Librarianship Masonic Circle Committee Report, by George Bolton.

[174] C.R. Sanderson to J.M. Mitchell (6 April 1927).

[175] C.R. Sanderson to the membership of the Circle (14 July 1928).

[176] E.g. in 1928 brethren had intended to invite the President of the Library Association to be President of the Circle also, until it was discovered that he was not a member of the Craft. C.R. Sanderson to J.M. Mitchell (3 July 1928).

[177] C.R Sanderson, Circular to membership of Librarianship Masonic Circle (17 January 1927).

[178] Ballinger's opinion related by C.R. Sanderson to J.M. Mitchell (24 August 1927).

[179] Three lists are deposited in the records of the Circle: those who attended the Craft dinner in Leeds in 1926; a typed list of members circulated by C.R Sanderson (14 July 1928); and a printed list produced for the gathering in Blackpool in September 1928.

[180] Mitchell Report, op. cit.

[181] C.R. Sanderson to J.M. Mitchell (19 September 1928).

[182] *The Librarian and Book World* 5:9 (April 1915), 260.

[183] The programme is simply entitled 'Librarianship Masonic Circle, Blackpool, 1928.'

[184] J.M. Mitchell, Manuscript notes on a speech to the 1931 gathering of the Librarianship Masonic Circle.

[185] M. Short, *Inside the brotherhood: further secrets of the Freemasons*, (London, 1989), 136.

[186] J.S.M. Ward, *Freemasonry: its aims and ideals* (London, 1923), 139, quoting J.H. Fussell, in Dudley Wright, W*omen and Freemasonry*.

[187] Ward, op. cit., 107.

[188] Ward, op. cit., 154.

[189] Ward, op. cit., 148-9.

[190] Ward, op. cit., 53.

[191] W. Wiegand, *Irrepressible reformer: a biography of Melvil Dewey* (Chicago, 1996), 48, explains that leading pioneers of librarianship in America were products of a socio-economic and cultural value system of white, Anglo-Saxon, protestant, middle-class males born and bred in the north-east of the country. It would probably be true to say, however, that the socio-cultural backgrounds of leading early librarians in Britain were more varied than this.

[192] Sometimes the network extended into the international sphere. C.R. Sanderson, who had left to work in Canada in 1929, contacted J.M. Mitchell by telegram (22 February 1931) to ask if he could arrange for the Grand Senior Warden of Ontario to attend a Scottish Rite or Craft on his visit to Britain, adding that the warden was a 'gentleman ... good speaker ... splendid ritualist ... and commodore [of a] yacht club.'

[193] B. Rogers, *Men only: an investigation into men's organisations* (London, 1988), 78-9.

[194] This is not to say that mobility was non-existent. Frank Atkinson, *Librarianship* (London, 1974), 90, commented that: 'Moving on may well be a sort of English fever. A generation ago [mid-century] one of the more lively aspects of the British public library scene was the continuous criss-crossing of librarians as they travelled south to north, west to east, highlands to midland, in pursuit of better-graded jobs.'

[195] Short, *Inside the brotherhood*, op. cit., 124.

[196] Lord Snell, 'The town council', in Laski, Jennings and Robson, *A century of municipal progress*, op. cit., 72.

[197] J. Harris, in E.F. Biagani (ed.), *Citizenship and community: liberals, radicals and collective identities in the British Isles 1865-1931* (Cambridge, 1996), 354.

[198] Laski, Jennings and Robson, *A century of municipal progress*, op. cit., 11.

[199] 'Books and men', op. cit.

[200] W.H. Swift, 'The work and influence of the borough library', *Cambridge Public Library Record*, 1:1 (November 1926), 7.

[201] 'Local opinions ... ', op. cit.

[202] Kenyon Report, 39-40.

[203] Kenyon Report, 40.

[204] *Preston Guardian* (28 January 1933), deposited in SRO, GD 281/81/16.

[205] J.M. Mitchell opening a library in Clacton Town Hall, LANC (February 1931 to January 1932).

[206] 'Great treasury of the public library', op. cit.

[207] Blyth Public Library, *Report*, op. cit.

[208] Glasgow Corporation Public Libraries, *What the Glasgow Public Library Service offers*, op. cit.

[209] 'Is a public library needful', *Denbighshire Free Press* (7 January 1922).

[210] SRO, ED 6/19, Scottish Library Association, Memorandum on Scottish Library Legislation (1933)

[211] 'Public libraries and education', *Yorkshire Observer* (1 December 1921).

[212] 'A public library: what is its chief aim and function?', *The Wicket: Magazine of the Sheffield Public Libraries Staff Association*, 6:1 (April 1936).

[213] B.J. Elliott, 'The social activities of the unemployed in an industrial city during the Great Depression', *Transactions of the Hunter Archaeological Society* 16 (1990). K. Nicholas, *The social effects of Unemployment on Teeside, 1919-39* (Manchester, 1986), 149-50, 184-5, 210.

[214] Baker, *The uses of libraries*, op. cit., 308.

[215] Sayers, 'Presidential address', op. cit., 291.

[216] 'Your library in 1931', news cutting deposited in SRO, GD 281/14/22.

[217] 'Prime minister in Manchester: ceremony at the new library', *Manchester Guardian* (7 May 1930).

[218] 'The poet's poor pay: librarian deplores materialism', *Yorkshire Observer* (20 August 1935).

CHAPTER FOUR

Bombs and Blueprints

1939-1945

Much more than in the First World War, between 1939 and 1945 the public library was able to show its worth as an institution of the people. After 1918, the public library continued to increase its presence on the cultural and social landscapes of Britain. The Second World War did nothing to interrupt that trend. On the contrary it accelerated it. Despite financial stringency, book shortages, the removal of staff to the armed forces and the considerable time and accommodation taken up in discharging civil defence and other official non-library duties, the war provided a marvellous opportunity for an expansion and extension of the public library service. In terms of policy-making, it acted as a powerful catalyst for planning reform, encouraging librarians to design and discuss radical blueprints for a modern, more popular and more efficient post-war public library system.

Wartime Damage and Shortages

As predicted before the war,[1] aerial warfare took its toll in terms of destroyed stocks and buildings. In the spring of 1941 branches were completely destroyed in Bristol and Chelsea. Around 100,000 books perished when Coventry's central library was bombed: it was reported in June 1941, in fact, that in the town 'the Central Library and many branches have been completely wiped out and the library service is almost at a standstill'.[2] Later in the year 75,000 volumes were lost in Plymouth and in Yarmouth the library remained open to the elements for several months, the roof having been blown off.[3] In 1942 Exeter's new library, built as recently as 1929 and described as 'one of the most palatial libraries in the country', suffered severe damage.[4] Further damage followed as a result of V1 flying bomb and V2 rocket attacks in 1944 and 1945: libraries in Bermondsey and Hackney being completely destroyed and others in Bethnal Green, Hampstead and Leyton receiving severe damage.[5] In total, between 1939 and

1945, some 50 branch and central libraries were destroyed or seriously damaged and around 750,000 books lost to enemy action.[6] For at least one public library regular, however, bombs actually improved the quality of his public library use: 'The library [in Eastbourne] received a direct hit in about 1942 and was destroyed, it soon re-opened in a large private house at the bottom of the road we lived in so I would go down to it on my own, it was also on my route to and from school.'[7]

Book shortages held back the public library during the war and was noted by the public. 'As a user of the Harrogate Public Library I can truthfully say that in the six weeks I have been such, I have never seen a new book [novel] ... As for the biography section, I do not believe a new biography can ever have reached that moth-eaten collection since the Dark Ages.'[8] It was estimated that by early 1942 the price of library purchases of books, periodicals and newspapers had increased by 10% since 1939 (despite the exemption of books from wartime purchase tax in 1940) and that of rebinding by 20% in the same period.[9] By the end of 1942 book prices were 30% above their pre-war level.[10] The scarcity of books was made worse, said librarians in Croydon, by the irresponsible behaviour of some readers who vandalised books, or carried books through the rain without protection, or who read at meals and squandered 'part of their meagre rations of preserves and fats on the leaves of books they have borrowed'![11] Shortages of books became more apparent as the war dragged on.[12] In October 1941 Rochdale Public Library Reported that 'of 139 titles still on order ... 72 are now quite unobtainable as a result of the blitz'.[13] In response to the crisis some libraries mounted salvage campaigns – such as the large salvage drive held in Bristol in 1942[14] – to attract donations from the public and from private collections.

Conscription decimated the public library's professional workforce. Librarians protested at the government's extraction of trained library personnel at a time when the volume of library service demanded by a public which was reading as never before was steadily increasing.[15] By 1945, nearly 2000 members, or approximately one-third, of the Library Association were serving in the Forces.[16] Bristol public library lost 9 members of staff to the Forces in the first six months of the war.[17] In London one-fifth of library personnel had been removed from service by September 1940.[18] The Library Association complained that 'gentlemen with academic and literary backgrounds have been put in charge of small county branches and the results are far from satisfactory or efficient'.[19] The war curtailed professional activities – such as book selection and cataloguing – considerably. 'All of us know', remarked Charles Nowell in 1944, 'that with every year of war the libraries are less and less an ordered array and more and more a collection of books'.[20] Yet, as in the case of a many other public services, the war generated a number of positive library developments: increased demand, energetic extension and outreach work, a new idealism in the library profession and, despite a lingering attachment to cultural control, a more popular appeal. 'Did any of us imagine for a moment that we should be so favourably placed after such a long struggle?', remarked Nowell a few months before the end of the war.[21]

Interest from Government and the Voluntary Sector

At a political level the Library Association operated pro-actively in the war, cultivating beneficial links with the Board of Education and the Ministry of Information, and winning backing from the Ministry of Labour. The Association's efforts to obtain support for the library service were made easier in the Second, than in the First World War, by virtue of the fact that after 1918 public libraries had become a much more familiar feature of social and cultural life, not least in the counties.[22]

At the very start of the war, the Library Association forged close links with the Ministry of Information. The Ministry was anxious to know that 'active steps were being taken to alleviate the boredom and lack of enthusiasm which a "static" winter [in 1940-41] would doubtless involve';[23] and it acknowledged public libraries as a means of distributing Ministry of Information material and providing premises for meetings and display areas for Ministry posters and other information. Librarians welcomed this type of war service and hoped that, by being enthusiastic in agreeing to undertake it, public library premises would not be requisitioned indiscriminately for purposes which had no informational or cultural dimension and which would prevent libraries from going about their normal business. As 'experts in indexing and filing and the maintenance of records', librarians also presented their credentials to the Home Office as willing candidates for undertaking such tasks as food control and national registration.[24]

From very early on in the war, unlike in the First World War, the government recognised public libraries as an antidote to psychological stress on the home front. In 1940, at the behest of a Ministry of Labour anxious to improve the welfare of industrial workers in the interest of production, the Board of Education issued a memorandum to library authorities, calling their attention to the importance of maintaining and, if possible, extending their services.[25] The memorandum (Circular No. 242) explained that:

> The public libraries afford recreation and instruction to vast numbers of readers and, when the hours of darkness come and the possibilities of outdoor recreation are less, increasing numbers will find in books a relief from the strain of war work and war conditions. Nor is the service which the public libraries can render confined to the supply of books. The library is often, and might still more generally become, a centre for the organisation of study circles, listening groups, play reading circles and similar activities. It is hoped, therefore, that all [local] authorities in the exercise of their powers under the Libraries Act will do all they can to enable their libraries to make the fullest possible contribution to a service which may so materially assist the national effort.[26]

The effect of the memorandum on the ground is difficult to gauge. Some library authorities clearly viewed it as an endorsement of existing or planned extension work.[27] Others regretted not being able to do all that the government was asking of them: 'No one will question', it was stated in Burnley in response to the memorandum, that:

libraries are playing their part with the splendid facilities they have at their disposal, and the decision of the committee to allow two books to each borrower ... illustrates their appreciation of the fact that in reading many people obtain the amusement and relaxation they need during the winter months. What the [library] committee regret is that they cannot go a step further and organise study circles and listening groups ... This is on account of the fact that the rooms which could have been utilised for such purposes have been taken over by the Ministry of Food.[28]

There is also evidence of some friction between the Ministry of Labour and librarians, the latter accusing the former of using labour exchanges to poach female library assistants for work of 'national importance'.[29] In general, however, librarians were pleased that 'a ray of light has crept into Whitehall', viewing the declared interest of a major government department as an opportunity to advance the library service.

Interest in the role libraries could play in raising morale was also shown by the Central Consultative Council of Voluntary Organisations (CCCVO) which was concerned that 'adequate facilities for recreation are available for workers engaged in war work'. It duly hoped to see promoted 'all means whereby workers can be assisted to make pleasant and profitable use of their leisure time'; facilities, for example, 'for concerts, play-reading, amateur dramatics, holidays, education, group discussions and physical training'.[30] The Council recognised the role libraries could play in meeting this objective, and its Recreation Group officially received a note on the matter from the Library Association. This note is worth quoting at length as it illustrates the extent to which libraries were prepared to *engage* in wartime society:

The services which public libraries, municipal and county, can render ... are in the main an intensification of their normal peace-time activities. The provision of a wide range of books, cultural, vocational, recreational, is made, but further efforts can and should be made to bring these facilities to the notice of the public. As a corollary, the library is a natural centre for the organisation of study circles, listening groups, play-reading societies, natural history and topographical study, etc., since all these activities can be carried out with books and guidance on the use of books close at hand. Machinery also exists through these libraries for obtaining sets of books for class use and special books for advanced study. One special problem may be that factory development has caused a growth of population in otherwise undeveloped districts and it may also be that circumstances of time or distance may make it difficult for factory employees to attend the library. In such cases it should be possible to arrange for deposit stations at the factory, the books being provided by the appropriate public library and exchanged at intervals, the issue of books being in the hands of a volunteer or a member of the factory welfare staff under the supervision of a qualified librarian, who would arrange a periodical exchange of books and regular visits for contact and advice.[31]

With regard to deposit stations in factories, the note went on to point out that these may in some areas place a great strain on local library services and that some extra funding would perhaps be necessary.

In fact the Library Association further backed away from the idea of providing factory collections when its note was formally discussed at a meeting of the CCCVO's Recreation Group. At this meeting the Library Association also distanced itself from Sunday opening of public libraries, as this would inevitably require staffing by volunteers, an arrangement which in the past 'had not been found to be satisfactory'.[32] It is unclear how many, if any, book deposit collections were set up in wartime factories.

The Reading Boom

War brought with it a boom in reading, from which the public library benefited accordingly. The escalation in public library use did not occur everywhere. Some centres saw a fall in issues. In country areas, where many service points were in schools and institutes that could not be blacked-out, restrictions on opening hours reduced demand.[33] However, in general, the black-out and air raids produced a minor revolution in public library opening hours: earlier opening, reduced half-day closing and, despite the reservations of the Library Association noted above, some Sunday opening. Further flexibility in operating services was evident in the availability of extra lending tickets and the prolongation of loan periods.

The reading boom, paralleling the phoney war itself, took time to get underway. With regard to general reading, in early 1940 Mass-Observation referred to 'a static and slow-changing habit'.[34] By October 1940, however, the organisation was able to report a large increase in the reading of books from public libraries: 'Most libraries, particularly the better class sort, report a shortening of the time people retain a book, and also an increase in the number of books taken out together.' An increase in non-fiction reading was observed. Libraries which stayed open during air raid warnings or which supplied two books on a single ticket were said to be doing especially well. Issues were also increased by people whose libraries had been bombed and who, because they now had to travel long distances to get their books, made the most of their journies to substitute libraries by borrowing more than usual.[35]

The growth in popularity of libraries during the war, and the reasons for it, were outlined in Keighley:

The outbreak of war and the consequent 'black-out' conditions have been responsible in a way for the increase in reading ... The curtailment of hours in the first few weeks of the war meant a decline in issues, but from the time normal hours were resumed there has been a steady increase in all classes of reading. It is rather early as yet to determine what effect the war will have on libraries and reading, although the general indications are, that with the restrictions on social activities and entertainment, reading will increase, and libraries will become a very important service in the lives of the people during wartime. It is needless here to recapitulate the benefits that are to be obtained from the use of books, but it cannot be too strongly emphasised that all the arguments for public libraries are one hundredfold stronger now than in normal times.[36]

The reading boom appeared to maintain its momentum throughout the war: 'Blitz or no Blitz – the demand for books goes up', trumpeted the *Daily Express* in 1944.[37] In 1942-3 Hyde Public library achieved a record number of issues, an increase of 10% over the previous year.[38] Large queues were regularly seen at Harrogate Public Library in 1943.[39] That same year, Sowerby Bridge Public Library was able to announce that 38% of the population were registered borrowers, compared with around 30% before the war.[40] In 1944 record annual issues were reported by Accrington and Gateshead.[41]

The early months of the war even witnessed the opening of new premises in some places. In Huddersfield one user contrasted starkly the town's pre-war library and the new building opened in April 1940: 'The old library was a poky, smelly place. It was so dark in places you could hardly see the titles of the books. Here it is all so different; plenty of light and room and plenty of fresh air.'[42] Despite the hostilities, resources were found for a new lending library in Cardiff, accommodated in what had previously been the central library's reading room.[43] However, sparkling new wartime buildings were mostly the result of plans laid before September 1939[44] and were soon to become a thing of the past as financial cuts began to bite. The new library in Swindon (1943) was one of the few new buildings both planned and opened during the war, the town having adopted the Public Libraries Acts only the previous year.[45]

The public library was believed to have an important role to play in relieving the stresses and strains of war. The editor of the *Library Association Record* wrote in the depths of the national crisis of May 1940 that: 'Books in war time can be a refuge into which we make our way to escape the slings and arrows of outrageous conflict ... a storehouse from which to draw sure knowledge and rich emotion to clarify our minds and strengthen our souls for the tasks to which we have set our hand.'[46] In Halifax it was claimed that: 'Books are the most important arm in the nation's civil defence programme. The reading of books helps the public to combat the black-out, to escape from the stress and strain of war news and war work, and to tide over the waiting, watching hours so much a part of present day conditions.'[47] In Preston it was recognised that:

The chief need for the majority of people in this period of strain and anxiety is for distraction. A few of the bolder and more restless spirits find it outside, but a far greater number put their trust in the familiar atmosphere and well-tried security of the fireside. To these a book to fit the mood is a priceless boon. The libraries provide the medium through which this morale-reinforcing relief can be obtained.[48]

In Lowestoft a local newspaper told its readers: 'As a means of passing the time between the air-raid warning and the all-clear signal, as an antidote to grievous news, as a source of inspiration, books are a boon to all, playing an important part in educating public opinion, and maintaining the stout heart of the people.'[49]

The increased demand for books came from several sources. Children, deprived of playing in the streets in the evenings, were seen to be turning to reading instead. Soldiers' wives, it was said, were finding in literature an antidote to loneliness.[50] Moreover, absent husbands enabled the average married woman, announced H.L. McGill, a female librarian in Manchester, to replace her household chores with more leisurely pursuits like reading: 'For the first time since she married, she can look forward to an evening of leisure, in which a pile of darning and mending does not reproach her idle fingers.'[51] People on civil defence and other official out-of-hours duties looked to reading to while away the time. Collections of books found their way into Report Centres, Auxiliary Fire Service Stations, First Aid Posts and Air Raid Wardens' Posts. London's first mobile library service was put into operation by the Borough of St. Pancras in 1941, its main aim being to serve the needs of civil defence workers, balloon barrage units and the Home Guard.[52]

The reading boom was not confined to local residents but resulted in part from the displacement of large sections of the population. It was reported in Halifax that good use had been made of the book stock by evacuees and refugees, as well as soldiers billeted in the town.[53] Evacuation was looked upon as an opportunity and a challenge as much as a problem.[54] After a month of war Luton Public Library reported that 15,000 children had entered the town, with a consequent increase in the use and popularity of local libraries.[55] By the end of 1939, under pressure from overburdened libraries in areas receiving evacuated children, the Government had begun to acknowledge that: 'The importance of reading to children transferred from their homes to the unfamiliar environment of reception areas has become more pressing with the approach of winter and the long dark evenings.' Hence it was proposed that financial help be given to libraries sending books and to libraries in reception areas.[56]

Public libraries in Salford, Manchester and Liverpool forwarded books directly to the schools where evacuated children were located. It was also reported that branches in the Manchester area were supplying sets of books to military and civil defence units of various types (500 books to one particular military camp), while 'visitor' members of the armed forces were also given the same borrowing facilities as local civilians (one branch had issued 226 tickets to members of the RAF stationed nearby).[57] 'The men on the balloon barrage have a special need for books', remarked Shoreditch's librarian, having arranged an 'inter-availability' scheme with 134 other towns to facilitate loans to displaced personnel.[58]

As people in Britain's large cities took to shelters for protection against air raids, the library service was gifted a sudden opportunity to extend itself to what was in effect a captive audience. Mass Observation noted that: 'Librarians have often been asked lately for something to read in the shelter. They think people are settling down to their nocturnal dwellings and [the shelters] are now providing light good enough to read.'[59] Librarians also took services directly *to* readers in their shelters. Library services to London 'shelterers' in particular, especially in Underground stations, are well documented. In October 1941 a service point offering a stock of 4000 volumes, operated by regular library staff working on a rota system, was opened in Bethnal Green Underground station. Shelters other than Underground stations also had libraries; by January 1941, for example, collections had been set up in 49 shelters in St. Marylebone. Shelter libraries were also to be found in Shoreditch, St. Pancras, Deptford, Islington, Westminster and Richmond-on-Thames.[60] These underground environments were highly conducive to pastimes like reading,[61] the library collections themselves aiming broadly 'to maintain the ordinary man's freedom of thought, spirit and comment'.[62]

Library services in shelters appeared to underline the public library's community role. It was observed that shelterers had developed 'a unique style of existence' and a 'social life has grown up, with a code of behaviour embodying rules for the better ordering of this new life'. In such an ordered culture,[63] the rationally oriented public library service could not help but flourish. The environment also suited the public library's missionary, idealistic credentials. Like clerics, librarians were quick to see the possibilities which the shelters offered, endorsing the strategy that: 'If the people can't come up to us, then we must go down to them.'[64]

But what were people reading in shelters and elsewhere that accounted for the wartime boom in library activity? In the opening months of the war, librarians observed an increased interest in books about current affairs, although a falling off in this interest occurred in early 1940.[65] A. Piper, librarian of Richmond (Surrey), noted a sudden demand for books on 'the political realities of Europe, the Great War, on the ethics of war and on the ideologies of the totalitarian states'.[66] Increased interest was noted regarding practical books – for example, information was required to respond to public information initiatives, such as the 'Dig for Victory' campaign.[67] Thus, borrowing from the work of Kipling, Tottenham Public Library entitled its gardening list, 'Dig till you gently perspire'.[68] The demand for 'books on engineering, mathematics, machine tools and aircraft maintenance', believed the librarian Edmund Corbett, 'is also a wartime phenomenon highly encouraging to the librarian and essentially work of national importance'.[69] It was believed that readers were realising 'as never before the value of the non-fiction stock of a public library'.[70] The increase in serious reading, although not to the detriment of levels of fiction consumption which rose rapidly, was reflected in the growing demand for Hitler's *Mein Kampf*.[71] In Keighley it was observed that: 'The standard of reading in Keighley remains high, and a marked feature of the year's reading has been the interest shown in international affairs. The demand for books of a 'crisis' nature has been most noticeable.'[72]

However, for all the usual celebration of serious reading, the vast majority of public library 'business' in the war remained in the area of imaginative literature. 'Nearly all the evidence points to the fact that fiction reading goes on the same, war or no war', noted a Mass Observation report in 1940.[73] Consequently, librarians remained as vigilant and as critical as always with regard to the people's reading. G.R. Gatland, librarian of Clapham, believed that the trend in reading was towards a lower class of literature: earlier in the century books were fewer but much better.[74] Another librarian observed that: 'As literacy has increased, so has the standard of light reading depressed itself to something approaching the nadir of imbecility.'[75] The librarian of West Sussex warned of the dangers of 'dope reading' – that is, 'reading material whose effect was in the long run to put the mind of its readers to sleep' – and recommended that 'all who wished to take their reading seriously, to apply themselves, as a matter of discipline as well as enjoyment, to the classics'.[76] Librarians were pleased to announce that the classics remained popular in Harrogate.[77] In Liverpool, although the classics were in demand, the greater demand was for 'a lighter type of reading – especially detective,

Western and romantic stories'. This was said to be appropriate in the circumstances, to offset 'the dreariness of the blackout years', but it was hoped that after the war readers' tastes would be uplifted, the war having served a purpose in getting new readers started.[78]

Some librarians believed that the quality of reading generally was in decline, complaining that 'bookstalls are flooded with worthless trash, not worthy of the dignity of print'.[79] Particular worry was expressed about teenage magazines. The CUKT contacted the Library Association about the dangers of 'doubtful' juvenile literature, which was said to fall into two types: the pseudo-health type (such as *Health and Strength* and *Health and Efficiency*) and the 'erotic blood' type (such as *Red Letter*, *Crystal*, *Miracle* and *Family Star*). A further example from the second category was *Red Star Weekly*, in which one issue (28 October 1944) contained a story entitled 'One girl, so many men', about a nineteen-year-old girl who found herself shipwrecked with a boat-load of men, most of them Nazis.[80]

The consumption of popular literature in the Armed Forces appears to have deeply concerned the library establishment.[81] In the same way that reading was deemed useful for maintaining morale on the home front, so also in the Armed forces books and other literature were regarded as a means of maintaining psychological stability. 'If you had seen, as I have seen on my many visits to the forces', wrote Winston Churchill in support of a drive to collect books for the troops, 'the need for something to read during the long hours off duty and the pleasure and relief when that need is met, you would look, and look again, through your bookshelves and give what you can.'[82]

Early in the war, the Library Association put forward what was described as a 'grandiose plan' for library provision for the Services, which commanders rejected as 'unsuitable to the conditions of modern war'. The Library Association's aim had been to set up a network of properly equipped libraries for the Services at home and abroad, 'with all the usual paraphernalia of tickets, records, etc', run by librarians currently in the Services who would be relieved of all other military duties. 'Consideration of man-power, accommodation and security and difficulties of administration made such a scheme impracticable', said Forces' chiefs; moreover 'there was a danger of the Forces being given what was thought good for them and not what they wanted'.[83] A list of recommended reading for the Forces – 'Books for the Services' – was criticised by some as highbrow and wholly inappropriate.[84] The informal supply of books to the Forces that ensued no doubt irritated library leaders who had hoped to see a centrally and bureaucratically controlled system along the lines seen in public libraries.

Some libraries continued to censor what they considered to be anti-social or anti-war material. In the summer of 1940 Stepney Public Libraries banned the Communist newspaper *The Daily Worker*, an act which one observer described as a 'reactionary and anti-democratic measure' and which led him to conclude that 'there is obviously a movement on foot to stifle all criticism'.[85] The newspaper was also banned by Merthyr Public Libraries on the grounds that, like the Fascist press, it was intent on destroying democracy – a decision which engendered similar protests to those in Stepney.[86]

Running parallel with the traditional propensity for cultural control, however, was a new sense of liberation about the public library. A radio talk on the BBC's Home Service by the librarian of Falkirk attempted to assure the public of a new openness in public library service:

Indeed, it's just possible that you feel a public library is rather a sombre place – cheerless, inhuman. The rows of books on the shelves seem a bit alarming – surrounded by them you become bewildered. You want something to read, but you are lost in a maze. You want to look up a reference – you don't know how to start. Now this is all wrong. Your library exists to help you. It's a social service for your benefit. The librarians are there to answer your questions.[87]

Pledges such as this had been made before, but the war somehow gave them an added, genuine meaning.

Other Responsibilities

Surprisingly, the exigencies of war enabled the public library to dispense a range of services and fulfil a number of roles beyond its 'normal' remit. At the start of the war, in Poplar, the 'circulation of books was varied by the distribution of gas helmets for babies and small respirators for young children, hundreds of these being fitted and handed out by the libraries' staff over a period of six weeks'. In addition, for much of October 1939 the majority of the staff were engaged in writing ration books. Thereafter several libraries continued to be involved in time consuming food control business.[88] Harrogate Public Library established a casualty information centre for people searching for lost relatives.[89]

Across the country the Ministry of Information established Local Information Committees, headed by an Information Officer. The prime purpose of the Committees and their officers was to distribute information to pre-selected display points in an emergency, when ordinary forms of communication – post, wireless, telegraph, railway – had broken down. The second day-to-day purpose of the system was 'to maintain the spirit of the people by affording ... to people facts and such assistance as the Government can give them'.[90] In some areas librarians undertook such work, either as officer-in-charge or as a Committee member. The Library Association believed that librarians should aspire to serving in such capacities because it was the 'one sphere pre-eminently suited not only to his training but to the many sources of knowledge and information with which he is surrounded'.[91]

Later in the war, the Ministry of Information sent a circular to local education authorities suggesting that they should collaborate with library authorities to provide information rooms in public libraries, along the lines of the successful rooms provided on most Royal Air Force (RAF) stations. Such rooms provided the type of materials seen in most public libraries, but did so, said the Ministry, in a much more attractive way, the RAF format possessing 'several qualities which many public libraries notably lack, namely comfort, visual appeal, and the consciousness that printed matter can be made an exciting and vital factor in the life of ordinary men and women'.[92] The Library Association, not surprisingly, was sceptical about such provision, believing that the practical details required close consideration to avoid the past experience with news rooms and magazine rooms:

Some effective steps would have to be taken to ensure that Information Rooms do not degenerate in the way that News Rooms did before they were, in many cases, abolished. The tramp and the betting man used the News Room far too much, and there is a sort of Gresham's Law in these matters – the bad citizen drives out the good.[93]

Despite the rejection at the start of the war of the librarian-led scheme for Services' Libraries, public libraries made considerable efforts to supply the Forces with books, firstly by signing up service personnel stationed locally, and secondly, by working with the National Book Recovery Campaign, launched in 1942 and supported by the Library Association. They also sent stocks of books and periodicals directly to camps and other installations. One unnamed Royal Army Ordnance Corp camp in the south of England housing a battalion of men, was served by the local county library service which lent five hundred books to form the backbone of its collection. To these were added another five hundred books obtained from the Services Book Depot, and a further 2300 from private donations and withdrawn stock given by local municipal libraries. The majority of books were fiction and over 17,000 items of all kinds were issued in the course of 1944. The library also supplied daily and Sunday newspapers, as well as periodicals like *The New Statesman and Nation*, *Radio Times*, *The Listener* and *Picture Post*. A small reference section was also provided: almanacks, timetables, maps, local information and copies of *Hansard*. When not open to borrowers the library was used for educational purposes.[94]

Mirroring programmes of education for citizenship run in the Forces, it was proposed that public libraries facilitate the same kind of education on the home front. Frederick Cowles, librarian of Swinton and Pendlebury, mapped out an authentic 'public sphere' role for public libraries:

Public libraries supply readers with books which help to educate them in the responsibilities of citizenship, and there is a welcome increase in the demand for such volumes. But it should be possible through public libraries to organise classes in the essential subjects followed by debates in which individuals freely widen their views through frank discussions and gain experience and confidence in public speaking.[95]

Thus, during the war 'many public libraries found themselves acting as cultural centres to a degree which they had never previously envisaged, and with resources which they had never hitherto been able to command'.[96] At Southfields Public Library in Leicester newsreel, documentary and information films were shown throughout the war, under the direction of Harold Jolliffe, the future leading advocate of extension activities in public libraries.[97] Heavy air raids on Cardiff in 1941 and 1942 led to slightly decreased issues, but did not prevent the city, it was said, from 'maintaining and increasing its many extension activities'.[98] Around the country public libraries not only progressed in terms of their traditional constituency of book-lending, but also in their extension programmes, including provision for reading circles and wireless discussion groups.[99]

Frederick Sinclair, librarian of St. Pancras, believed that while not seeking to usurp the functions of the social club, the public library could complement it by providing public lectures, educational film sessions, gramophone recitals, discussion groups, play reading groups and music and art circles, and other activities associated with the term 'Social Centre'.[100] Edward Sydney, Chair of the Library Association's Post-War Planning Committee and leading advocate of 'libraries for citizenship', believed that this wider function reinforced the traditional role of promoting reading:

There is a quite considerable body of evidence that the library which does participate in adult education and does make the library a centre for local societies with intellectual and cultural aims, reaps a reward of public appreciation, increased opportunities of personal service to citizens, and official financial and other support leading to development in library adequacy and efficiency ... The library which is a focal point of local cultural activity seems to possess a dynamic in book use not present in other libraries.[101]

This philosophy found support outside the library movement. In 1944 the *Times Educational Supplement*, having investigated the work of a public library in an impoverished part of London, ran an article on the theme of the public library as a cultural centre: if large enough, libraries should have lecture theatres, meeting rooms and exhibition space to facilitate various educational and arts activities. Moreover, 'the public librarian in a mass-technological democracy must be much more than an efficient and learned storekeeper; he must be dynamic in the encouragememt of the use of books.'[102]

Wartime Portsmouth's public library experience provides a good example of the opportunities war gave to *extend* services. In 1941 the city librarian was appointed Emergency Information Officer and thereafter library service points operated as emergency information bureaux after air raids. Between May 1942 and May 1945 several members of the library staff volunteered for the YMCA's mobile library service to fifty service units in the Portsmouth area. The library authority also promoted a successful series of lunch-time classical concerts under the auspices of the Council for the Encouragement of Music and the Arts (later the Arts Council) – an experiment which continued after the war to ameliorate 'austerity with music'.[103]

Nottinghamshire's War

The general picture of increased reading, assumption of auxiliary responsibilities and disruption to services is vividly reflected in the wartime experiences of Nottinghamshire's county library system.[104] When war was declared, plans were in hand for the building of three new branch libraries and the opening of several other service points in new or converted premises. These plans had, of course, to be abandoned and it was not until the early 1950s that new buildings could be considered again. Pre-war plans to expand the service incorporated the necessary projection of an enlarged professional staff. Before the war most qualified staff were employed in the county library's headquarters and with the exception of two sites, the employees at all branches were without professional qualifications. The onset of war brought the development of the service's professional base to an abrupt halt, the situation deteriorating after the middle of 1940 when library staff began to be called up for national service.

A month after the outbreak of war the library committee decided that economies should be made in the service and that future estimates should not exceed those of 1939-40. Later, however, it was realised that libraries in Nottinghamshire were providing a vital service and, consequently, an increase in expenditure was in fact imperative. Thus, annual expenditure increased between 1939 and 1945 from £16,834 to £29,619. Extra money was required to meet the increased demand for books across the county, especially early in the war when the problem of supplying evacuees with books arose suddenly.

Not surprisingly the war interrupted the normal pattern of service provision. Fortunately little damage was caused to library property by air raids. However, additional responsibilities were imposed on libraries. In addition to regular services, the county's libraries were called upon to discharge certain civil defence and other duties: premises being used to house Citizens Advice Bureaux, WVS Centres, Auxiliary Fire Services and Air Raid Patrol Centres.

During the war it was deemed wise to disperse the bookstock as much as possible away from large urban centres to minimise the risk of damage by air raid. Following on from this, it was decided to regionalise the system. The county was divided into around half-a-dozen regions, each under the control of a qualified librarian and containing branch libraries and school and adult centres. First introduced as an expediency, regionalisation became a permanent feature of the county's system after the war. The problem of providing services over such a large county none the less remained. Before the war travelling stocks of books and inter-library loans had been delivered to centres by haulage contractors. After the outbreak of hostilities, however, this arrangement came under pressure, the majority of books (certainly to branches) being delivered thereafter by the County Librarian in her private car! It was not until 1943 that the County invested in a small van for making such deliveries.

At the end of the war the County had a book stock smaller than in 1939 and there was a marked shortage of trained librarians. But in other respects the work of the library had greatly increased during six years of war. The number of branches had increased from 9 to 15; the number of adult and junior centres from 291 to 480; the number of readers from 61,000 to 116,000; and the annual total of books issued had risen from 1,400,000 to 2,700,000. Yet these improvements had been carried out with a relatively smaller increase in income, to the detriment of the standard of service offered; this was especially true in respect of the quality of the bookstock and the staff administering it. However, as the source of this typical story of wartime county provision observed:

Although the ideals of librarianship could not be achieved [during the war] they were never forgotten. The work done during the war did not merely satisfy the day to day demand but laid the foundation upon which an improved service could be built when more favourable conditions returned.[105]

From Crisis to Renewal

The crisis that befell Britain in May and June 1940 – as the German army swept through France and the Low Countries, forcing the British Army to flee in disarray from the beaches of Dunkirk – shook the nation out its complacency, invigorating it with purpose and propelling it towards a programme of social renewal in anticipation of victory. Almost immediately, the demand for social reform 'sprang up as suddenly as a gust of wind on a still day and continued to blow with increasing force' for the rest of the war.[106] Henceforth, the war was to be conducted with planning for needs taking priority over the financial correctness demanded by the Treasury. Social reform became a beneficiary of the new strategy: for example, free or subsidised school milk for the under-5s and their mothers was introduced barely days after the last troops disembarked from their cross-Channel retreat in June 1940.[107] Reform, and the planning for reconstruction that went with it, was obviously good for the morale of public and the Services alike. But it was also based on the need to build a healthier nation, physically and mentally, capable of winning the war and generating a future society shorn of the vast inequality, waste and injustice of the pre-war years.

Although it is dangerous to over-romanticise the spirit of liberation, collective solidarity and socio-political consensus of the war years,[108] the emergence of a 'Dunkirk spirit' and a sense of 'equality of sacrifice' – the feeling that if 'dangers were to be shared, then resources should also be shared'[109] – is difficult to deny. As one historian has put it:

Few stood on their dignity when crammed together in air-raid shelters; queues were a great leveller; there was a common topic of conversation in the war news ... Locking the iron gates to the gardens in privileged London squares was suddenly intolerable ... Saving for victory, digging for victory, sewing for victory – this was a war in which everyone could 'go to it' and do their bit on the 'home front'.[110]

This emergent egalitarian spirit provided the ideal soil in which fresh plans for the intrinsically democratic public library could be sown and nurtured. R.H. Blackburn, librarian of Chorley, typified the new commitment to a better future when he contrasted the heretofore 'poverty of ideology' in public library provision with the commitment and evangelical fervour of the Victorians in respect of reading and learning:

We have lost something of that vital and tense atmosphere of discussion and enquiry which marked the educationalist of the nineteenth century. I often think of my great grandfather who held a post in a village colliery in the north and of his efforts to act as teacher to some of the village lads by providing evening classes in reading and writing. I haven't the slightest doubt that in the mystery of learning, in the stirring of youthful imagination, he saw a new heaven and a new earth, even among those grim surroundings.

Following the disillusionment brought about by two world wars and by mass unemployment, the time was now ripe, preached Blackburn, for a 'new movement' in librarianship. 'Is it too much to expect', he asked, for

a revival of hope and confidence in many spheres of social life? That the humiliation and cynicism of the previous decade might be forgotten? That we should see again something of the idealism which inspired earlier reformers and social "well-wishers"? That we should be emphatic in our idealism and make no apologies for our enthusiasm?[111]

In opening Swindon's new library in 1943, R.H. Tawney similarly invoked the spirit of Victorian idealism when he described the institution as 'a mighty lighthouse of knowledge'.[112]

Libraries thrived on the war's ideological fight against authoritarianism. For J.H. Wellard, the significance of the public library, which he regarded as having come of age in the war, was in its 'contribution to the general welfare of democracy'. The war, which had thrown up 'certain disagreeable and extremely bewildering problems' constituting a challenge to democracy', was revealing the public library to be a truly 'social force', a 'living organism' rather than an 'established institution'. Public libraries (and libraries in general) were, in common with the free church, free school and free press, 'the instruments of those democratic ideas which Fascism abhors'.[113] At the height of the crisis of 1940 the editor of the *Library Association Record* proclaimed that the 'war is a conflict not only of arms but of wills'. Hitler, he reminded his audience, had paved the way to power 'by fouling the mind of the opponent with personal falsehood', hence 'the well-stocked mind is proof against such infection'. Consequently, he concluded, libraries were 'rendering signal service to the national cause'.[114] Reports of cultural atrocities in Eastern Europe, such as the systematic destruction of large and historic libraries in the Ukraine, were publicised to emphasise the fact that the Nazis were the enemies of science, books and learning.[115]

Voicing a similar ideological fervour, and reflecting on the place of libraries during and after the war, the librarian Norman Pugsley declared in Churchillian style that:

Never were firm convictions and clearly envisaged ideals more needed than now. The qualities of leadership must show in many or we shall fail. Librarians have a magnificent opportunity if only they can sufficiently and in the right spirit persuade themselves of its magnificence by understanding its nature. We must be sure of what we stand for and stand unshakable in our faith in what we know to be our task. If we are not sure of what we are trying to carry through and maintain, we shall have failed ... Now is the time for a fundamental reconsideration of all that librarianship means. We look for clear and vigorous statements of belief and policy, searching analyses of basic values. Most of us feel, if we do not always openly admit, that the library movement is at a critical stage. The age of the pioneers has passed and with it much of their spirit. It takes more imagination and ability to-day to be a pioneer, because the ground has shifted and become harder. The phase of technical experiment is closing. Methods have become stabilized. Gadgets still exert their fascination, but there is a more general realization that their charm is no panacea nor substitute for wide knowledge and hard thinking.[116]

Continuing this ideological 'call to arms', Pugsley stated that librarians needed 'to develop both as a body and as individuals a greater sense of responsibility, a larger and keener vision'. Public librarianship, he urged, 'has need of militancy'.[117]

The library world sensed the change of public mood, one librarian commenting that 'a silent revolution is going on in this country, in other words the War has caused people to re-orient their ideas on things ... and if our social system is to stand, those in positions of responsibility must keep pace with the people and subject themselves to self-examination'.[118] Not to contribute to the spirit of enquiry which had arisen during the war would be to repeat the mistake made during the First World War when too little thought was given to post-war reconstruction, thereby causing, hypothesised one librarian, the inter-war generation to fail.[119] It was in keeping with this sense of renewal that public library initiatives like the McColvin Report should be viewed.

The McColvin Blueprint

Reacting to the spirit of national reconstruction, the Library Association asked its Honorary Secretary, Lionel McColvin, Westminster's librarian, to conduct a survey of the state of, and prospects for, public libraries. It was said that McColvin was the right person for the job as he had an 'unrivalled knowledge of the conditions of British librarianship',[120] his work on the Library Association's large pre-war survey of public libraries having given him the authority to undertake further, more exhaustive research.[121] McColvin's investigations, funded by the CUKT, were carried out largely in the second half of 1941 and were reported on in late 1942.[122] It was planned that he should spend a total of 70 nights away from home, travelling the length and breadth of the country visiting libraries of all types, some in the remotest of places. The McColvin Report, as it became known colloquially, galvanised debate on public library policy both during the war and for years after it.[123]

The tone of the Report was its most compelling characterisic. Idealistic, committed, ideological even, the Report in many ways resurrected the burning faith in the importance of self-realisation through the public library which had marked the discourses of the service's Victorian pioneers. Philip Whiteman, an expert on the Report, has described it as 'wholly uncompromising, its author taking the risk that his ideas would be taken as impracticable, even outrageous'.[124] The publisher Geoffrey Faber's view of McColvin was that he was 'a very enthusiastic, able librarian', but 'like many of his kind rather apt to think that libraries are the backbone of civilisation'.[125] The grand, optimistic view of the social role of libraries, even if over-stated, none the less suited the mood of the times, focused as it was on the urgent need to plan a better post-war world. McColvin wished to promote the idea that libraries were 'a great instrument and bulwark of democracy', civilisation [which Nazi Germany had abandoned] and books being inevitably intertwined. [126]

McColvin painted a sorry picture of existing provision: 'The outstanding impression of the library service gained throughout this survey is that it is badly organised.'[127] Book stocks and staffing was often inadequate and, although there were some 'oases in the desert',[128] most libraries survived in poor premises with lamentable facilities. 'All libraries should be to all men an opportunity and an inspiration', he observed, but in Britain, 'too many are a disappointment and a failure'.[129] Some of the examples McColvin reported were nothing short of 'library nightmares'. One small library he found was

housed in imposing council premises, unfortunately right on the outskirts of the borough ... The interior does not, however, live up to the promise of the exterior; the lending stock is very poor, the juvenile absolutely poverty-stricken, the reference department completely derelict.[130]

One central library he visited he discovered to be 'shockingly crowded ... with no possibility of providing even separate sections for children's books or reference books, no store room, no work room, no office for the Librarians, no place for the staff to hang up their coats'.[131]

However, as the *Times Educational Supplement* commented at the time, the main importance of the Report was 'not its criticism of the present – though that is useful – but its suggestions for the future'.[132] McColvin's key ingredients for fashioning a more efficient library service was the establishment of a national body with responsibility for libraries and with the power to administer direct grants from central government. Of equal importance in the Report, but much more controversial, was the proposal to reduce the existing total of 604 library authorities in the United Kingdom to 93 (78 in England, including 9 in London; 9 in Scotland; 5 in Wales; and 1 in Northern Ireland). Larger authorities would deliver economies of scale, reduce the damaging distinction between town and country and produce a more efficient system of inter-library co-operation.

Months before the publication of the Report, the 'McColvin line' was leaked to the wider cultural community via the *Times Educational Supplement*, which announced that:

Public libraries should be considered as a national service. The smaller boroughs and urban districts have not been able financially to support an adequate library service, and the work of the larger boroughs and county boroughs requires greater co-ordination, as does the work of the county library systems which fall under the control of the county educational authorities. This would involve some form of regionalisation and nationalisation on the lines of that already existing for education ... Grants should be made from the Central Government to public library authorities, consisting of 50% of expenditure on salaries, books and extension work.[133]

McColvin's proposals caused consternation among librarians concerned about the loss of autonomy threatened. Many still clung to the compromise that had been worked out between the wars: to co-operate but retain independence; or in the words of Sir Frederick Kenyon, 'to continue to be locally autonomous, but to think nationally'.[134] The Library Association advertised McColvin's five-shilling report with a disclaimer: 'The Council of the Library Association, in publishing this report, do not commit themselves to the policy or the recommendations which have been submitted for their consideration.'[135] None the less, when in the following year the Association published its official blueprint for post-war public libraries,[136] it came to accept virtually all McColvin's recommendations. However, in merely proposing that 'local government areas should be re-arranged to give the best results',[137] the Association's proposals unsurprisingly rejected the idea of forming *ad hoc* library authorities in advance of the general local government reform which would deliver the larger units upon which library structures could be more solidly built. In 1946 the Association dropped the idea of larger library units, *ad hoc* or otherwise, and spent the next two decades holding the line in the fight between the 'enlargers' and the 'parochial-minded'.[138]

One of the first commentaries on the report was by Richard Wright, librarian of Middlesex, who announced that McColvin had 'given the profession a detailed *blueprint* [my emphasis] of a new library service.' However, in suggesting the scrapping of many library authorities, although McColvin was in effect leading the way in local government reorganisation, Wright believed many would think that: 'Here he is taking liberties, his defences are open to superior forces'; for many librarians believed regionalisation, promoted by the war, was as far as loss of autonomy should go.[139] Shoreditch's librarian, A.C. Jackson, typified the suspicion levelled at McColvin's plan when he wrote: 'One realises that standards must be raised in the backward areas, but unfortunately minima tend to become maxima. My experience in large systems leads me to believe that they are admirable shelters for a flat level of mediocrity, with little opportunity for the outstanding.'[140]

In the long debate which followed the publication of the Report, in a plea to continue to fight for the 'common cause', McColvin reminded readers of the *Library Association Record* that:

There are still far too many isolated public libraries, serving communities too small and too poor to be able to contemplate (even if they were aware of its existence) paying for the sort of service now being given by the public libraries of most of our great towns. If the Library Association's proposal for post-war reconstruction take effect, their isolation will be ended, and they will be brought into organic relation with the centres which do give a full service.[141]

McColvin belittled 'those who prate about liberty, interference, bureaucracy, remote control and the like'.[142] He was impatient with library authorities, such as that in Rugby, that sought to retain autarky, calling instead for a 'wider vision', a 'broadening of outlook, a willingness to extend and to co-operate' in the pursuit of a 'truly nation-wide service'.[143]

McColvin was not alone in his fight against the parochial mentality. Irritated at the opposition generated by the report, Raymond Irwin scoffed at the dangers which some saw lurking behind the proposed system of 'remote control', the spectre of which he believed to have been misrepresented as 'unenlightened and unsympathetic administration'.[144] Others welcomed the statist tone they perceived in the Report. It was E.V. Corbett's view, for example, in pondering the question of users resident in one library authority using the services of others, that the trouble with the inter-availability of tickets was just one problem which made nationalisation necessary.[145] At a practical level the merger of library authorities appeared to make sense. In Newcastle the City Librarian reported that:

As administrative work (including the ordering of various supplies, accountancy work, cataloguing and classification etc.) common, in varying degrees, to each of the nine libraries in the system is centralised in one building, considerable progress may be expected in the direction of co-ordinating the organisation and administration of the libraries system and its control in the interests of efficiency and economy of working.[146]

By 1944 McColvin's proposals were being discussed by government. A Ministry of Education memo that year estimated that since the end of the First World War there had been about a dozen suggestions – from the Library Association, various library authorities and local education committees and the National Library of Wales – for direct grants to public libraries from central government. However, it was reported that financial stringency and the library community's fear of loss of autonomy, and a dislike of inspection as the corollary to grant-aid, had combined to ensure that central funding never went beyond the drawing board.[147] Yet central funding for library provision was not without precedent. To provide extra services to evacuated children in country areas, the Board of Education had given grants early in the war to libraries via local education authorities, which in county areas controlled public library operations.[148] Calls for direct grants came from some surprising quarters. The Archbishop of Canterbury, aware of the slowness of library reform and the danger of 'failing to keep pace with the social and educational developments to which we are looking forward', pressed the President of the Board of Education, R.A. Butler, to establish 'a ministry, or department of ministry, which could be charged with doing for public libraries what the Board does, and has still more to do for education'; but he added that public libraries should remain locally controlled and that because their field was wider than that of formal education the Board should not be the ministry chosen to control them.[149] In reply, Butler dismissed the suggestion, claiming that the time was not 'opportune for us to embark on consideration of these issues'.[150] Other government departments appeared more amenable to the idea of centralisation. The Minister of Health was advised in 1944, in the context of the need for greater involvement by local libraries in the hospital library provision, that 'public library services will sooner or later have to be placed on a more rational basis than at present and that some form of central direction and control may be necessary'.[151]

Plate 1: Poster (1920s) promoting the public library as a dynamic, multi-purpose institution for the nation.

Plate 2: Surveillance by design (1922). Radical arrangement of book stacks provided permanent 'supervision' of the public from the library counter.

Plate 3: Storytelling for children (1930). Librarians knew that if they grabbed readers when they were young, they had a better chance of attracting them to libraries as adults.

Plate 4: The public library network in Hereford (1938). A component of the 'library grid' that librarians constructed between the wars.

Plate 5: William Benson Thorne (1878-1966) retired in 1942 having worked for Poplar Public Libraries for over 40 years, the last eight as chief librarian.

Plate 6: An army camp library in the Second World War. Such libraries were often supplied by public libraries.

Plate 7: Edinburgh Central Library Lending Department (1954). This photograph illustrates the time-consuming, manual-intensive nature of borrowing and returning books before the arrival of computers.

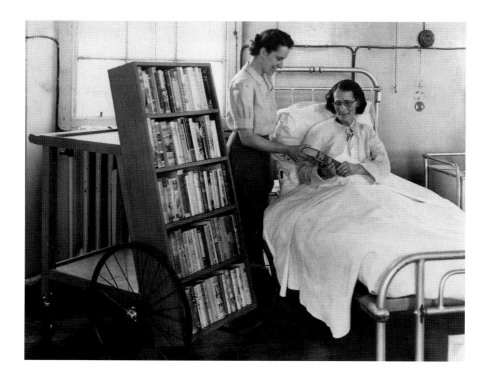

Plate 8: Outreach (1950). In the post-war years public library work reflected closely the public service ethos of the welfare state.

"...and this is the dark-room, where we do our most interesting experiments."

Plate 9: Always a place of social interaction, this cartoon from a library staff magazine in the early 1950s shows how public libraries could also provide the ideal, relaxed setting for romantic liaison, whether between staff or public.

Plate 10: Self-improvement (1962). The facilities of a large reference library being used mostly for the purposes of private study.

Plate 11: Behind the scenes (1962). Fordist, assembly-line production in the cataloguing department.

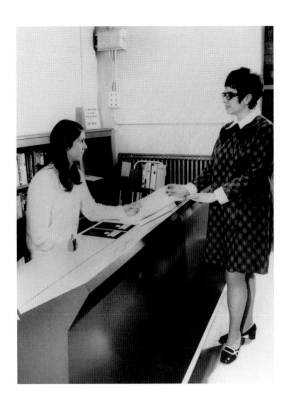

Plate 12: The first operational computerized book-circulation system, Brighton (1969).

Plate 13: Information on-line (1980s), precursor of the 'electronic super highway' technologies which became increasingly visible in the 1990s.

A Wartime Retirement: W.B. Thorne, Public Service and the Self

The closing weeks of 1942 witnessed the 'end of the beginning' at El Alamein and the publication of William Beveridge's ground-breaking *Report on social service and allied services* and of the less momentous (though not in the library world) McColvin Report. They also saw the retirement of one of the country's most dedicated, long-serving and respected librarians, William Benson Thorne, whose professional life is worthy of extensive coverage here because of the way it reflects various core principles of twentieth-century public librarianship.

Born in 1878 in Stoke Newington, London, Thorne began work as a *Victorian* librarian, entering the library of the St. Bride Foundation Institute, off London's Fleet Street in 1895, progressing to librarian-in-charge by the end of his time there. In 1902 he was appointed to Poplar Public Libraries as librarian of the Bromley (at Bow) Branch Library, becoming the Borough's deputy librarian in 1928 and chief librarian in 1934, a position which he occupied until his retirement on 30 November 1942, the day before Beveridge released his Report. He died, aged 88, on 17 November 1966.

Thorne joined the Library Association in 1899, served on its Education Committee for several years and was elected to the Association's Council in 1919, of which he remained a member for 18 years. For a period he chaired the Publications Committee and during the formative years of the Association's London and Home Counties Branch he acted as Secretary-Treasurer. He was an examiner in library administration and organisation for the Library Association from 1918 to 1931 and an external examiner for two years for the School of Librarianship, University College, London. Between 1902 and 1904 he edited the *Library Assistant*, a task he was forced to give up as a result of his time-consuming work in Poplar. He also served as Honorary General Secretary (1915-20), first President (1906-9), Honorary Fellow (1916) and Chairman of the Library Assistants' Association. In 1904 he co-authored (with George Roebuck) *A Primer of Library Practice*, which was re-written and issued in a second edition in 1914. He also wrote two pamphlets for the Library Assistants' Association: *First steps in library routine* (1915) and *First steps in library cataloguing* (1917). Reflecting his respect for order and bureaucratic method he wrote *Honorary Secretaryship* (1926), published by Isaac Pitman and Sons. His interest in local history generated several articles on Poplar's past in the *Poplar Libraries Quarterly Record*. In 1938 he was elected an Honorary Fellow of the Library Association in recognition of his services to librarianship.[152]

Judging by the reaction of close wartime colleagues, his decision in 1942 to bring to an end almost half a century of service to libraries and their public was viewed in the library profession as premature and a matter of sadness.[153] His contribution to the profession was widely recognised as having been considerable. 'You are rather an institution ... and things won't be the same without you', wrote C.M. Jackson, librarian of Shoreditch.[154] His work for the Library Association 'was assiduous and conducted with an unobtrusive efficiency'.[155] He was 'a great Association man', remarked George

Roebuck.[156] 'Scarcely a meeting dealing with librarianship in or near London', it was said, 'has been held at which he has not been present.'[157] After he retired Thorne was described by a colleague as 'one of the outstanding personalities of my generation in the library world ... he has played a leading part in the organisation of the profession and the raising of the status of librarians'.[158] On his death he received further acclamation: 'Public librarianship at the beginning of the century was a new and struggling profession and it was due to the efforts of men like Benson Thorne that it has reached the standing that it commands today.'[159]

Thorne was anxious that a proficient scheme of training for librarianship be maintained and developed, complaining that library posts should not be filled by people without library qualifications.[160] He was a leading promoter of the library education system, 'endeavouring to give instruction ... to distant brethren'.[161] Few could rival him as a letter writer and 'every recipient felt himself honoured'.[162] Indeed, the 'extraordinary felicity of his phraseology', makes one realise 'just how thrilled librarians were to receive a letter from him'.[163] It was said that Thorne publicised Poplar's libraries not merely by the work he did there but also 'by his voluminous correspondence, written in a beautiful regular hand, to brother assistants all over the world';[164] he was 'one of the best letter-writers of his time, letters helping and inspiring his fellow librarians'.[165]

Thorne's pursuit of fellowship in the professional sphere was matched by his idealistic stance towards libraries and their users. Thorne's humanity was widely commented upon. When he retired it was said that: 'His geniality, complete sincerity and sympathetic readiness to advise all who appealed to him will long be remembered.'[166] Munford has described him as an 'exceptionally kindly, helpful and hospitable librarian of the old school'.[167] His kindness and social idealism were reinforced by strong religious convictions; on his death his local church paid tribute to him, stating that: 'His tall, upright figure and old-world charm and courtesy would be sadly missed.'[168]

From the outset Thorne practised librarianship in a context of social fellowship. The St. Bride Foundation Institute, which he joined the year following its foundation in 1894, displayed an unequivocally idealistic aim: 'the inhabitants and employees of the parish were to be provided with educational [including general, reference and typographical libraries], physical and moral training, with public lectures, musicals and other entertainments, and exhibitions of art and industry, at such charges and under such regulations as would make them available for the poorer classes.'[169] In his early career he undertook work in connection with Toynbee Hall and other settlements in the East End of London: 'He has always had a high sense of the importance of his job', wrote A.C. Piper:

and has been eager to do all he could for his readers, especially those less fortunate than himself. His lot was caste mainly among such people and he used his opportunities as few would have done ... Benson

Thorne has a rare enthusiasm for libraries and a wide and idealistic vision of their potentialities ... His ideals and his faith in the mission of libraries has never wavered.[170]

Thorne *believed* in the library service:

It was one of the fundamental things that he had been able to believe in, and no matter what people said to the contrary, whatever the argument or the criticism, nothing shattered the conviction that the libraries were an essential service to the people of the nation, and only by their wise and intelligent use would the people grow better in their ideas and outlook.[171]

Libraries for Thorne, although partly recreational, were essentially educational places:

It had been his constant endeavour to persuade people to attempt something better in the way of reading. There were people who looked upon reading as a pleasant way of passing the time. He had no use for those type of people. He thought that books should inform, stimulate and encourage people, and it had always been that class of book that he had endeavoured to get before the residents of the Borough.[172]

He fully accepted that people read partly for relief from the strains of the world but he saw reading very much as a source of information and education, 'the needs of the serious student being, as always, specially considered'.[173] Thorne embraced the ethic of individual improvement wholeheartedly, making strenuous efforts to encourage readers to make the most of their potential: 'It was one of the joys of his life' to be able to tell his family, 'that "So and So" had passed this exam, won that award, gained a good promotion, or whatever, as a result of reading books from the Library, and using their intelligence'.[174] In the spirit of idealistic fellowship Thorne constantly strove to bring librarian and reader into closer proximity. He was keen to give talks about the importance of reading, and was 'always glad of an opportunity for explaining to the uninitiated the value of the right use of books and libraries, believing that through the medium of books people may be led to enjoy fuller and happier lives'.[175] His public lectures, into the preparation of which it was said he put a tremendous effort, included philosophical and educational subjects such as *What is education?*, *Reading techniques*, *The mind*, *Static vs. dynamic: positive vs. negative*; as well as less serious subjects like *English humour: an hour with 'Punch'*, *Leisure* and *Sleep*.[176] In addition he ran library study circles and was a regular contributor to the Poplar Public Libraries readers' magazine *Books to Read* (originally entitled *The Readers' Review*), in which his comments were always 'a model of erudition'.[177] His openness towards readers was clearly demonstrated in a letter written to the author of a book on reading for girls, assuring them that 'you need not, either because you do not like to give trouble, or from fear of your application being resented, hesitate to make enquiries'.[178] Such was the strength and memory of the links that Thorne forged with his local community that in 1955 a new block of Poplar flats was named after him.[179] It was said that he gave 'effective leadership to the community',[180] and nowhere was this more apparent than in the Second World War when he served as a Deputy Food Control

Officer for the Borough. It was 'largely due to his initiative', remarked a local newspaper at the time, 'that the people of Poplar owe the ease with which Food Control problems have been solved.'[181]

In fact it was 'the combined forces of German iniquity and Food Control' which made early retirement (albeit merely a few weeks before his 65th birthday) an attractive proposition.[182] Although sad to relinquish his librarianship and wartime administrative duties, he none the less did so in the full knowledge that his life had been one of giving service to others. Libraries and the 'service they render', he wrote to a colleague, had been the chief interest of his life,[183] and he was unequivocal in his perception of public libraries as a truly *public service*.[184] He was 'quite convinced that there was a glorious opportunity for the future of the library services',[185] agreeing with the sentiment of a friend (Bristol's librarian) that the McColvin Report was an 'admirable document and should have enormous influence on post-war development'.[186]

The values which Thorne embraced and taught throughout his life, and which he so clearly brought to bear on his public library work, were at a premium in the Second World War when visions of a New Jerusalem came to dominate the agenda for post-war society. New Jerusalemers, according to Barnet,[187] were both 'tender-hearted and highminded', their objectives strongly flavoured with a religious social mission. Thorne was not a member of the liberal intelligentsia – the 'enlightened Establishment – which mapped out the terrain of the New Jerusalem, but he did share its roots of nineteenth-century romanticism and Victorian idealism. These urged the need to recognise the innate good and potential for improvement residing in every individual and claimed that social ills could be banished by 'the creation of an ideal society founded on justice, virtue and good feelings'.[188] As much as the work of liberal elites striving to build a better post-war Britain, Thorne's work with individuals and the local community drew on John Stuart Mill's 'vision of a community of individuals seeking freedom and pleasure, yet capable of acting for the common good'.[189] Citizenship in the tradition of classical liberalism emphasised both the rights and obligations of the citizen. It was this definition which formed the foundation of the welfare state in the Second World War and which, at the relatively humble level of public library provision, librarians like Thorne endeavoured to put into practice. Libraries would help provide the security, or the means, of self-improvement, action by the state encouraging self-realisation.

For H.L. McGill of Manchester Public Libraries the main challenge of the war was the need to protect the identity of the individual self in the face of unprecedented social flux. In her opinion:

Now there is no security anywhere and the safe world has slipped its cable and is spinning into unknown universes. In such world-shaking events the only defiance that the artist can make is to re-affirm his faith in the value of the individual. If man is to be helpless in the face of outward events, his sole hope of sanity lies in his ability to keep inviolate the central self that is his claim to individuality.[190]

During the war, libraries certainly continued to offer an escape from harsh reality by allowing people to engage spiritually with the 'souls' of recorded culture. Frederick Sinclair viewed the public library as a 'centre ... for mental relaxation and intellectual renewal amid the great community of minds enshrined in its books'.[191]

The careers of idealists like Thorne not only spanned the period from high Victorianism to mid-twentieth century modernity, they also provided a link - a line of ideological continuity - between the moral conviction and evangelism of Victorian idealism and the state-driven welfarism and quasi-socialism of the Second World War. This tradition preached that individuals and 'individualism' could only thrive if given the opportunity to do so by effective communal provision. As the McColvin Report stated,

democracy depends upon the universal existence of the ability to participate in democratic government and its cardinal aim is to give equality of opportunity. No other qualities can avail if access to so important a means of individual development is not full and universal. The maintenance of a sound public library service is therefore as important to the community at large as to each of its members.[192]

McColvin reiterated librarians' belief, as shared by professionals like Thorne, that their job was to create 'whole personalities' and work on 'the minds and souls' of individual citizens. Equally, he believed better libraries 'will materially help to reveal to every person his responsibility for service to his fellow men, which alone can be the basis for a new community'; they were promoters of 'true citizenship – of the community, of the nation, of the world ... the basis of sound social co-operation'. Libraries, McColvin reminded his audience in an idealistic tone, can 'enable a person to develop to the fullest extent any abilities which he may possess that will be of benefit to society in so far as they can be developed by books'; they helped to develop 'those abilities which will be of benefit to himself', which 'also should be of benefit to society'[193] – a marriage, in effect, between the intangible inner-self and the very visible progress and needs of the 'social whole'. As another librarian put it at the time: good books provided through libraries was 'the movement of the soul of the people'.[194]

Notes and References to Chapter Four

[1] H. Meyer, 'Air raid precautions for record offices, libraries and museums', *LAR* 40 (May 1938), 204-9.
[2] SRO, GD 281/13/45, Library service for evacuees (6 June 1941).
[3] See the following issues of *LAR* 43 (May 1941), 93; (August 1941), 147; (October 1941), 186.
[4] *LAR* 44 (June 1942), 75.
[5] A. Esdaile, 'Annual report of the Library Association', *LAR* 47 (August 1945), 147.
[6] T. Kelly, *A history of public libraries in Great Britain and Ireland 1845-1975* (London, 2nd edn., 1977), 327.
[7] MOA, The Public Library (Summer 1999), A883.
[8] 'New books', *Harrogate Advertiser* (30 November 1940).
[9] D. Gray, 'Public library finance in wartime', *LAR* 44 (April 1942), 42. See G. McAllister (ed.), *The book crisis* (c. 1943), produced for the National Committee for the Defence of the Book, deposited in SRO GD 281/17/13.

[10] T. Kelly, *A history of public libraries*, op. cit., 327.

[11] 'The library service: scarcity of new books but careless usage', *Municipal Journal* (23 July 1943).

[12] 'Appeal for books', *Manchester Guardian* (20 March 1944).

[13] *LAR* 43 (October 1941), 186.

[14] J. Ross, 'Books salvage drive at Bristol', *LAR* 45 (January 1943), 6-7.

[15] L. McColvin, 'Women in the library service', *LAR* 44 (January 1942), 1.

[16] *LAR* 47 (January 1945), 1.

[17] PRO, ED 80/20.

[18] 'Library service in the London area', *LAR* 42 (September 1940).

[19] SRO, GD 281/13/45, P. Welsford to Board of Education (31 October 1941).

[20] C. Nowell, 'Post-war libraries and librarians', *LAR* 46 (June 1944), 101.

[21] C. Nowell, 'The Library Association in wartime', *LAR* 47 (February 1945), 30.

[22] D. Russell, 'The promotion of public libraries in the Second World War', *Library History* 15 (May 1999), 42-3.

[23] PRO, INF 1/260, Ministry of Information to A.R. Boyle (6 August 1940)

[24] *LAR* 41 (September 1939), 460-3.

[25] 'A call to public libraries', *Times Educational Supplement* (24 August 1940). 'Public libraries and welfare work', *Publishers' Circular* (24 August 1940).

[26] *LAR* 42 (September 1940), 243.

[27] D.C. Russell, *A social history of public libraries in London 1939-45*, unpublished MA (Information Studies) dissertation, University of North London (May 1995), 33.

[28] 'An essential service', *Burnley Express and News* (24 August 1940).

[29] SRO, GD 281/13/45, P. Welsford to the Board of Education (28 October 1941).

[30] PRO, LAB 26/32, Recreational facilities for workers engaged on work of urgent national importance: general note, CCCRG(40)1 (1940)

[31] PRO, Lab 26/32, Public libraries: note prepared by the Library Association and circulated to the members of the [Recreation] Group for information, CCCRG(40)5 (1940).

[32] PRO, LAB 26/32, Central Consultative Council of Voluntary Organisations, Recreation Group, Minutes (7 August 1940).

[33] 'Libraries and the black-out' (July 1940), LANC.

[34] 'War-time reading: Mass Observation', *The Library Assistant* 33 (1940), 103.

[35] MOA, Air Raids, Box 7, File D (18 October 1940).

[36] Borough of Keighley Public Libraries, *Annual Report* (1938-9).

[37] *Daily Express* (24 February 1944).

[38] *LAR* (July 1943), 129.

[39] 'Harrogate sets up books record: library queues', *Yorkshire Evening News* (3 March 1943).

[40] *LAR* 44 (May 1943), 85.

[41] *LAR* 46 (October 1944), 188.

[42] 'What they think of the new library', *Huddersfield Daily Examiner* (17 April 1940).

[43] 'New lending library for Cardiff', *Western Mail* (13 June 1940).

[44] As was the case in Stretford, Manchester: W. Threlfall, 'New Stretford library', *LAR* 43 (March 1941), 43-7.

[45] J. Swift, 'Swindon Public Library', *LAR* 45 (October 1943), 178-80.

[46] R.D. Hilton, 'A message to librarians', *LAR* 42 (May, 1940), 133.

[47] 'Halifax reading boon for all classes', *Bradford Telegraph and Argus* (10 January 1940).

[48] 'Reading as a relief from strain and anxiety', *Preston Guardian* (28 September 1940)

[49] *Lowestoft Journal* (24 August 1940).

[50] 'Lonely wives turn to books', *The Star* (24 August 1940). Women were *said* to be more nervous about air raids than men, which meant they stayed at home for longer period and were presumably able to read

more: MOA, Air Raids, Box 7, File D (21 October 1940).

[51] H.L. McGill, 'Reading tastes in wartime', *LAR* 45 (February 1943), 24-5.

[52] F. Sinclair, 'London's first mobile library', *LAR* 43 (May 1941), 86-8.

[53] 'Public libraries and welfare work', op. cit. (24 August 1940).

[54] R. Howarth, 'Evacuation: a problem and an experiment', *LAR* 42 (January 1940), 15-16.

[55] *LAR* 41 (October 1939), 520.

[56] PRO, ED 80/20, Board of Education Circular, Supply of books for evacuated children (15 December 1939). See also in this file several letters from local authorities to the Board of Education outlining the difficulties involved in meeting increased demand from evacuees. For example, Bath, a prominent reception area, experienced a 20% increase in registered readers in 1940. Mansfield, another reception town, issued 57% more books in July and August 1940 compared with the same months the previous year. Material on libraries and evacuees can also be found in SRO, GD 281/13/45.

[57] 'Libraries and the black-out' (July 1940), LANC.

[58] 'This ticket is good for 134 libraries', *Evening Standard* (17 April 1940).

[59] MOA, Air Raids, Box 7, File D (18 October 1940).

[60] Russell, 'The promotion of public libraries ...', op. cit., 44. In the St. Marylebone shelters, collections ranged from 50-550 volumes, many of them Penguin paperbacks and other sixpenny series; books could be borrowed for home reading: *LAR* 43 (March 1941), 46. Westminster had 150 shelter libraries with a total collection of 5000 volumes: *LAR* 43 (April 1941), 73. See also, S. Snaith, 'A tube shelter lending library', *Library Review* (Spring 1942).

[61] Mass-Observation noted in one shelter, however, that what reading was being done was mostly of magazines, while the majority sat doing nothing, staring into space and occasionally exchanging remarks: T. Harrison, *Living through the Blitz* (London, 1976), 115.

[62] C.M. Jackson, 'Shoreditch shelter libraries', *LAR* 43 (April 1941), 71.

[63] The authorities had feared that shelters would be a source of civil unrest, detracting from the war effort: see Harrison, *Living through the Blitz*, op. cit., 112.

[64] R.D.H. Smith, 'Libraries underground', *LAR* 43 (February 1941), 19.

[65] 'War-time reading: Mass Observation', op. cit., 104.

[66] *Bradford Telegraph and Argus* (16 October 1939).

[67] 'Popular libraries', *Yorkshire Observer* (8 October 1941).

[68] *LAR* 43 (May 1941), 93.

[69] E.V. Corbett, '1940 and after: a review of the public library service after fifteen months of war', *LAR* 43 (January 1941), 5.

[70] *Lowestoft Journal* (24 August 1940). Government too noted an increased demand for books on science, economics, history and sociology: PRO, ED 80/20.

[71] 'Fiction more popular', *The Yorkshire Observer* (21 October 1939).

[72] Borough of Keighley Public Libraries, *Annual Report* (1938-9).

[73] 'War-time reading: Mass Observation', op. cit., 104.

[74] 'Our taste in literature', *Clapham Observer* (4 February 1944).

[75] H.L. McGill, 'Reading tastes in wartime', *LAR* 45 (February 1943), 25.

[76] 'Books and the library service', *Chichester Observer* (16 March 1940).

[77] 'What Harrogate is reading: popularity of the classics', *Harrogate Herald* (31 December 1941).

[78] 'Reading in war-time', *Liverpool Daily Post* (21 September 1944).

[79] L.R. McColvin quoting a public librarian's annual report: 'No place for rubbish', *LAR* 45 (December 1943), 209.

[80] SRO, GD 281/82/66, J. Wilkie to P.S.J. Welsford (13 October 1944).

[81] M. Hung, *Change and resistance: public libraries in the Second World War*, unpublished MA dissertation, Thames Valley University (August 1999).

[82] PRO, WO 32/10436, A letter to you from the prime Minister (October 1942); it was estimated that

100,000 new books a month were needed to meet the demands of the Services: Supply of recreational and educational books for the army (17 April 1942).

[83] PRO, WO 32/10437, H. Creedy, The Services Libraries and Book Fund (1 December 1943).

[84] *LAR* 41 (December 1941), 569-70.

[85] 'Stepney libraries and the *Daily Worker*', *City and East London Observer* (27 July 1940).

[86] 'Councillor tore up communist newspaper', *Merthyr Express* (13 July 1940).

[87] T. Brown, 'Your public library – How it can help you', *LAR* 43 (February 1941), 21.

[88] 'Poplar libraries and the war', *East End News* (31 May 1940).

[89] *Harrogate Herald* (3 July 1940).

[90] R.D.H. Smith, 'Local information committees', *LAR* 42 (October 1940), 261.

[91] Ibid., 261.

[92] L.R. McColvin, 'Information rooms', *LAR* 47 (September 1945), 173.

[93] PRO, ED 171/1, P.S. Welsford to R. Wood (12 July 1945). Gresham's Law stated that bad money will tend to drive out good money.

[94] R.G. Roberts, 'A RAOC camp in the south of England', *LAR* 47 (April 1945), 72-3.

[95] *Manchester Evening News* (8 March 1943).

[96] Kelly, *A history of public libraries*, op. cit., 334.

[97] H. Jolliffe, 'The library and the film – a Leicester experiment', *LAR* 47 (March 1945), 48-51. See also, H. Jolliffe, *Public library extension activities* (London, 1962).

[98] *LAR* 44 (February 1942), 18.

[99] C. Nowell, 'The Library Association: annual report of the Council', *LAR* 43 (July 1941), 122.

[100] 'The library as a social centre', *LAR* 47 (June 1945), 115.

[101] E. Sydney, 'Design, planning and equipment of buildings for residential and non-residential adult education' (October 1944), deposited in PRO, ED 171/1.

[102] 'The library as a cultural centre: experiments in a London area', *Times Educational Supplement* (29 July 1944).

[103] J.G. Ollé, 'Portsmouth Public Libraries: the last fifty years 1935-1974', *Library History* 15 (May 1999), 52.

[104] As recalled by J.N. Taylor, 'County library history: the library in war-time', *Grapevine: Staff Magazine of the Nottinghamshire County Library Service* (December 1967), 2-4.

[105] Ibid., 4.

[106] P. Addison, *The road to 1945: British politics and the Second World War* (London, 1975), 108.

[107] R.M. Titmuss, *Problems of social policy* (London, 1950), showed how government concern for social issues was galvanised by the war.

[108] A. Calder, *The myth of the Blitz* (London, 1992). B. Pimlott, 'Is the post-war consensus a myth?', *Contemporary Record* 2:6 (1989), 12-14.

[109] Titmuss, op. cit., 121.

[110] P. Clarke, *Hope and Glory: Britain 1900-1990* (London, 1996), 207.

[111] R.H. Blackburn, 'The dangers of being a librarian', *LAR* 46 (January 1944), 5-6.

[112] 'A mighty lighthouse of knowledge', *Evening Advertiser* (16 August 1943).

[113] J.H. Wellard, 'The public library comes of age' (London, 1940), preface, 16, 190, 194, 196.

[114] R.D.H. Smith, 'A message to librarians', *LAR* 42 (May, 1940), 133.

[115] *LAR* 45 (January 1943), 8.

[116] N.S.E. Pugsley, 'Our place in this war and after', *LAR* 42 (May 1940), 134.

[117] Ibid., 135.

[118] R. Wright, The McColvin Report, *LAR* 44 (October 1942), 144.

[119] Ibid., 144.

[120] SRO, GD 281/13/45, P. Welsford to P. Morris (c. 4 July 1941).

[121] L.R. McColvin (ed.), *A survey of libraries: reports on a survey made by the Library Association*

during 1936-37 (London, 1938).

[122] SRO, GD 281/13/45, J. Wilkie to P. Welsford (27 August 1941).

[123] L.R. McColvin, *The public library system of Great Britain: a report on its present condition with proposals for post-war re-organization* [The McColvin Report] (London, 1942). See SRO, GD 281/13/45 for archive material associated with the survey that underpinned the Report. The Report made a wide impact, to the extent that it was discussed in the *Times* (15 October 1942), the *Manchester Guardian* (19 October 1942), the *Times Educational Supplement* (24 October 1942), the *Municipal Journal* (30 October 1942), the *Publishers' Circular* (7 November 1942), *Public Opinion* (27 November 1942) and *Nature* (20 March 1943).

[124] P. Whiteman, *Public libraries since 1945: the impact of the McColvin Report* (London, 1986), 1.

[125] PRO, ED 171/1, G. Faber to H. Brooke (27 October 1944). Faber added that libraries were 'at any rate, an important part of its [civilisation's] anatomy'.

[126] McColvin Report, op. cit., 1, 5.

[127] Ibid., 109.

[128] Ibid., 81.

[129] Ibid., 195.

[130] Ibid., 43.

[131] Ibid., 45.

[132] *Times Educational Supplement* (24 October 1942).

[133] 'Public library reconstruction: some necessary reforms', *Times Educational Supplement* (10 January 1942), deposited in SRO, GD 281/81/18.

[134] Speaking at the Library Association's annual conference in 1927: 'A national library service', *The Scotsman* (29 September 1927). At the same conference, and reported in the same article, the opinion of Lord Elgin of the CUKT was that: 'The spirit of the library service was the spirit of liberty. It had grown up by individual initiative and local support, and they [librarians] did not wish to sacrifice one particle of that spirit of local independence and of local responsibility.'

[135] *LAR* 44 (October 1942), 145.

[136] Library Association, *Proposals for the post-war reorganisation and development of the public library service* (London, 1943).

[137] Ibid, paragraph 10.

[138] Whiteman, *Public libraries since 1945*, op. cit., 152.

[139] R. Wright, The McColvin Report, *LAR* 44 (October 1942), 144-6.

[140] Tower Hamlets Local Studies Library, C.M. Jackson to W.B. Thorne (10 November 1942),.

[141] L.R. McColvin, 'The common cause', *LAR* 46 (December 1944).

[142] L.R. McColvin, 'Decline and fall', *LAR* 46 (August 1944), 131.

[143] L.R. McColvin, 'The wider vision', *LAR* 46 (June 1944), 95.

[144] R. Irwin, 'Remote control', *LAR* 46 (August 1944), 134.

[145] Corbett, '1940 and after ...', op. cit., 5.

[146] Newcastle-upon-Tyne Public Libraries Committee, City Librarian's Monthly Report (19 December 1941).

[147] PRO, ED 171/1, Public libraries: previous requests for grant-aid (20 December 1944).

[148] D. Gray, 'Public library finance in wartime', *LAR* 44 (April 1942), 40.

[149] PRO, ED 171/1, Archbishop of Canterbury to R.A. Butler (21 March 1944).

[150] PRO, ED 171/1, R.A. Butler to the Archbishop of Canterbury (4 April 1944).

[151] PRO, ED 171/1, Memo from N.D. Bosworth Smith (March 1944).

[152] PWBT, Curriculum vitae of William Benson Thorne. Obituary, *LAR* 68 (December 1966), 458-9. W.A. Munford, *Who was who in librarianship* (London, 1987), 79. *The Library Assistant* 41 (January-February 1948), 5-6. 'Poplar's new librarian ...', *East London Advertiser* (29 December 1934).

[153] 'William Benson Thorne, FLA', *LAR* 44 (December 1942), 186-88. The high esteem in which he was

held was demonstrated by the fact that at the lunch given by the Library Association to mark his retirement around forty librarians attended, many more havingt to be turned away: *LAR* 45 (January 1943), 16-17.

[154] Tower Hamlets Local Studies Library, C.M Jackson to Thorne (10 November 1942).

[155] Words of W.C.B. Sayers, *LAR* 44 (December 1942), 188.

[156] *LAR* 44 (December 1942), 186.

[157] 'Our new Honorary Fellow', *LAR* (July 1938).

[158] Words of A.C. Piper, *LAR* 44 (December 1942), 187.

[159] 'Former Poplar librarian was Honoured by the Library Association', *East London Advertiser* (23 December 1966)

[160] SRO, GD 281/13/82, Thorne to A.L. Hetherington (16 October 1918).

[161] 'Our new Honorary Fellow', *LAR* (July 1938).

[162] Munford, *Who was who in librarianship*, op. cit., 79.

[163] Correspondence from Winifred Thorne, W.B. Thorne's daughter (12 July 1998).

[164] 'Our new Honorary Fellow', op. cit.

[165] Words of W.C.B. Sayers, *LAR* 44 (December 1942), 188.

[166] *Books to read: the 'quarterly' of the Poplar Borough Public Libraries* No. 31 (January 1943).

[167] Munford, *Who was who in librarianship*, op. cit., 79.

[168] *Viewpoint* [Newsletter of St. Peter's Church, Harold Wood] (December 1966).

[169] *St. Bride Foundation Printing School souvenir of 'coming of age'* (Session 1914-15), St. Bride Printing Library, London

[170] Words A.C. Piper, *LAR* 44 (December 1942), 187.

[171] 'Poplar's librarian to retire', *East London Advertiser* (12 September 1942).

[172] Ibid.

[173] 'Poplar library service', *East End News* (4 August 1940)

[174] Correspondence from Winifred Thorne, W.B. Thorne's daughter (26 April 1998).

[175] 'Poplar's public library service: Mr. W.B. Thorne takes charge', *East End News* (21 December 1934).

[176] List deposited in PWBT.

[177] 'Poplar's librarian to retire', op. cit..

[178] C. Kernahan, *The reading girl: saunters in bookland and chats on the choice of books and methods of reading* (London, 1925), 17.

[179] 'Change of name', *Evening News* (30 November 1955).

[180] Words of A.C. Piper, *LAR* 44 (December 1942), 188.

[181] 'Poplar's librarian to retire', op. cit.

[182] Thorne to H.E. Dennis (20 July 1942), Tower Hamlets Local Studies Library.

[183] Ibid.

[184] W.B. Thorne, 'Valedictory', *Books to read: the 'quarterly' of the Poplar Borough Public Libraries*, No. 31 (January 1943).

[185] 'Poplar's librarian to retire', op. cit.

[186] Tower Hamlets Local Studies Library, James Ross to Thorne (23 November 1942).

[187] C. Barnet, *The audit of war: the illusion and reality of Britain as a great nation* (London, 1986), 11.

[188] Ibid., 12.

[189] K. Faulks, *Citizenship in modern Britain* (Edinburgh, 1998), 33.

[190] McGill, 'Reading tastes in wartime', op. cit., 26.

[191] 'The library as social centre', op. cit., 115.

[192] McColvin Report, op. cit., 1.

[193] Ibid., 4, 5.

[194] Frank Hugh, in Halifax Public Libraries, *Reader's Guide* (August 1940).

CHAPTER FIVE

Welfarism and Modernisation

1945-1976

In the thirty years following the Second World War the public library in Britain gradually took on a modern pose, drawing inspiration and, eventually, considerable funding from an interventionist state. Although not strictly speaking a facet of the welfare state – which originated as a combination of provision for social security, housing, health, full employment and formal education[1] – the public library increasingly defined itself, notwithstanding some librarians' suspicion of state planning, less in terms of civic society and more according to the principles of welfarism: universalism; heavy investment by central government; and top-down services delivered by professionals committed to the public service ethos. The public library underwent a steady, yet extensive, process of modernisation, so much so that whereas in 1945 the institution was widely characterised by remnants of Victorianism, by the mid-1970s it had in many places and in many respects modernised itself beyond a point that would have been immediately recognisable to a library user of the nineteenth century.

From Austerity to Affluence

Following the war, which was seen as much as a triumph for freedom of thought as a military victory, the Library Association confidently predicted that public libraries in Britain had a central role to play 'in the unfolding story of twentieth century democracy'.[2] It was to be some years, however, before the public library was fully able to justify this confidence, hampered as it was by the austerity which marked the immediate post-war years. 'Legislation after the Second World War', Jose Harris has written in respect of new arrangements to combat poverty and disadvantage, 'created in Britain one of the most uniform, centralised, bureaucratic and "public" welfare systems in Europe, and indeed the modern world'.[3] In the heights of industry, in transport and communication, in health and in education the state also became highly interventionist.

Even in the field of culture the state declared an interest, the Arts Council being established in 1946.

Public libraries, on the other hand, attracted little attention from the state for a decade or more. When they did, moreover, the agenda which was set effectively excluded the proposals for quasi-nationalisation which McColvin and his supporters had argued for during the war. In the post-war years public libraries appeared to fit neatly into the political consensus which emerged around the welfare state. At the local level they had frequently aroused animosity between economisers and liberals. At a national level there were signs that the war had helped to reduce the tension between money-saving Gradgrinds and expenditure-minded advocates of culture. Towards the end of the war, in a letter to the publisher Geoffrey Faber (copied to the Minister of Education, R.A. Butler), the Conservative Henry Brooke suggested that his fellow Tories might like to familiarise themselves with the public library issue for 'immediate' political gain. He observed that the Conservative Party was being depicted as 'interested in nothing but money-bags', and supporting a 'cultural subject' like public libraries could be attractive to 'people not normally in close touch with party politics'. He believed public libraries could be a weapon to help people realise 'that the Conservative Party is catholic and not narrow in its aims and purposes'.[4] In reply, Faber wrote of the importance to a renaissance of conservatism of taking every opportunity to kill the reproach of Philistinism, to show:

that the [Conservative] Party is concerned with the 'imponderables' of art, science, and all the rest. Indeed I think it is a matter of necessity rather than importance, if conservatism is to be the political force we hope it will be. Unhappily we haven't much of a record to show in the cultural field. It is to that fact I attribute a very great part of the leftward drift ... Instead of being regarded as the party of Philistinism, we ought to be regarded as par excellence the enemies of Philistinism. On the level of minor performance, nothing could do more of itself to contribute to this desirable change in public opinion that for us to take us, deliberately, the aim of strengthening the libraries. These librarians are men, very often indeed of very considerable influence. They arrange meetings, invite speakers, lead discussions, and take part in innumerable local intellectual activities. These are breeding-points of public opinion, and it would make a very perceptible difference, in a few years time, if the librarians began to come over to our side. I should guess that, at present, they are nearly all left-inclined.[5]

The extent to which Faber's desire to see a drift towards the centre ground of politics in respect of the public library issue was fulfilled is difficult to say. However, reflecting on the post-war library scene, it is the opinion of a former leading post-war public librarian that librarianship mirrored the general, moderate political disposition of the nation: 'This country doesn't like extremes. We don't like "outside-Rights", or "outside-Lefts". We like "inside-Right" Labour and "inside-Left" Tory'.[6] This said, however, librarians hardly appeared unified in their attitude to the growing influence of the state after the war. Although welcomed by many, the increasing emphasis on state planning undoubtedly worried a vocal group of librarians who wished to preserve as much local autonomy as possible and, moreover, viewed ideologically the growth in state power as damaging to the self, to the individuality and initiative they saw as prime products of public library use (more about this later). Further, libraries were certainly not immune from the rough and tumble of adversarial politics. For example, the challenging view of a government opponent in 1962 that 'the library service is deteriorating under our eyes', was met by a predictable ministerial reply: 'I have no evidence', countered Sir David Eccles, 'that the library service is deteriorating. Within the last two months, I have visited a number of libraries and have found them in excellent shape.'[7]

Despite the general agreement among the political parties that public libraries were generally a good thing and, therefore, worthy of attention, if only for the political benefits this might bring, support for public library renewal did not show itself until the late 1950s. As late as 1959, Harrogate's public library users were told that: 'People tend to have a guilt complex about the spending of public money on cultural services.'[8] Fear of stagnation in public library development in the post-war years was mixed with remnants of the optimism generated by the public library movement during the war. Writing to his friend William Benson Thorne in 1940, the librarian George Roebuck wondered:

how things will go during the depression which is likely to follow the Peace. Poor old Social Services may suffer ... There may be the need to economise later on. There are times when I'm glad to have lived through those 'best years' [between the wars]'.[9]

Looking at the general picture of library provision in the immediate post-war years, Roebuck's fear appeared justified, as another librarian writing to Thorne in 1958 demonstrated with regard to library provision in Poplar:

Remembering the libraries in the pre-war days, they are in a sad state now. Issues are steadily dropping, staff is at a minimum, as is cash, which means we are no longer giving a real service and have become practically dispensers of books.[10]

In many places, and in various facets of their operation, public libraries displayed a backwardness reminiscent of Victorian provision. In Nottinghamshire in the early 1950s, the voluntary village centre which was the basis of the rural library service, could not, in most cases, provide an adequate library service: 'The choice of books was often limited to 100 changed three times a year and advice on books and reading was given by a voluntary librarian who although probably very keen, had a limited knowledge both of books and the resources of the library.' Elsewhere in the county, shortages of books, especially standard works, continued for many years; as did the use of converted and temporary premises instead of permanent, purpose-built libraries, the construction of which was not permitted. Branch libraries were opened in a bewildering variety of non-library institutions: in sports pavilions, hospitals, village institutes and halls, shops, chapels, and in one instance even in a 'fish and chip saloon'. Staffing in Nottinghamshire's libraries improved as former employees returned from war service, but immediate work requirements had to be juggled with long-postponed professional training.[11]

The situation appeared much worse in some remote areas of Scotland. C.S. Minto, Deputy Librarian of Edinburgh, reported in 1948 that in Lossiemouth, although readers were admitted to the shelves, a Cotgreave indicator was still being used for the purpose of issuing books; moreover, the library was in the charge of the town hall caretaker. In Tain, he found that 'the stock is moribund, unclassified, unlettered, unlabelled and without discernible shelf order. What good books there are there is no evidence of recent use'.[12] In Keighley, peace did not result in the expansion of use anticipated at the end of the war. Whereas total issues rocketed from 267,000 in 1937-8 to 524,000 in 1945-6, by 1956-7 they had fallen to 518,000.[13] A major problem underpinning the problem of stagnating issues was identified as a severe shortage of books following the barren years of the Second World War, when barely a volume was purchased or bound.[14] This picture of austerity and desolation was reflected by Kingsley Amis in his 1955 novel *That Uncertain Feeling* (later made into the film *Only Two Can Play*, starring Peter Sellers), in which in one scene the wife of the chairman of the library committee in a Welsh town visits the central public library, only to be horrified by what she saw. The narrator describes how:

She looked about with the irritated wonder of one being shown a very ancient and boring ruin. We came to two adjacent doors. One of these led to a room ostensibly dedicated to book-repairs, but nobody used to do very much of that in my time, and the place was actually three-parts full of junk, the peculiar detritus, almost but never quite totally useless, thrown up by a large public library. I opened the other door and went in. This was where Jenkins catalogued the non-fiction. Nobody had been cataloguing the fiction since the outbreak of war, and after the war nothing had happened to make starting again seem desirable. Here too, there was plenty of junk, much of it powdered with dust and plaster, but no Jenkins.[15]

A similar sense of stagnation was identified in nearby Ilkley where, although the public library gave 'a general impression of efficient operation in the spirit of public service', and was seen to occupy 'an important place in the life of the town' (36% of the population were registered readers), the overall feeling given in a survey conducted in 1956 was of a static, unchanging service. Restrictive practices such as Wednesday afternoon closing, the provision of separate tickets for fiction and non-fiction and a twopenny charge for each ticket were still to be seen. Further, proposals were made to improve the service in the minds of the public: the appointment of a designated children's librarian; personal name plates to be displayed at the readers' advisor desk; and the encouragement of telephone enquiries.[16]

From the late 1950s, however, a more optimistic outlook for public libraries appeared. In July 1957, a few months after becoming Prime Minister, Harold MacMillan, in a now famous passage, told the British public: 'Let's be frank about it; most of our people have never had it so good. Go around the country, go to the industrial towns, go to the farms and you will see a state of prosperity such as we have never had.'[17] Over the next two decades public libraries were to reap the benefits of this perceived age of affluence. In 1955, the Public Libraries Act (Scotland) ushered in a new era for library provision north of the border by abolishing the rate limit (at the time threepence in the pound) on library expenditure.[18] A series of enquiries in the late 1950s and early 1960s demonstrated a renewed interest in public libraries on the part of government,[19] culminating in fresh legislation for public libraries in 1964. Expenditure on libraries, museums and the arts, out of which public libraries took their fair share, more than doubled between 1961 and 1967.[20] Such was the explosion in library activity in Britain that news of it appeared to travel far and wide. In opening a new library in Allerton in 1961, Evelyn Evans, Director of Ghana's library service, said that: 'Whereas in the past it had been common practice for overseas librarians to go to Scandinavia or America to learn about library services and techniques, things had now changed and they were now visiting Britain for such information.'[21] This period was, in the opinion of some, the 'golden age' of public library development. 'The 1960s was a notable decade in British library history', wrote James Ollé: 'For the first time in more than a hundred years it had become common, rather than exceptional, for public libraries to be both resourceful and attractive, offering appropriate services to all ages and many specialized interests ... Even the county libraries had begun to flourish.'[22]

Evidence of the growing popularity of public libraries is seen in the decline of the private circulating libraries. Mudie's Library had been the first to go in 1937; but the 1960s saw the sudden collapse of the remaining leading players in the field: the W H Smith Library, the Times Book Club and the Boots Book Lovers' Library disappearing in 1961, 1965 and 1966 respectively. By the mid-1960s the vast majority of the twopenny libraries (which had emerged between the wars in response to a popular market that many public libraries, and librarians, had turned their backs on) had also disappeared. Writing out of sheer desperation to the Prime Minister in 1957, the owner of the Mill House (twopenny) Library in Dovercourt, which he had established in 1937, had no hesitation in identifying the cause of his library's financial ruin: the public library. He argued that public libraries were funded by ratepayers on the understanding that they were educational institutions, whereas in reality, he was keen to point out, 'the bulk of the volumes they lend are the doubtful and trashy type' – presumably of the kind his library had supplied over the years.[23]

Despite the paperback revolution and the competing attractions of the mass media, most notably television, the appetite for borrowing books from public libraries and using them for various educational, cultural and informational purposes gradually increased. However, expansion created new pressures on the delivery of services. In Darlington in 1969 it was reported that:

There are more students requiring ever more esoteric books and articles, and better facilities for using them. Industry and commerce are asking for a more sophisticated information service for their local library. The ordinary reader is perhaps beginning to think of his library, not just as the place to acquire his weekly or fortnightly reading matter, but as a possible centre for local artistic life – concerts, lectures and exhibitions.'[24]

As awareness of the improved capability of any service becomes better known, the demands made upon it inevitably increase. In the third quarter of the twentieth century, as the population became more educated and articulate in matters of culture, what was *asked of* the public library not only escalated but also became more complex. 'Especially notable this year', it was observed in relation to Nottingham Public Library in 1968:

has been the ever-increasing variety of demands made on our services. It is increasingly apparent that the vague and generalised approach of our enquirers is being replaced by one more highly specialised, intensive and articulate. We are faced by sections of the community who are making explicit demands on us *as* sections of the community. The more demanding they are the better they come to know us. The staff, too, are becoming less maids-of-all-work and more specialised departments.[25]

More sophisticated use emanated in particular from the expansion and improvement of education especially in the tertiary sector.[26] Speaking in the debate on the second reading of the Public Libraries and Museums Bill in 1964, A.E.P. Duffy explained that:

The library service was having to take the strain of an over taxed educational system. In any town accommodating a university, a college of advanced technology, a college of technology or a training college, it was obvious that students spilled over quite freely into libraries.[27]

On the one hand, heavy student use was palpably a good thing for libraries. On the other, it reinforced in the minds of some the image of educational seriousness – perhaps even stuffiness – which prevented the institution from reaching down into the lower layers of society. Addressing the Library Association in London in 1950, Eric Clough, deputy librarian of Brighton, observed that:

All our reference libraries suffer from the aura of scholarship with which we have contrived to surround them in the past hundred years. As a result all we have succeeded in doing is frightening a large section of the public away and leaving it in the hands of a small group of scholars and students, and a large group of highly respectable idlers and time-wasters.[28]

Interviewed for BBC Television News in 1957, on the occasion of the centenary of the Westminster Public Library, Lionel McColvin dismissed the notion that libraries served a relatively narrow stratum of society. Asked what people were reading nowadays he replied:

They are reading about everything. We cover the widest possible range of material. We try to provide books on everything in which people are interested, and our readers cover every type and class of person, from the Members of the Houses of Parliament across the road, to the children from the nearby housing estate.[29]

This pluralistic line was later echoed by Thomas Kelly who, arguing that in the immediate post-war decades the public library moved decisively into a fully modern phase, wrote that these were years when: 'The last vestiges of the old working-class image now rapidly faded, and the library became in a real sense the possession of the community, even though it was still only a minority of the community that made regular use of its services.'[30]

Arguably, such history arises more from wishful thinking and seduction by the idea of community, than from a precise reporting of the historical record. During the era of the classic welfare state, public libraries may well have jettisoned part of their 'soup kitchen' reputation, but this was not replaced by a new sense of comprehensive social class use; rather by a strengthening of the institution's respectable, 'deserving' and middle-class constituency. Indeed, this proposition is in keeping with the theory that with the coming of the welfare state, the middle-classes began to enjoy a disproportionate share of universal services like health and education.[31] In the case of the public library, of course, the benefits accruing to the respectable, educated, 'deserving' classes from a flourishing public library service are obvious. Effectively, therefore, the increased spending on public libraries in the era of the classic welfare state reinforced middle-class interest in, and influence on, the public library – an enduring characteristic of provision which can be traced back to the inception of the public library movement when proposals were made with the need to satisfy middle-class cultural needs very much in mind. By the 1970s, some librarians began to highlight the middle-class trajectory of public libraries and to suggest policies which might reduce the partiality of use and encourage greater participation among the disadvantaged (more about this in Chapter 6).

Size Matters

Although the government had recognised their social importance during the war, it quickly lost interest in public libraries once peace arrived, making little attempt to realise the grand plan which McColvin and the Library Association had formulated. Whereas vast areas of both the economy and social provision were placed under common ownership after the war, never was the nationalisation of public libraries seriously contemplated.[32] In 1945 the Minister of Education was advised to show sympathy towards the grand plan, but to deflect pressure for public library reform until the effects of educational reform had worked through.[33] The government appears to have explored some of the key components of the plan. For example, the Ministry of Education sounded out the Treasury on the issue of central grants to public libraries, and the possibility of fresh legislation *was* discussed. However, other reasons holding back legislation resided not with the government but with the library world itself. It was not only that the huge number of library authorities in existence made the task of administering grants extremely difficult, but also that many of these authorities shied away from the idea of the government inspection and loss of autonomy which both central grants and larger authorities would mean.[34] Faced with a divided opinion in the public library world, therefore, it is hardly surprising that government ignored the draft new Public Libraries Act which the Library Association drew up in 1948.[35]

The post-war public library was in many ways a confused and fractured national institution, in terms of both the library system and librarians' views on the best way forward: 'The present structure of the library service is a jungle of overlapping and conflicting spheres of responsibility', observed Lord Hailsham, the Minister of Education, in 1957.[36] That same year, the Library Association emphasised the 'good deal of disparity in resources and efficiency of public libraries. An improvement in standards all round, making them a bit better and more uniform in character, would be a benefit to the country'.[37]

For many post-war public librarians size mattered a lot. The question of the optimum size of public library authorities at times dominated professional debate. Those in favour of larger authorities pointed out that 'a good library service cannot be achieved with libraries starved of necessary material, because their resources are too small'; and hoped that smaller authorities would not regard the larger authorities that were to absorb them as seeking 'the aggrandisement of our own system at their expense'.[38] Noting the increasing size of enterprises in the commercial sphere, advocates of enlargement stressed the economies of scale which could be achieved. In addition to this economic reasoning, certain 'political' issues were also at play. Librarians realised that larger authorities would mean a less complicated system. This would increase the possibility of obtaining direct Treasury grants (much needed in the big city libraries which needed to provide expensive services to industry, for example),[39] thereby increasing central government involvement in library services, and, importantly reducing the influence of local politicians, some of whom were 'definitely against' public libraries: 'We do not believe any more in local enthusiasm and local initiative', remarked T.E. Callander, Librarian of Croydon, in 1961.[40]

Those in favour of sweeping away small and inefficient library authorities gained official support in the form of a Ministry of Education inquiry in the late-1950s, led by Sydney Roberts (later Sir Sydney), Master of Pembroke College, Cambridge. The general thrust of *The Structure of the Public Library Service in England and Wales* (the Roberts Report) was the need to significantly reduce the number of library authorities in existence: parishes should cease to be library authorities and others bodies should give up their library functions if they fell below certain thresholds of expenditure on books and population served.[41]

As in the Second World War, the suggested gathering together of smaller authorities into larger units created a great deal of opposition, as well as anxiety.[42] 'The disease of giantism is abroad', declared one opponent, the librarian and library educator Raymond Irwin in 1949. 'Wise administration', he believed:

may overcome some of the difficulties of great size. But present-day experience of administration of swollen organisations such as the coal, electricity and transport services in Great Britain suggest that skilled administration cannot always be bought ... there is a great deal of evidence to show that the most successful of all general libraries are those of a moderate size – the middle town library which is large enough to stock most of the students' tools, and yet not so large that the personal factor in its administration is overwhelmed by the complexity of the machinery ... librarianship is above all an individual service; there is no reason for standardisation in the goods it supplies or the services it performs.'[43]

The 'keep it local' lobby once again found its voice in the late 1950s, as proposals for enlargement gained momentum. Surprisingly, the librarians of some of the country's largest cities collectively voiced the opinion that where there was a compact community it should have a local library service and should not become part of a larger reorganised unit: 'The public library is an organic growth in response to a community need; its character, therefore, reflects the community it serves ... in the large industrial cities the community is complex and varied and the public library services are of a like kind.'[44] Less surprisingly, smaller public libraries themselves were vehement in their desire to remain local, and thereby closer, in their view, to their readers. A 'Smaller Public Libraries Group' urged that a number of points be considered before any decision was taken to restructure the service. These included: the 'desirability of the public library service, which is essentially a personal and local service, being administered by as "local" an authority as possible'; the proposition that the 'coherence of a community served by a public library unit may be more important than the question of the administration of that unit'; and the suggestion that co-operation 'can solve many of the existing problems'.[45] Others sought a compromise on the issue of size, arguing that combination was important, but only for the provision of specialist services to meet minority needs and interests.[46]

The debate on size was eventually overtaken by events (although it was never quite laid to rest entirely).[47] Changes in the structure of local government, largely outside the sphere of influence of the library world, eventually forced the issue. Local government reorganisation came first to London. From 1965 the London County Council was replaced by the Greater London Council, comprising 32 boroughs (plus the City of London) and covering a much wider geographical area. Many smaller boroughs disappeared: in London's East End, for example, Bethnal Green, Poplar and Stepney were amalgamated to form a single borough, Tower Hamlets. Reorganisation followed in the rest of England and Wales with effect from 1974, and in Scotland with effect from 1975. The structure of library authorities fell in behind this reorganisation, realising much of what McColvin had advocated decades before. The net result of reorganisation in England and Wales reduced the number of separate library authorities from 385 to 121; and in Scotland from 80 to 40.[48]

Some saw the move to large authorities as beneficial in terms of both efficiency and urban regeneration. In Bradford the prospect was welcomed because the city would have the opportunity of becoming the cultural and commercial centre of a larger area where new facilities, including libraries, 'could provide a welcome boost to what is at present a dying city'.[49] South Tyneside public libraries, having been formed from two smaller authorities, reported in 1975, a year after amalgamation, that: 'It would be a lie to say that either service was eager for the marriage although quite clearly each had much to offer the other.'[50] In Newcastle upon Tyne, where a larger authority was also formed, no drop in standards was found and the amalgamation was said to have avoided the 'traumatic experience which it has been in some other areas of the country'.[51] Such a positive experience may have had less to do, of course, with the size of the problem in hand, and more to do with the poor economic conditions – certainly compared to the time when London reorganised – of the day. The economic and political instability of the mid-1970s was a poor environment in which to rework the public library system. Successful or not, reorganisation was a fact of life for public librarians, and henceforth the conflict between those who believed 'small is beautiful' and those who proclaimed the benefits of economies of scale faded quickly.[52] Thus, after over 30 years of professional debate and conflict – what Thomas Kelly called the 'battle of the boundaries'[53] – the conservatism of the parochial-minded perished in the flames of modernisation and Fordist 'giantism'.

Modern Times

Against the backdrop of post-war austerity, the public library slowly dragged itself into the modern age. In 1953 Wakefield Public Library took down its Victorian silence notices.[54] In 1951, in Keighley, as if to mark the passing of post-war harshness and the arrival of modern times, librarians took the radical step of introducing reservations for works of fiction! Grounds for optimism were evident in the early 1950s. In 1950 the public library movement celebrated its centenary, the movement taking the opportunity to promote itself as 'democracy at work'.[55] Libraries around the country joined in the celebrations. In Leeds, for example, the public library held an exhibition on social growth, providing information on developments in education, housing, public health and, indeed, on the library movement: the 'library tributary' to the stream of social growth was described as modest, but one which had never dried up, going 'on from year to year increasing in volume and sustaining power'.[56]

The national mood was lifted by the Festival of Britain (1951) and the arrival in 1952 on the succession of a new monarch, of what contemporaries hailed as 'a new Elizabethan age'. But authentic 'modern times' did not arrive until the early 1960s. Pop culture, a general opening up of social mores, England's triumph in the 1966 soccer World Cup and an increasing standard of living infused much of the nation with a sense of social optimism only fleetingly glimpsed later in the century. Technology too had a part to play in fashioning a forward-looking mentality. In 1963, Harold Wilson declared that his Labour Party was restating its socialism 'in terms of the scientific revolution', and a new Britain would be 'forged in the white heat of this revolution'.[57] In terms of technology, despite lingering anxiety concerning the underlying strength of the economy, the 1960s was an era of notable British 'firsts': the vertical take-off jet, the hovercraft and in association with the French, the supersonic passenger jet, Concorde.[58]

The public library reflected these optimistic, modern times. 'The period ahead holds great promise for British librarianship', remarked one public library report in 1964.[59]

Even before the 1960s, during the era of austerity, public libraries continued to build on their tradition as serious providers of technical and commercial information for a modernising economy, acknowledging that 'commerce and industry thrive on information'.[60] Librarians appeared to be aware of Britain's fragile economic position. Eric Hinton, Librarian of Newcastle upon Tyne, warned in 1948 that the 'relatively careless enjoyment by a creditor nation of a seller's [world] market', which had marked the pre-war years was no longer possible: 'light-hearted inattention to research, to methods and to markets can only lead to disaster, to our complete financial, political and social ruin', he added. Hinton was thus anxious to 'stress the importance of factual information and emphasise the necessity of studying the possibilities and new methods, and their application in improving the quality and the design of our industrial products'. He was pleased to announce that his own library was rich in information pertinent to business: patents and British Standard specifications; reports on German industry and on commercial conditions and opportunities in other countries; official trading returns; statistics of various kinds; and some 120 commercial and technical periodicals. A new development in his library was the acquisition of 'Copycat' apparatus to provide within minutes, photographic copies of documents.[61]

On the hundredth anniversary of the Public Libraries Act (1850), the Library Association re-asserted its faith in the public library's economic role as a dispenser of commercial and technical information, declaring that 'Information is an Export'.[62] By 1952, Sheffield's 'Organisation for the Interchange of Technical Publications', established in 1933, included four libraries, four institutions, four government departments and twenty eight firms, lending among themselves thousands of items each year. At the heart of the organisation was Sheffield Public Library's Science and Commercial Department whose staff maintained 'regular and personal contacts with those engaged in productive industry' in order to assemble a stock of materials responsive to local industrial requirements.[63] Librarians were keen to stress that economic information in public libraries was available on a bewildering variety of activities. For example, the resources of the Commercial Science and Technology Library in Leeds were used to produce a booklet entitled 'Who makes jam in Amsterdam?'[64]

By the late 1950s commercial and technical provision had become a serious component of public library work and a reflection of the public library's commitment to economic modernisation. The leading exponent of commercial and technical services, J.P. Lamb, librarian of Sheffield, viewed that their future would be 'profoundly affected by the emphasis now being placed on scientific and technical education and practice'.[65] Librarians believed their collections appealed to a wide variety of economic sectors in any given locality and also made up for the over-specialisation of library provision by the industrial research associations (which had begun during the First World War). Public technical and commercial libraries were also said to be important because libraries in many firms were still young, lacking out-of-print books, long runs of periodicals and government publications.[66] In 1964 the Director and Principal Librarian of the British Museum, Sir Frank Francis, advised that: 'The local library should ally itself to local industry and give the craftsman, the foreman and the manager the chance to improve his know-how ... To cater for local business and commerce is a really constructive job, requiring energy and imagination.' He warned, however, that local businesses were too often 'dependent on the enterprise of an over-worked librarian, and we are only beginning to see ways of helping this important service'.[67] Nonetheless, a government report on standards of service in public libraries in 1962 urged that the institution 'must play an essential and increasing part in the scientific, technical and cultural advance of the economy'. Here we have once again a firm declaration of faith in the public library's dynamic ability (or at least endeavour) to bridge the gap between science and culture. As in the nineteenth century the public library, after the war, ambitiously set out to embrace the two cultures – that of the 'literary intellectuals' and the 'natural scientist' – between which C.P. Snow, in his famous discourse in 1959, believed there to be a large gulf, born of mutual suspicion, ignorance and incomprehension.[68]

The public library's modernity in this period was also defined by a Fordist mode of operation. Fordist production is characterised by, amongst other things, economies of scale, standardisation, vertical integration, division of labour and mass production. These characteristics were also visible in the post-war public library, and are discussed systematically here.

Regarding the quest for standardisation and economies of scale, in the absence of the national structure advised by McColvin during the war, co-operation was the next best thing. The co-operative library network begun between the wars was strengthened after 1945. W.C.B. Sayers wrote in 1947 that:

a librarian regards every library as a branch of the national library service ... Every public library in England is within one of nine regional library systems which cover the country ... Behind the regions lies the National Central Library, which has as its outliers several government and special libraries belonging to the learned societies, industrial institutions, universities, colleges and schools; the whole system based on the assumption every library will be willing to lend to every other – the National Central Library acting as the sponsor and co-ordinating agents of all. Through this machinery, which is much simpler than this rather complex statement would imply, any book ... that can be spared for a brief time can be lent to any library in any part of the British Isles; and the borrowing libraries in turn are willing to lend ...any of their books.[69]

The spirit of universalism was also seen in the growth of ticket interchangeability schemes. In 1950, in Newcastle upon Tyne, where visitors had for some time been able to obtain books from the town's libraries on the ticket of their home towns, the library committee anticipated 'the day when library tickets may be useable throughout the country'.[70] The universal accessibility of knowledge via public libraries was glowingly praised by a reader in Cambridge:

Rather half heartedly I recently applied at the central library for half a dozen rare and costly books published over a century ago. To my intense gratification they turned up after a very short wait; they came from various libraries in East Anglia and the Central Midlands. It was not long before I was sending in requests for German books.[71]

Standardisation was discussed energetically and became the focus of a government enquiry in 1962.[72] Shortly after, a new Public Libraries Act (1964) ensured (for England and Wales only, as Scotland was not included in the Act) a fundamental level of standardisation by *compelling* local authorities to provide an public library service, one which was, moreover, 'comprehensive and efficient'.[73]

Although vertical integration in its true sense was not a feature of public library provision, the welfare state provided the opportunity for various public services to be integrated in poly-purpose centres. In Nottingham, for example, a number of libraries were opened in complexes shared by health services. In Carlton-in-Lindrick a 'three-in-one' premises was opened in 1962, housing a health clinic, chiropody service and a library.[74] Libraries also formed parts of large new educational and recreational complexes, such as in the Abraham Moss Centre in Manchester.[75]

A detailed division of labour is endemic in library work – the 'army system of delegated responsibility works well in a library', McColvin once remarked[76] – and remained so during this period. If anything it was accentuated by the increasingly defined separation of professional and non-professional work, the former improving its position by moving to fully-fledged graduate status in the 1960s and taking advantage of the expansion in full-time education for librarianship. Labour specialisation among qualified librarians themselves was articulated by the removal of the distinction between reference and lending functions and the emergence in the 1960s, in some of the country's larger libraries, of subject departments – for example, business; commerce and technology; arts and humanities; social sciences; sciences; music and gramophone; popular; children's; general enquiries – requiring professional staff 'dedicated' to various areas of knowledge.[77] It therefore appeared that, because it was trying to be all things to all people, the large public reference department had had its day. However, the traditional reference department, originally fashioned in the Victorian era, was to prove more resilient than promoters of subject specialisation predicted.

By the mid-1970s the public library in Britain was, like most large-scale enterprises in the private sector, subject to a strict Fordist regime of operation. The public library was confirmed in the efficacy of this, moreover, by the emergence in the early 1970s of Fordism at the top of the library hierarchy. In 1973, the British Library was formed, drawing together the operations of the British Museum Library, the National Central Library, the National Lending Library for Science and Technology, the National Reference Library of Science and Invention and the British National Bibliography.

The public library's commitment to a modern future was evident in tentative steps taken towards the computerisation of library facilities. Libraries had long been anxious to mechanise their operations, punch-card technology (peek-a-boo retrieval) having first been experimented with between the wars. In the late 1950s came book-issuing by camera (photo-charging machines).[78] The next step was automation. Computers in libraries made sense: the new technology lent itself well to the repetitive, routine tasks characteristic of library work, the processes of cataloguing and book-issuing being the main beneficiaries of computerisation. The earliest computer work in public libraries was in cataloguing. The amalgamation of library authorities in London in the mid-1960s prompted the combination of catalogues on computer files.[79] The first operational (non-laboratory) computerised book-issue system appears to have been installed in the lending department of Brighton public library in 1969. By that date the manual system in Brighton was said to have 'reached a point of total breakdown, so heavy were the demands made upon it'. Having adopted an automated system the town's librarian was pleased to report that: 'The dull repetitive and routine tasks associated with this aspect of our work were from that time relegated to machines, and staff have been able to spend more time in giving a direct service to our readers.'[80] By January 1974, some 35 individual libraries were operating computerised circulation systems, and another 120 were awaiting installation having ordered the new technology.

The age's passion for streamlining found favour with the librarian K.C. Harrison, who pointed out that it had become a prime concern for him and his fellow professionals 'to streamline their organisations for the convenience of readers'.[81] Harrison, along with many others, was a fan of the modern, uncomplicated systems (administration) and lines (buildings) of Scandinavian libraries.[82] The Scandinavian example proved very influential, particularly in the case of library designs. Clean lines, uncluttered space and well-lit premises provided, in many places, library environments a world away from the Gothic and Classical designs of earlier generations. The lighter feel to many of the new library buildings of the 1960s was illustrated vividly in the design of the Bradford Central Library in 1967:

Vast rows of windows flood the building with light ... Especially pleasing is the glass-fronted entrance hall with its elegant canopy. The interior of the hall is spacious and its marble floor, walls and columns, together with pendant clusters of tubular lights, all help to make it an aesthetic delight.[83]

The Newcastle upon Tyne public library built in the late 1960s was advertised unequivocally by the city's librarian as nothing less than a reflection of 'the space age'.[84] Others, to be fair, were less enthusiastic about the shift to modern forms in library design: 'a supermarket library designed to wipe out the human element', commented a librarian on a new branch library in Nottinghamshire in 1971.[85] But generally modernism was enthusiastically embraced by librarian and reader alike.

Popular Culture

It is a paradox that the post-war decades, particularly after the mid-1950s, witnessed a substantial increase in state patronage of arts and culture, including public libraries, and at the same time the growth of an alternative culture, often vigorously anti-establishment in its philosophy and practices.[86] During the post-war period the public library became increasingly popular: queuing in and, indeed, outside pre-computerised libraries at peak times was not an uncommon site in the 1950s and early 1960s.[87] But was the modern, post-war public library truly popular in the cultural sense? How quickly, and to what extent, did it respond to the cultural revolution of the time?

The issue of censorship continued to raise its head. In 1960, Harrogate Public Library Committee banned *Lady Chatterley's Lover*, not even allowing it to be kept 'under the counter', the alternative suggested by the chief librarian. The Committee was duly criticised for having 'taken upon itself the paternal task of deciding what the people of Harrogate should read'.[88] The Committee was also lambasted for keeping the music library too elitist. Selection was confined to recordings of classical music: 'The ordinary resident would like to borrow these', explained a local newspaper, 'but also other records as well. A much wider choice of music will be needed, folks say, musicals and jazz included, before the residents of Harrogate will be willing to join.'[89] Eventually, of course, audio materials became fairly widely accepted as a natural feature of public library provision, but not without opposition from a strand of opinion in the library profession which regarded music recordings as 'an unaffordable extravagance'.[90]

In the days before the licensed betting shop, the popular pastime of gambling and the pursuit of the racing news needed to facilitate it, remained a target for librarians' wrath. In Nottinghamshire, in 1957, library staff were given lengthy guidance on the best way to deal with 'our bettors':

Establish the identity of the bookmaker's runner. He is the colourless individual who moves around the table from newspaper to newspaper instead of remaining in one position and snatching them. Usually he will wear a hat ... When you see a betting-slip actually being made out do not at once reproach the reader but wait until the vital paper has been passed to its recipient ....Catch them in the act. This can be done very effectively in this manner: the bookie's runner will be wearing a belted fawn raincoat of the Central-European-Fascist-Revolutionary pattern...Throw him out and keep him out.[91]

This advice might have been 'tongue in cheek', but it was none the less indicative of a gulf existing between the public library and 'the popular'. This gulf was also evident in the never-ending battle between advocates of highbrow literary culture and those who were more tolerant of popular literature. Despite the expansion of education, public library patrons mostly remained tied to imaginative literature. In 1957 in Keighley, it was reported that fiction accounted, broadly as in previous years, for 75% of loans,[92] despite earlier efforts to boost 'serious' reading by giving readers a non-fiction ticket in addition to their general ticket, on which both fiction and non-fiction could be borrowed.[93] Some librarians were worried that too much of a taste for fiction was inappropriate and damaging, and were unconvinced by the argument that reading 'trash' was often merely a preparation for the consumption of finer literature.[94]

The desire to oversee public morals remained strong. The librarian Richard Gordon, addressing fellow librarians in 1947, was reported to have asserted that: 'With the increase in the number and decline in the quality of books the public needed guidance and protection from the tendentious presentation of information.'[95] In 1951 John Stuffins, librarian of Harrogate, was anxious to point out that, as he saw it:

The demand is for "pure" books, books that can be read by anyone in the family ... It is surprising how many people make a point of this ... Some of them say they dare not turn a page in many of the books they read, for fear of what they will find. Most Harrogate readers definitely dislike books with any suggestion of sex and sadism. Yet the old sweet love stories are getting harder to find.[96]

Parts of the library profession were clearly uncomfortable with the emergent popular culture of the 1950s and 1960s. In 1952, a correspondent to the *Library Association Record* echoed growing concern about the influence of American comics, which, with their 'graphic descriptions of murder, armed hold-ups, bashings, floggings, torture, [and] sexual depravity',[97] were seen to be ousting more acceptable productions, like the *Beano* and the *Dandy*. In 1955 librarians and teachers met together at a conference to criticise comics as 'short-winded reading' which damaged the ability to hold onto long stories. They were also suspicious of the effects of television, seen in some quarters as a dangerous 'eternal music hall'.[98] Even popular literature for children of the gentlest kind came under fire. In 1971 a newly appointed librarian in Nottinghamshire was amazed to find that the County Library had banned the *Rupert Bear Annual* on the cultural and intellectual grounds that it was 'insufficiently stimulating to the juvenile intelligence'.[99]

Such was the continuing vitality of the popular literature question that it was debated and commented upon at the highest level. In 1953 John Profumo, later scandalised for lying to Parliament over an issue of national security and sexual propriety, was anxious to supply the Minister of Education with a letter he had received from a public library user objecting to the large supply of fiction by public libraries in the counties:

I am informed that about 90% of the books delivered to the door free of charge to people in rural areas are *fiction*, and really I must say that I sympathise with people who are forced to pay for luxuries which they do not use themselves.[100]

When the new Public Libraries Bill came before Parliament in 1964, much of the debate was given over to the supply of role of works of fiction by libraries. Advocates of charging for the loan of fiction were vocal. One MP argued that 'free lending libraries were an out-moded Victorian concept. It was not reasonable ... that people should be able to borrow fiction *ad lib*. at no cost whatever'. Another:

asked the House seriously to consider what principle required the state educated and prosperous wage-earner to obtain free from his public library books of romance and adventure, detectives, westerns and humour at the expense of the elderly widow's rate, when he quite properly paid for all these facilities when he enjoyed them on television and at the cinema.

But defenders of free core services were equally strident in their contributions to the debate. 'If there were charges', claimed the Minister of Education:

libraries would tend to provide mainly what was most in demand by the majority and reduce expenditure on the materials needed by the minority. There would be a tendency to discriminate in favour of books for the mass, and not to cater for a number of minority tastes.

The Minister also pointed out that: 'In the matter of discrimination between fiction and non-fiction ... how could it be said that a travel book was more meritorious than, say, a novel of Henry James or Proust?'[101]

Even more disturbing than the negative effects attributed to the widespread consumption of popular fiction was the potentially demoralising influence of television perceived in some parts of the library profession. In the post-war decades, television became a major vehicle of popular culture. Whereas in 1946 only 15,000 homes owned a television licence, by 1958 there were 6.4 million licence holders; and by 1964 this figure had swollen to 12.8 million. Watching television became the largest leisure activity, occupying about a quarter of the leisure time of men and women in England and Wales by the late 1960s.[102] Reactionaries believed television would 'create mental and physical inertia, mass hysteria and mass emotions', and would become a 'substitute for life'.[103] Another voice from the public library world was equally fearful:

Annual report soon comes round again and though we still increase our annual issue I think this will be the last year when we shall do so. Our buildings can take no more and the light fiction readers are looking in at ITV![104]

Others, however, believed television had a beneficial effect on reading and improved the quality of public library use. In 1956 in Keighley, it was reported that:

Television ... has certainly not kept readers away from the Libraries. In fact, plays, films, documentaries, and controversial subjects on television, have sometimes stimulated readers to such an extent that they have followed them up by reading the original play, or the book from which the play or film was adapted, and by reading books on some subject or controversial topic of the day.[105]

Whereas some libraries had experienced a slight falling away in issue statistics at the start of the television boom in the early 1950s, by the middle of the decade the belief among public librarians appeared to be that:

The sigh of the intellectual, thinking about the passive entertainment which is the feature of this age, need not be too heart-felt. Man, despite the bombardment of moving pictures, had not lost his desire to read...television is possibly not quite the devitalising monster that some believe. Indeed it can, and has, encouraged viewers to go to the non-fiction shelves.[106]

Consumption of the classics, in particular, was said to be a healthy spin-off of television drama.[107] This echoed the earlier endorsement, by some, of films and radio. In Nottinghamshire in 1950, before television exploded into national popularity, the belief was that:

Radio and films have their influence. A tremendous lot of those who hear a radio serial of Jane Austen or Hornblower say to themselves "I must read that" or "I must read that again", and were all very glad to hear that something is being done about announcing proposed serials in good time as this will help to prepare us.[108]

Thus, although perceived as being slightly damaging in its early history, certainly by the early 1960s, television (along with radio and the cinema) had, according to one librarian, 'ceased to be an adverse factor'.[109]

Given continuing doubts among some librarians concerning the legitimacy of popular cultural products like television, comics and light fiction, it is evident that the claim made by the Library Association in 1950, that librarians 'no longer think it necessary to excuse the popularity of novels', was extremely premature – even more so if one enlarges the fear of popular fiction to include the suspicion of popular culture generally. After the war, the public library in many respects modernised itself, but it was not able to throw off entirely its long-standing reputation as a site where culture was vigorously contested.

As a result of the cultural pressures of the 'swinging Sixties', however, a serious attempt was being made by the end of that decade to relinquish the 'image of librarians fostered by films and television, as narrow-minded intellectuals moving silently through a world of dusty books'.[110] Librarians busied themselves preparing for the age of leisure they perceived to be emerging. To this extent, the modern public library of the early 1970s had moved a long way from the (in many respects) Victorian-style institution of the 1940s and 1950s. However, it is debatable whether the speed at which the public library took on modern garb from the late 1950s onwards kept pace with the cultural revolution of the day. For all the glass, the concrete and bright lights, the carpeted floors, streamlined fittings and paperback books, the public library, by the early 1970s, appeared to many, including librarians, to be too out of touch with popular and working-class culture (more about this in Chapter 6).

Libraries in Society

In parallel with certain conservative forces influencing the post-war public library, librarians were anxious to do much more than they had in the past to extend the library *into* society and to reach out to their public. In 1966 librarians in Nottingham were quizzed by the BBC on the extent to which libraries were appealing to modern people and how they were selling the idea of using public libraries.[111] David Gerard, thye city librarian, replied that they were doing this by:

Getting in touch with local factories, schools, local groups, organisations, lecturing, talking, showing slides, having special exhibitions, linking up with various centres in the locality, in Nottingham for example, and the County, where people come, where they pass by, casually perhaps, but where they are, we are trying to reach them outside the library premises.

His colleague, Kenneth Stockham, the County Librarian, added that:

We're doing all sorts of things, from standing a mobile library in a market square and at the junior level by arranging inter-school quizzes, and quite a number of things which we hope will get at readers and of course in the County we are always prepared to go and talk to Women's Institutes and those sort of organisations, and they're usually very prepared to listen to us. We do what we can.

Pressed on the question of the public library's image as, in the interviewer's words, 'rather an austere place, a Victorian place almost' and, in particular, the Nottingham Central Library's 'Cathedral-like atmosphere', the two librarians explained that in smaller libraries it was much easier to build up a 'feeling of intimacy and friendliness' and this was helped by the arrival of modern buildings with pleasant furniture and good fittings, where, especially, 'young people feel very much at home'. In larger buildings, they claimed, there was an even greater premium on making interiors look attractive; but they stressed that:

the really attractive part of any organisation is the human beings who service it... the human aspect is all important and if your staff are of the right calibre, know what they are doing, like people, like to service people, like to talk to people, or like to get themselves involved with the public then you'll create an atmosphere which the public will want to be involved in.

This interview encapsulates the twin objectives which together formed a new 'library in society' strategy: improved in-library service to, and communication with, the public; and the further development of the long tradition of providing outreach and extension activities.[112] That public libraries had a long way to go after 1945 to win over large sections of the public is indisputable. The librarian R.B. Oliph Smith, addressing the Library Association's annual conference in 1955 (the theme of which was 'The Library in the Community') was of the opinion that: 'No one except ourselves gets excited about libraries...We are not too sure where we are going and no one else cares. We are taken for granted like other unexciting public services or utilities such as the dustman, or the milkman, the coal man or the postman.'[113] Complaints such as that received from a naval Commander by the Essex County Library Service in 1957 did not make this task any easier: 'A study of the rules of most libraries', he ranted:

will reveal that they are designed almost entirely for the benefit of the librarians and very seldom for the reader ... rather comparable to the old Storekeeper's "Haven't got it, what do you want?"... The entire underlying spirit needs changing to 'Up and Coming'.[114]

In Stepney in 1956, to counter such accusations of inefficiency, staff were told by the chief librarian that: 'The reputation of our library service rests upon the impressions gained by the public in their contacts with us', and that these impressions were influenced by four major factors: the cleanliness and attractiveness of buildings; the speed and efficiency in dealing with enquiries, whether for books or information; the neatness, alertness and courtesy of staff; and the adequacy (in quantity) and up-to-dateness of the book stock.[115]

Over the next 20 years, improvement was forthcoming nationwide in each of these areas of service, and certainly in respect of the most tangible aspects of service: buildings and book stock. The quality of the librarian user-interface is much harder to judge. However, as society liberalised and consumerism grew, what *can* be said is that librarians made strenuous efforts to improve relations with their clientele. In 1965 Eric Cave, city librarian of Cambridge, related that he liked 'to maintain personal contact with the public because I consider public relations are an important job'.[116] Indeed, public relations (PR) became a prominent feature of the librarian's job description, so much so that articles and books began to appear on the subject. 'Librarians of the future must become more PR conscious, and more expert in using PR techniques', K.C. Harrison felt able to advise in 1973.[117]

Researching users became a key ingredient of the new pledge to draw closer to the public. It was during this period, especially after about 1960, that librarians began to borrow heavily from the work undertaken by marketeers and academics and to make use of social science techniques that were being employed in other spheres to 'measure' a society growing ever more complex and sophisticated in its needs.[118]

However, merely accommodating unfolding demands in respect of core services like lending, reference and children's work was acknowledged to be insufficient in a society exhibiting rising expectations. Librarians recognised that they had to become more pro-active. Books with a 'library in society' theme gushed from the pens of librarians seeking a higher level of social engagement.[119] 'It is the function of a public library not only to satisfy, but to promote, the desire for books', asserted the Roberts Report in 1959.[120] In the mid-1950s, Glasgow public libraries appeared to be attempting to do just that. The 'other' services it provided included: books in homes for the elderly, exhibitions, group loans to educational bodies, hospital libraries, lectures and discussions groups, prison libraries, a photocopying service and assistance with an educational service for seafarers and residential schools for convalescent and disabled children.[121] This was a varied and valuable diet of services.

In examining the outward-looking aspects of library work, a distinction needs to be drawn between *extension* and *outreach* activities. Extension activities included such cultural activities as lectures, film shows, gramophone recitals, play and poetry readings, art exhibitions, concerts, adult education classes, discussion groups and art festivals. In Keighley, during the winter of 1961-2, over 2,000 children attended a programme of story evenings, film shows and lectures.[122] In the early 1960s, Retford public library was being used for farming lectures, WEA classes, public lectures, and meetings of the local photographic society and of the Townswomen's Guilds.[123] Across the country such services boomed in the 1960s;[124] although formal adult education provision, in terms of the traditional nineteenth-century model, became patchy.[125] In reviewing the state of extension work in Scotland, it was urged that:

The librarian must be an educationalist in the fullest sense of the term, going out into the highways and byways seeking out readers, listeners and spectators and creating conditions under which people will be unable to resist the appeal of the 'documents of every kind' which reveal the culture and learning of the world.[126]

However, the pursuit of extension activities came with a warning from the library establishment. It was the Library Association's opinion that:

It is not considered a proper extension of library functions for the librarian to initiate such activities as amateur dramatics, art exhibitions, pageants, concerts, formal instructional classes ... its function is not that of curator, concert manager, or entertainments manager.[127]

In providing new cultural materials and formats librarians were on slightly safer ground. The lending of long playing records eventually became commonplace and largely uncontroversial. Less understandable perhaps, from the public's point of view, were the experiments in toy libraries for children. One of the first of these, opened in a branch library in Brighton, was described as 'a natural step from play to literacy': young children attracted to libraries by toys would progress to books and reading. It appeared, moreover, that some kind of moral education would accompany toy collections. In the Brighton experiment children themselves, it was hoped, would be involved in the repair of damaged toys.[128]

Librarians also took it upon themselves to 'reach out' to readers and potential readers beyond the walls of the library. The most obvious manifestation of the outreach mentality was the mobile library. Mobiles had proved important before the war in rural areas. During and after the war their usefulness was demonstrated in urban areas also, where the public library building programme was curtailed for virtually a generation.[129] By 1962 around 70 urban libraries were using mobile vehicles, often to serve new suburban housing which had expanded faster than the social and cultural infrastructure needed to serve them.[130] Recalling the early post-war mobile service in Nottinghamshire, one librarian wrote of:

the thrill of working out the routes and of how quickly our visits became part of the life of the countryside so that the people look forward to our coming in order to tell us their news, how they brought the new babies to see us and how our first driver invariably asked them on the second visit 'Can that baby read yet?'[131]

In 1948 Westminster public libraries commenced a personal delivery service to housebound readers (adding to their existing service to Darby and Joan Clubs for the elderly).[132] This was the first systematic service of its kind; by the 1970s services to the housebound had become a familiar aspect of public library work. Housebound services came under the heading of clients with 'special needs', other groups being prisoners, the hospitalised and youth – even lighthouse keepers![133]

Reaching out to groups which were restricted from using public libraries services in the normal way, and providing special services accordingly, was hardly new. For example, since the nineteenth century many of the country's large public libraries had provided books (in various formats) for the blind.[134] But the years of the classic welfare state marked a new commitment on the part of the public library to serve clients who were unable to make use of the institution in the way that the majority were able to. The need to serve such clients coalesced, moreover, with a general desire on the part of the librarians to boost their presence in the community – a desire reflected in an on-going post-war discourse articulated in parts of the profession calling on their institutions to become community centres as much as libraries.[135] The extent to which libraries widely became authentic community centres is, however, unclear. Observing activity in small branches in Nottinghamshire in the mid-1960s, one librarian revealed that: 'The public spend little time in the building but come in and select their books and leave. The library has *not* [my emphasis] become a local meeting place for teenagers or a sort of common lounge where one comes to write a letter, or read while waiting to catch a bus.'[136] This observation obviously detracts from the romantic image of the small library as a place where 'community' thrived.

The Public Library and the Modern Self

During this period, modernity is considered by some commentators to have reached its zenith, thereafter giving way to a post-colonial, -industrial, -Marxist and -materialist (in terms of the rise of the ecology movement) world. Frederick Jameson has argued that: 'The 1960s are in many ways the key transitional period, a period in which the new international order (neocolonialism, the Green Revolution, computerization and electronic information) is … set in place.'[137]

Before the arrival of economic liberalism in the 1970s, modernity also 'peaked' in terms of both the level of state involvement in social and economic life and the development of a burning faith in the efficacy of public expenditure. In 1973 Daniel Bell, in his classic book *The Coming of the Post-industrial Society* (1973), reminded his audience that: 'The axial principle of the [modern] culture is the desire for the fulfilment and enhancement of the self.' At first glance such a desire would appear to be at odds with the supposedly stiffling control operating in societies with a heavy state presence. As Foucault argued, modernity has given rise to 'technologies of control' which serve to repress the self.[138] On the other hand, according to traditional liberalism, the state is crucial to the emancipation of the self, providing the 'security', or means, for self-help and self-realisation. Thus, far from being a time when the self suffered at the hands of an overbearing state which spent taxpayers' money wildly on public services, like free municipal libraries, the later post-war years might be considered to have been an era of great liberation for individuals and their life projects. This was true in terms of increased opportunities for learning and self-culture offered through a rapidly expanding public library system. On a larger scale, it was also the case in respect of citizens' modernist faith in science, belief in truth and trust in the expert – the endorsement by individuals of the 'grand narratives' of knowledge and culture, to borrow Lyotard's phrase.[139]

Just as the post-war years might be considered to be an era of intense modernity, so also during that same period, as noted above, the public library might be seen to have experienced *its* 'golden age', in which the interface between the public library and the self reached a new level of mutual association. In 1950 the publisher Raymond Unwin equated the role and philosophy of libraries with the individual freedoms and rights encapsulated in the ethos of the welfare state. But the latter, he believed, should not simply be concerned with bestowing rights and freedoms on the citizenry (the most important of which was the freedom of all not to be poor). On the contrary, the citizen should be called upon to play a larger role, to participate and discharge obligations. To balance the potential dangers associated with the state's increased influence in daily lives, the onus was on citizens to be more vigilant in protecting their independence, to think and reason for themselves. Public libraries, Unwin pointed out, had a long tradition of encouraging people to do just that:

The whole purpose and aim of libraries in a democratic society is to encourage individual citizens to learn how to think things out for themselves, freely and without pressure; how to base their reasoned opinions on observed facts; how to live a full creative life of their own, a life that is intellectually honest and independent.[140]

The strengthening of the self which Unwin recommended, and which he was convinced libraries had a central role in facilitating, does not appear to have been eclipsed by the burgeoning structures of welfarism in the minds of librarians, many of whom believed that the growth of a (local) state agency like the public library did not compromise individuality. David Gerard, a leading advocate of the 'library in society' strategy, epitomised this viewpoint: 'Public libraries should be connected to all portions of society ... Public libraries should exhibit socio-political awareness', he proposed. Public library professionals, he believed, should jettison notions of outright impartiality and 'get involved'. 'The gospel of neutrality is dead', he declared. At first glance this prescription might smack of cultural policing. However, Gerard was keen to point out that the ultimate aim of 'intervention' was very much the growth of the individual self:

The idea of an influential profession using its gift and resources, not only to nourish the laboratories of the technologists, but to nourish the heart and head of every man inside his laboratory, his sensibility, is gaining ground.[141]

Others, however, were suspicious of growing state power. In 1951 a report on libraries in Scotland[142] acknowledged that: 'Modern, civilised life, having become large-scale and complicated, needs planning as an alternative to chaos.' However, it was also hesitant about the effects of planning on the self, for planning:

discourages initiative on the part of the planned-for and assumes on their part an attitude of meek and grateful acceptance. Now, nobody with a healthy active mind wants to live, in a 'finished' world, a life that is completely portioned out for him … One arrives, therefore, at the paradox that the only justifiable form of planning is one that will give each individual an increased sense and opportunity of making his own plans. The other drawback of large-scale planning for other people is that it can never quite achieve the living quality of things that develop slowly and unconsciously and are adapted to the varied and changing needs of individuals. For this continuing development of personality, free access to the resources of a great library is one of the most important conditions.

'Joy's soul lies in the doing', the report observed. Post-war librarians librarians were thus clearly grappling with the problem of finding the ideal balance between state help and safeguarding the interests of the self, one of the fundamental functions of libraries.

Protecting the self appeared to take on added meaning, indeed, in an age of hectic technological and social change. Opening the new library in Ruddington in 1963, the government Chief Whip, Martin Redmayne MP, observed that: 'We are living in a fussy, conscious-struck, introspective, panicky age', in which people had lost the art of being calm. To restore calmness, he urged people to replace television with books.[143] K.C. Harrison similarly linked the value of public libraries in the modern age to the corrosive effects of new communication media on the individual self:

The pressures of mass-media – television, radio, high-circulation newspapers, public relations and advertising – already weigh heavily upon the thoughts and actions of the individual. There are very few strongholds of individual thought left, but one of them is the public library, a place where each member of the community can enter and browse freely, making up his own mind about the books and materials he borrows, whether it be for education, recreation or vocational improvement.[144]

As in the decades immediately preceding the First World War, when the pace of life hastened noticeably and the public library, partly for this reason, enjoyed an unprecedented expansion, so also in the busy and modernising 1960s their value as an antidote to social anxiety was strongly acknowledged. As the eminent American library theorist Jesse Shera wrote in 1970: 'the library, in a world that is growing increasingly raucous and cacophonous, is almost the last outpost of silence and the quiet stir of thought'.[145] The new buildings of the 1960s and early 1970s, much more spacious in most cases than those they replaced, became havens of the modern self. The tendency in designs towards a more open lay-out, as well as the blurring of the distinction between departments and functions that accompanied this, made for a new sense of freedom within the library space. Extra room for browsing underlined the importance of seclusion and reflection in the library experience. The quiet selection of one's reading was (as now) a serious and personal activity. One Harrogate reader reminded fellow library users in 1962 that: 'A book is a virgin field to be ploughed and assessed by the individual … Choosing a book is as important I would say as choosing a lover or a matrimonial partner.'[146]

However, this is not to suggest that the public libraries of the 1960s and 1970s were public spaces where individuals turned in on themselves in order to preserve the self from the harmful effects of a 'hurried' modernity. Progress-oriented individuals embraced the public as one means of realising their aspirations. Education was one of the requirements identified as essential to a modern Britain. Although increasing state provision and control in formal education might be pointed to by some as eroding individuality and choice, the same accusation cannot be laid at the door of public libraries, which remained committed to independent learning and to the proposition that education was, at base, aimed at self-realisation. Their status as informal agencies of education was based on their ability to facilitate *self-directed* enlightenment. As the philosopher Jacob Bronowski told the Library Association at its annual conference in 1957, the public library needed to be viewed as 'the storehouse of the best thought of the past and an instrument of education'; moreover, he was sure that 'the printed word and the public library remained for others, as they were for me, the most powerful means for self-education'.[147]

In the post-war years, therefore, the long-standing mantra that the library was the 'dispensary for the healing of the soul'[148] does not appear to have been diluted by the forces of a materialist modernity. At the time, however, technological advance must have seemed threatening to the public library's function as a place of quiet reflection. Reporting on a meeting called between librarians and computer experts in 1966 to discuss the automation of library services, Sir Frank Francis believed he could 'well understand the despair of the book lover at the thought of these developments. The idea of the library as the *healing place of the soul*, seems to belong to a different world from that now envisaged'.[149] But the plain truth was, he continued, that if automation did not proceed then libraries were 'in danger of atrophying through sheer bulk'.[150] Many agreed that automation would improve library services, thereby providing a new way of nourishing soul and self.

Others doubted the beneficial effects of technological advance (especially in the area of communications) on culture. Marshall McLuhan lamented the passing of the 'Gutenberg age', which had delivered the mass printed book and, hence, silent individualised reading, as opposed to the pre-modern practice of reading aloud in groups. He despised what he called the 'electric age', the 'acoustic culture' of modernity:

The printed book, by its stress on intense visual culture, is the means of detachment and civilised objectivity in a world of profound sensuous involvement. The printed book is thus the only available means of developing habits of private initiative and private goals and objectives in the electric age. These characteristics do not develop in the cultural milieu of electric sound and information, for the acoustic world ... is not private nor civilised but tribal and collective.[151]

If McLuhan was right in believing that tribalism and collectivism, expressed through the mass media and a globalised culture, are the inevitable outcome of advances in communication technology, then one would expect the last quarter of the twentieth century to have been a social and cultural dessert for the self, inside or outside the arena of the public library. As the final chapter shows, however, such predictions vastly underestimate the resilience of the self, certainly in the public library setting.

Notes and References to Chapter Five

[1] The contours of the welfare state are laid out by A. Land, R. Lowe and N. Whiteside, *The development of the welfare state: a guide to documents in the Public Record Office* (London, 1992). Town and country planning, nursery provision and care for the elderly and disabled might also be added to the list.

[2] Library Association, *A century of public libraries 1850-1950* (London, 1950), 27.

[3] J. Harris, 'Political thought and the welfare state, 1870-1940: an intellectual framework for British social policy', *Past and Present* 135 (May 1992), 116.

[4] PRO, ED 171/1, Henry Brooke to Geoffrey Faber (25 October 1944).

[5] PRO, ED 171/1, Geoffrey Faber to Henry Brooke (27 October 1944).

[6] Interviewed January 1996.

[7] Hansard, *Parliamentary Debates* (12 July 1962), copy deposited in SRO, ED 6/33.

[8] *Harrogate Advertiser* (28 February 1959).

[9] PWBT, George Roebuck to W.B. Thorne (2 July 1940).

[10] PWBT, A.H. Gardner to W.B. Thorne (9 April 1958).

[11] 'After the war', *Grapevine: Staff Magazine of the Nottinghamshire County Library Service* (December 1967), 4.

[12] In T. Kelly, *A history of public libraries in Great Britain 1845-1975* (London, 2nd edn., 1977), 347.

[13] Borough of Keighley Libraries and Museums Committee, *Annual Report* (1956-7), 19.

[14] 'Bradford book shortage', *Bradford Telegraph and Argus* (27 September 1947).

[15] K. Amis, *That uncertain feeling* (London, 1984), 16.

[16] Leeds School of Librarianship, *Report on a survey of the organisation and methods of the Ilkley Public Library* (1956), Bradford Local Studies Library.

[17] In D. Childs, *Britain since 1945: a political history* (London, 4th edn., 1997), 80.

[18] For background evidence on the Act, see SRO, ED 6/41.

[19] Ministry of Education, *The structure of the public library service in England and Wales* [Roberts Report], Cmnd. 660 (1959). Ministry of Education, *Standards of public library service in England and Wales* [Bourdillon Report] (1962). Ministry of Education, *Inter-library co-operation in England and Wales* [Baker Report] (1962).

[20] Central Statistical Office, *Social trends* (1970), 46.

[21] *Nottingham Evening Post* (1 June 1961).

[22] J.G. Ollé, 'Portsmouth public libraries: the last forty years', *Library History* 15:1 (May 1999), 55.

[23] PRO, ED 171/4, H. Elliot to the Prime Minister (24 September 1957).

[24] County Borough of Darlington Public Library, Art Gallery and Museum, *Annual Report* (1969-70), 2.

[25] *Nottingham Public Libraries: a century of service* (1968), Nottingham Local Studies Library.

[26] For documents indicating that public libraries were increasingly becoming part of the new educational direction of the country, see PRO, ED 171/2.

[27] *LAR* 62 (March 1964), 107.

[28] 'Libraries deal with "so much rubbish and literary froth"', *Bradford Telegraph and Argus* (21 September 1950).

[29] BBC Television News, 10.45 pm (11 March 1957), transcript deposited in Westminster City Archives.

[30] Kelly, *A history of public libraries*, op. cit., 535.

[31] R. Lowe, 'The welfare state in Britain since 1945', *ReFRESH [Recent Findings of Research in Economic and Social History]* 18, 4.

[32] PRO, ED 171/2, Ministry of Education to G.H. Bushnell (21 May 1948).

[33] PRO, ED 171/1, 'F.B.' to Minister of Education (4 October 1945).

[34] PRO, ED 171/1, A.E. Miles Davies to R.T. Tyas (20 June 1947); and report by W.R. Elliot on the Library Association's annual conference (15 May 1946).

[35] PRO, ED 171/2 contains two copies of the draft.

[36] PRO, ED171/7, Lord Hailsham to S.C. Roberts (1 July 1957).

[37] P.S.J. Welsford quoted in 'Inquiry into structure of library service', *Times* (4 September 1957).

[38] PRO, ED 221/97, G. Foster to E.C.G. Boyle (12 September 1962).

[39] PRO, ED 171/8, Committee on public libraries: discussion with representatives of the chief librarians of large cities (1957).

[40] PRO, ED 221/97, Notes on a meeting arranged by the association of Assistant Librarians at the House of Commons (13 December 1961).

[41] Roberts Report, op. cit.

[42] 'Threat to status of independent libraries', *Harrogate Advertiser* (21 February 1959).

[43] R. Irwin, *Librarianship: essays on applied bibliography* (London, 1949), 116, 117, 118.

[44] PRO, ED 171/8, Memorandum to Roberts Committee from the city librarians of Birmingham [and other large cities] (13 November 1957).

[45] Papers of Frank Gardner, Library Association Archive, Smaller Public Libraries Group: answers to the Committee [on Public Libraries in England and Wales] questionnaire (2 November 1957).

[46] J.F.W. Bryon, 'Small town libraries', *Manchester Guardian* (3 October 1957).

[47] A. Midwinter and M. McVicar, *The size and efficiency debate: public library authorities in a time of change* (London, 1994).

[48] L. Paulin, 'Recent developments in the provision of public library services in the United Kingdom', *Library Quarterly* 48:4 (1978), 513-4.

[49] *Rumpelstiltskin: Magazine of the Bradford Public Libraries Staff Guild* 2 (June 1970), 4.

[50] South Tyneside Libraries, *Annual Report* (1974-5), 2.

[51] Newcastle upon Tyne Public Libraries, *City Librarian's Annual Report* (1974-5).

[52] R. Shimmon, 'Reorganisation – is it working?', *Assistant Librarian* 68:3 (March 1975), 41.

[53] T. Kelly, *Books for the people: an illustrated history of the British public library* (London, 1977) 193.

[54] 'The dynamic librarian of Wakefield', *Bradford Telegraph and Argus* (13 March 1953).

[55] G. Jefcoate, 'Democracy at work: the Library Association's "centenary assessment" of 1950', *Library History* 15 (November 1999).

[56] Leeds Public Libraries, *Public library centenary: one hundred years of social growth* (Leeds, 1950), 4.

[57] In T. Wilkie, *British science and politics since 1945* (Oxford, 1991), 73-4.

[58] Childs, *Britain since 1945*, op. cit., 127.

[59] Ealing Public Libraries, *Respice – Prospice: a report on the Ealing Public Library Service* (1964), 6.

[60] R. Haxby, 'Municipal commercial and technical libraries', in J.D. Stewart (ed.), *The reference librarian* (London, 1951), 85.

[61] E.A. Hinton, 'Industrial, technical and commercial information: the contribution of the public library', *Aslib Proceedings* 2:2 (1948), 53, 63, 65.

[62] Library Association, *A century of public libraries 1850-1950* (London, 1950), 15.

[63] 'The public library and industry: developments in Sheffield', *Manchester Guardian* (23 December 1952).

[64] Leeds Public Library, Local Studies Department.

[65] J.P. Lamb, *Commercial and technical libraries* (London, 1955), 269.

[66] PRO, ED 171/8, Memorandum to Roberts Committee from the city librarians of Birmingham [and several other large cities].

[67] 'Library's role as aid to industry', *Yorkshire Post* (10 May 1965).

[68] C.P. Snow, *The two cultures*. With and introduction by Stefan Collini (Cambridge, 1993).

[69] W.C.B. Sayers, *The province and the purpose of the public library* (Croydon Public Libraries, 1947).

[70] Newcastle upon Tyne Public Libraries Committee, *A short history of Newcastle upon Tyne Public Libraries 1854-1950* (1950).

[71] 'Tribute to Cambridge City Library', *Cambridge Daily News* (31 October 1958)

[72] Bourdillon Report, op. cit.

[73] Aside from formally permitting public libraries to provide non-book formats and services, the Act also officially enabled library authorities to collaborate with each other and to form joint authorities if they so wished.

[74] 'It's a three-in-one, says county chief', *Worksop Guardian* (17 December 1962). Nottinghamshire County Council, *East Leake County Library and Health Centre* (1969) and *Cotgreave County Library and Health Centre* (1969), both deposited in Nottingham Public Library, Local Studies Department.

[75] T. Kelly, *Books for the people* (London, 1977), 226.

[76] L.R. McColvin, *Library staffs* (London, 1939), 118.

[77] M.A. Overington, *The subject departmentalized public library* (London, 1969). R.J. Duckett, 'Subject departments: their rise and fall at Bradford Metropolitan Libraries', *Art Libraries Journal* (Summer, 1985).

[78] E.V. Corbett, *Photo-charging: its operation and installation in a British public library* (London, 1957).

[79] Department of Education and Science, *The staffing of public libraries. Vol. 1.* (London, 1976), 125-6.

[80] Delegates to a conference on computer book-charging were reminded that the 'reputation of the library is made or lost at the issue counter': *Proceedings of a symposium on computer book-charging held at Leeds Polytechnic* (Leeds, 1970).

[81] K.C. Harrison, *Public libraries today* (London, 1963), 12.

[82] B. Hjelmqvist, *Swedish public libraries in pictures* (Stockholm, 1956).

[83] 'A paradise for book-lovers', *Bradford Telegraph and Argus* (17 April 1967).

[84] City of Newcastle upon Tyne, *Report of the city librarian* (1968-9), commentary accompanying photograph of the inquiry hall in the city's new library building.

[85] *Grapevine: Staff Magazine of the Nottinghamshire County Library Service* (Autumn 1971), 40.

[86] A. Marwick, 'The arts, books, media and entertainments in Britain since 1945', in J. Obelkevich and P. Catterall (eds.), *Understanding post-war British society* (London, 1994), 184. R. Hewison, *Too much: art and society in the Sixties, 1960-1975* (London, 1986), xiii, reminds us that the 'swinging Sixties' was an era characterised not just by an oppositional political ideology, but also by a materialist culture of hedonism which revolved around pop art and music.

[87] 'Saturday queues at library', *Harrogate Advertiser* (28 December 1957).

[88] 'Lady Chatterley not for the library', *Harrogate Advertiser* (9 November 1960).

[89] *Harrogate Advertiser* (19 November 1960).

[90] L. Swaffield, 'Oh, what a library war!', *LAR* 100 (August 1998), 402.

[91] 'The branch librarian's handbook', *Nottinghamshire Public Libraries Staff Magazine* (May 1957).

[92] Borough of Keighley Libraries and Museums Committee, *Annual report* (1956-7), 12.

[93] Borough of Keighley, *Annual Report of the chief librarian* (1947), 13.

[94] 'Reading "trash" leads to finer literature', *Sussex Daily News* (24 June 1950).

[95] 'Librarians' conference: the individual mind', *Times Educational Supplement* (21 June 1947).

[96] 'Readers prefer good clean novels', *Harrogate Advertiser* (5 May 1951).

[97] Quoted in L. Swaffield, 'The strife-torn struggle for solidarity' *LAR* 100 (July 1998), 353.

[98] *From comics to classics: report of a conference held on 3 November 1955 at Church House, Westminster*, sponsored by the Library association and the Comic Campaigns Council. Fear of the influx of American culture, especially horror comics, is discussed by V. Neuburg, 'Comic strips and books', *British Book News* (April 1985).

[99] *Grapevine: Staff Magazine of the Nottinghamshire County Library Service* (Spring, 1971), 7. The question of comics in libraries endured: M. Wakeman, 'Why don't libraries buy comics?', *LAR* 93 (June 1991), 402.

[100] PRO, ED 171/3, J. Profumo to K. Pickthorne (9 December 1953).

[101] David James, T.L. Iremonger and Sir Edward Boyle (Minister of Education) respectively, quoted in *LAR* 66 (March 1964), 106, 107-8, 109. Although the government of the day came out against charging for core services, the issue *was* discussed, the Treasury exploring the possibility of fees for borrowing

adult fiction and discovering that £1.1 per annum would be raised in revenue if such a scheme were implemented: PRO, ED 171/5, J.A.C. Robinson to J.F. Embling (10 January 1962).

[102] P. Clarke, *Hope and glory: Britain 1900-1990* (London, 1996), 253.

[103] *LAR* 62 (April 1960), 125.

[104] PWBT, P.A. Barnett to W.B. Thorne (23 April 1958).

[105] Borough of Keighley Libraries and Museums Committee, *Annual report* (1955-6), 12.

[106] 'No decline in reading because of TV', *Harrogate Advertiser* (12 January 1957). See also, 'Television does not reduce reading', *Harrogate Advertiser* (26 March 1960).

[107] Borough of Keighley, *Report of the chief librarian* (1958-62), 5.

[108] 'Your library', BBC radio broadcast (30 November 1950), Nottingham Public Library, Local Studies Department.

[109] 'Harrogate spends less than average on libraries', *Harrogate Advertiser* (23 March 1963).

[110] B. Rawlins, '*Topic* talks to the city librarian', (September 1969), Nottingham Public Library, Local Studies Department.

[111] 'Shire talk: national library week', BBC radio broadcast (15 March 1966), Nottingham Public Library, Local Studies Department.

[112] Objectives noted by Harrison, *Public libraries today*, op. cit., 116.

[113] 'Librarians pool their ideas', *Times* (21 September 1955)

[114] PRO, ED 171/4, J.M. Sharpey-Shafer to Essex County Libraries, the National Central Library and the Minister of Education (12 September 1957).

[115] 'Stepney Public Libraries Staff Bulletin' (August 1956).

[116] 'Cambridge ideal city librarian', *Cambridge News* (21 May 1965).

[117] K.C. Harrison, Public relations for librarians (London, 1973), 102.

[118] E.g. M.B. Line, *Library surveys* (London, 1967) and B. Groombridge, *The Londoner and his library* (London, 1964).

[119] E.g., E. Sydney and R.F. Ashby, *The library in the community* (London, 1956); K.C. Harrison, *The library and the community* (London, 1963); G. Jefferson, *Libraries and society* (Cambridge, 1969); R.C. Benge, *Libraries and cultural change* (London, 1970); B. Luckham, *The library in society* (London, 1971); *Libraries and the community: papers read at the week-end conference of the London and Home Counties Branch of the LibraryAssociation* (London, 1973).

[120] Roberts Report, op. cit., 8.

[121] Corporation of the City of Glasgow, *Public libraries 1874-1954* (Glasgow, 1955), 36-7.

[122] Borough of Keighley, *Report of the chief librarian* (1958-62), 2.

[123] *Grapevine: Staff Magazine of the Nottinghamshire County Library Service* (Spring, 1965), 4-5.

[124] As quantified by B. Luckham, *The library in society: a study of the public library in an urban setting* (London, 1971), 13. H. Jolliffe, *Public library extension activities* (London, 1962), 3-5, outlines the various activities but said extension work varied from place to place.

[125] PRO, ED 171/29, Public libraries and adult education [questionnaire to public libraries].

[126] SRO, GD 281/94/39, Advisory Council on Education in Scotland, Committee on Libraries, Notes by D.M. McIntosh (11 June 1948).

[127] Library Association, *Memorandum of evidence ... [to] the Minister of Education to consider the structure of the public library service in England and Wales* (London, 1958).

[128] Brighton Public Libraries, *The public library service in Brighton: a five year survey* (1973), 4.

[129] PRO, ED 171/3, P.S.J. Welsford to M. Davies (24 May 1950).

[130] Kelly, *A history of public libraries*, op. cit., 363.

[131] P. Whiddon, 'The day they took away the whale', *Grapevine: Staff Magazine of the Nottinghamshire County Library Service* (March 1974), 5.

[132] City of Westminster, *Report of the Public Libraries Committee* (1948-9).

[133] Library Association, *A century of public libraries*, op. cit., 20. L.R. McColvin, *Public library extension* (Paris, 1950), 77-9.

[134] 'A lending library for the blind', *LAR* 2 (February 1900), 113-4.

[135] PRO, ED 171/2, Library Association statement on libraries as community centres (1948).

[136] *Grapevine: Staff Magazine of the Nottinghamshire County Library Service* (Spring, 1965), 5.

[137] F. Jameson, 'Postmodernism and consumer society', in A. Gray and J. McGuigan (eds.), *Studying culture* (London, 1993), 193.

[138] M. Foucault, *Discipline and punish: the birth of the prison* (London, 1991, first published in French in 1975).

[139] J-F. Lyotard, *The postmodern condition: a report on knowledge* (Manchester, 1984, first published in French in 1979).

[140] R. Unwin, 'The library service in the welfare state', in D. Gerard (ed.), *Libraries in society* (London, 1978), 24, originally published in *Library World* 53:8 (August/September, 1950).

[141] D. Gerard, 'Face to face', *LAR* 68 (November 1966), 387, 389.

[142] Scottish Education Department, *Libraries, museums and art galleries*, Cmnd. 8229 (1951), 9.

[143] 'Let's be calm the Chief Whip says', *[Nottingham] Guardian Journal* (8 July 1963).

[144] Harrison, *Public libraries today*, op. cit., 14

[145] J.H. Shera, 'The quiet stir of thought or, What the computer cannot do', *LAR* (February 1970), 37.

[146] 'The obnoxious borrowers', *Harrogate Advertiser* (6 January 1962), letter to the editor.

[147] 'The library as an instrument of education', *Harrogate Herald* (18 September 1957).

[148] Harrogate library supporters were reminded of this in '1906 – Then and now – 1956', *Harrogate Advertiser* (28 January 1956).

[149] 'Libraries call in computers to catch up on knowledge', *Times* (29 June 1966).

[150] Ibid.

[151] M. McLuhan, in B. Baumfield (ed.), *Do books matter?*, (Leeds, 1973), 35.

CHAPTER SIX

Cuts and Computers

1976-2000

Notwithstanding the danger that the history of a period so recent in the memory might be written with less than the objectivity required to identify key issues and to form a balanced assessment, four themes featured strongly in the history of the public library in the last quarter of the twentieth century: cuts, class, corporate culture and computers. The first and the last of these are the most important in terms of public visibility.

From the viewpoint of the general public, public libraries changed a great deal in the period under consideration in this final chapter. The importation of new media formats and the harnessing of new information and communication technologies, especially in the 1990s, was plain for all to see. Equally apparent to the average public library user would have been the constant under-funding of the service, which manifested itself in disappointment over decreasing opening hours and a declining state of book stocks relative to expectations. The issue of social class in the public library context, and the anxiety which many librarians felt concerning the inability to reach lower socio-economic groups, gave rise around 1980 to a new model of service known as community librarianship, but which by the 1990s had lost much of its original radicalism and professional appeal. Despite its positive impact in some places, as well as its extensive coverage in the library press, community librarianship was not a mode of operation readily or widely recognisable outside the library profession. A discussion of it is none the less important, and is duly undertaken below, because of the light its rise and fall throws on the general ethos and direction of the public library in the late-twentieth century. Similarly, the implementation of management techniques drawn from the corporate sector, although largely an unknown process as far as the general user was concerned, is worthy of coverage here because of how the embracing of management ideology helped define the status aspirations of public librarianship yet, paradoxically, also highlighted the profession's distrust of the Gradgrindism perceived to be inherent in management theory and culture.

Cuts

This chapter begins in 1976 because this was one of the most significant years in the history of Britain's post-war economy. The impact of the decisions taken in 1976 in response to the economic crisis of the time was to have serious consequences for public library services – in the short term in respect of the expenditure cuts immediately imposed; in the long term in respect of the pattern and example these initial cuts set for unremitting pressure on the resourcing of public libraries thereafter.

In the 1960s and early 1970s, under the influence of a benign and expanding welfare state, the public library had flourished. The mid-1970s, however, marked a turning point in the development of the welfare state and the Keynesian demand management and deficit spending that had funded it. The quadrupling of oil prices overnight helped push inflation to 27% in 1975, exacerbating the existing problems of rising unemployment (which had breached the million mark four years earlier) and declining economic performance on the world stage.[1] Such was the depth of the crisis, that some believed Britain might slide into circumstances more in keeping with that of an ungovernable 'banana republic', where democracy, including public sphere institutions like public libraries, is normally sacrificed on the altar of economic stability.[2] Commentators observed a 'Britain in decline'[3] and predicted the break-up of Britain,[4] or, less pessimistically, asked: 'Whatever happened to Britain?'[5]

Nothing symbolised Britain's vulnerability and weakness at the time more than the negotiations which followed between the government and the IMF in 1976. A three billion dollar loan was agreed, but only on the condition that swingeing cuts in public expenditure were put in place. These amounted to one billion pounds in 1977–8, and one and a half billion pounds in 1978-9.[6] Later, the then Chancellor of the Exchequer Denis Healey was to describe the economic information which he and his negotiators had worked with as "unforgivably misleading". According to Treasury calculations, which the IMF used in their own analysis of Britain's economic situation, public spending in Britain had reached a massive 60% of GDP. When, later, public expenditure was costed as in other countries, where, crucially, benefits arising from social insurance contributions were excluded, public spending in Britain fell to 46% of GDP.[7] Assisted by mis-information, therefore, the monetarist cat leapt relatively unhindered out of the economic bag. Monetarism arrived in Britain under a Labour government, three years before the 'Thatcher revolution'. Despite an upswing in the economy in the late 1970s (by the end of 1978 inflation and unemployment were well down, growth had risen to 3.5% per annum and the balance of payments had returned to surplus), the precedent for large cuts in public sector activity had been set. The strong medicine Britain swallowed in 1976, and the apparent recovery this had brought, strengthened the position of those who had been arguing for decades that too much investment had been directed into so-called non-marketable services – like public libraries – thereby 'crowding out' productive economic activity.[8] Even before the New Right came to power in 1979, therefore, the efficacy of public sector retrenchment was, for some, demonstrable. This eased the way for a sustained restraint, experienced to this day, on the funding of public sector institutions like public libraries; a strategy continually reinforced by an awareness of Britain's steady descent down the world's league table of economic performance (by the early 1990s it had sunk to 18th place in terms of GDP per head).

Pressure on public expenditure in areas like libraries increased markedly in the early 1980s as the country's economic indicators plummeted.[9] A survey by the Library Association in 1980 found that 25 out of 29 English libraries who replied had experienced a cut in expenditure in that particular financial year. Cuts, in real terms, in book funds of up to 30% were reported. Vacancies were being frozen or delayed and early retirement schemes were being speedily deployed. Many libraries were looking to new automated systems, in circulation and bibliographic access, to ease work-loads and to pave the way for staff reductions. Cuts were also reported in Scotland by 10 out of 31 replying library authorities: book funds had been slashed by anything from 19% to 30%; spending on furniture by up to 50%. The charges for overdue items, reservations and loans of recordings had been increased by up to 100%, 100% and 300% respectively.[10] Between 1979-80 and 1983-84, expenditure on public libraries did not fall, even in real terms. When capital (e.g. on buildings) and current (e.g. on salaries and books) spending were separated out, however, the picture looked 'altogether more gloomy'.[11] In Edinburgh, in 1980, the money spent on book stocks in the city's public libraries fell by 25%. The city's librarian was of the opinion that the 'book stock at many libraries was approaching the end of its useful life but funds were sufficient only for purchase of current publications'. Rationalisation in personnel in Edinburgh's libraries 'reduced staff to minimum levels'.[12]

In response to such stories, a pressure group calling itself 'The Library Campaign' was established in 1984 to convey information about reduction in services and to rally the support of librarians, as well as supporters of public libraries, such as writers, publishers, celebrities and library users themselves. A report on public libraries by the consumer magazine *Which?* in 1990 painted a disappointing picture of a lacklustre institution battling to improve against a backdrop of a decade and a half of under-funding.[13] Whereas the public library received a 'cautious thumbs up' in terms of its overall value, a number of specific criticisms were voiced: out-of-dateness in reference stocks; too few new books; and a poor range of audio-visual materials. Libraries were also criticised for their inconvenient opening hours and inefficient marketing.

In 1992 Timothy Renton, Minister for Libraries, confidently remarked that: 'There is no crisis in the public library service. It remains dynamic, accepting new ideas and adapting to new ideas from users.'[14] That public libraries progressed and changed in the last quarter of the twentieth century, despite the economic problems confronting them, is undeniable. For example, roughly 300 new public libraries were opened during the 1980s,[15] including a new central library in Cardiff.[16] But as the century drew to a close, the argument employed by some in authority, that there was little wrong with public library provision, was based more on political posturing that on reality. At any given moment, a key indicator of the health, usefulness and public visibility of public libraries is the length of time their doors are open to the public. In 1974, 229 libraries were open for 60 hours or more a week, a figure which had fallen to just 18 by 1992. More recently, between 1992-3 and 1997-8, the number of libraries open for 45 hours or more a week fell from 797 to 713. Reduced opening hours also contributed to a decline in the number of books borrowed from public libraries in the 1980s and 1990s.

In the late 1990s the threat of closure continued to be experienced by many libraries. The *Sunday Times* reported in early 1999 that at least 50 libraries were at risk of being shut, thereby 'adding to the 500 [or 10% of the total] ... which have been closed over the last 10 years'. It was predicted that by March 1999 only 21 libraries would be open for 60 hours or more a week.[17] In 1997 the Audit Commission found that although expenditure on public libraries was actually increasing, money was being channelled into capital expenditure and hidden costs such as staff pay, rather than into books and other materials. This is why, 'people feel very much that their services are being cut', explained a representative of the Library Association.[18]

Cuts in public libraries certainly sparked a reaction amongst the general public. A volunteer for Mass Observation in 1988 wrote:

I am incensed by the lack of funding for local libraries. They are the best front-line, classless, unjudgemental, accessible social service this country provides. They are also productive, helping unemployed people further their knowledge and education, providing stimulating, warm environments for old age pensioners and children and mothers. I have written to my councillors, my local MP, and phoned radio stations in support of libraries. I am horrified at the thought of losing a free access to books and knowledge – every working class person I know has made use of the library without qualm. It amazes me when people talk of it as a middle class service! I think this may happen if charges are introduced! But what more can one do? I feel the tide rising against this service and feel helpless in its defence. The deterioration in staff morale is really noticeable as their jobs are cut back, their duties extended, their professionalism undermined.

Another declared: 'I am a member of the public library. Very much so; and have recently signed a petition when jungle drums gave the message that some libraries were heading for closure. DISGRACEFUL.'[19]

In the late 1990s, users remained just as bitter and annoyed about cuts in library funding, as the following statements show:

I stopped going to my local branch library long before I abandoned the central one, because they started opening on three half days only, and it meant I couldn't just pop in on the way home from work.

Some things have not changed for the better: opening hours for instance. Most areas have less access time than they used to. Also, many small branches have been closed which is a great loss to communities.

Cuts in public spending over the last twenty years have affected library services. Small branch libraries have closed and others are open for shorter hours on fewer days. Therefore it is less easy for people like myself who are in employment and working long hours to use the facilities. This may become a vicious circle with further reductions in services as usage falls due to poor availability.[20]

Class

Despite its faults and limitations, the public library, certainly in recent decades, has been an institution which has generated a fair amount of public goodwill. Leaving to one side the inevitable debates on funding and policy, the existence of the welfare state – which in the second half of the twentieth century did much to further the cause of the public library – has encouraged an uncritical assessments of those services which offer universal access. Generally, the public library is a *relatively* popular institution. The public library is (mostly) free at the point of use and open to all, and is used by a wide spectrum of the public. It is symbolic of the ideological essence of the welfare state. Enshrined in the philosophy of the public library is the principle of equality of opportunity, the efficacy of which mid-nineteenth-century liberal-utilitarian pioneers of the institution argued with such force and success. The public library is widely viewed as an institution which has consistently displayed liberal credentials of emancipation and inclusion.

This said, in respect of *social class*, the public library is an institution which has under-performed in relation to its liberal ideals. The public library has always found difficulty in attracting users from the very lowest social groups. Moreover, although working class readers have very much featured – to a greater or lesser extent depending on place – in the public library's readership, they have generally done so in lower numbers than one would expect if the proportion they represent in the population as a whole is taken into consideration. Because of its inherently contentious nature, class is a question which supporters and providers of the ostensibly *neutral* public library have for the most part approached at a superficial level, hoping that assurances of continuing universal access would in some way make the question go away. Yet class is something which, for 150 years, the public library in Britain has failed to address successfully. Occasionally, librarians have attempted to raise and discuss the issue of class in the public library context.[21] However, the tendency has generally been to quietly push the issue to one side. In the 1970s and 1980s some librarians attempted to revive the class issue. Their efforts to do so will be described and analysed below, but in order to do this it is useful to see how in the more distant past class intersected with public library philosophy and practice.

Since the first proposals for public libraries in the 1830s and 1840s, class has been a near permanent facet of discussions on the social value of the public library. But the 'everyday' view of the history of the public library – certainly within the library profession – tends to simplify the institution's past in respect of class. This is certainly the case with regard to the institution's origins, the discussion of which is often diverted down a tidy avenue into the temperance issue: middle class reformers provided libraries to counter-attract workers from the drink which increased crime, secondary poverty and expenditure on policing and other measures of containment. However, this interpretation ignores the main reason why nineteenth-century reformers wished to see an end to working-class drinking (or indeed other kinds of irrational recreation and intellectual idleness), namely, to prevent dangerous association and the spread of radical ideas.[22] Municipal libraries not only offered an alternative to the dangerous liaison of the public house; they also acted as a counter-attraction to independent working-class libraries, which were often located, if the example of Nottingham is anything to go by, in public houses.[23] It was hoped that the 'sober' literature found in *free* local libraries would entice workers away from pernicious 'socialist' literature. It is no coincidence that the push for public libraries occurred at a time of great upheaval and protest, seen most obviously in the demands of the Chartist for various basic political rights. Public libraries originated as antidotes to working class aspirations at a time of immense social and political tension. So fundamental was the attempt to appease radical opposition that this motive of public library provision re-surfaced time and again over the next hundred years, as earlier Chapters here have shown.

Over-simplified explanations of the public library's controlling past divert attention from what has been the institution's key class dimension: the influence of the middle classes on the institution's operation and purpose. The social control thesis stresses the middle-class provision of public libraries for the working classes. In fact public libraries have historically been promoted by the middle classes to a large degree for themselves. An assessment of occupational classification in ten medium and large late-Victorian municipal libraries has revealed that 'the professional and non-manual element was considerably over-represented in comparison with their proportion in the population at large'.[24] Further, it should be recalled that the Select Committee on Public libraries (1849) reported that: 'A great Public Library ought, above all things, to teach the teachers, to supply with the best implements of education those who educate the people, whether in the pulpit, the school or the press.'[25] A prime role of the early public library, therefore, was the service it provided to scholarship among the respectable classes.

In the inter-war period the social class complexion of the public library began to change. An expanding 'new middle class' of white-collar workers increasingly featured in library membership profiles. During the economic depression of the 1930s, which affected most occupational groups, middle-class readers found *free* library use extremely attractive. Suburban drift created a reservoir of readers for new outlying branch libraries to tap into. By 1939, Stanley Jast believed the public library had finally given up its working-class, soup-kitchen image, thereby permitting middle-class readers to enter 'its hospitable doors'.[26]

The increasing attraction of middle class readers to the public library accelerated after the Second World War. As the public library drew nourishment from a growing welfare state, middle-class users of the institution – as in many other aspects of post-war social, cultural and welfare provision – benefited proportionately more than groups further down the social scale. In a survey of reading in Tottenham in 1946,[27] it was shown 'how little compared with the middle class, the working class has been penetrated by consciousness of the public library', some 53% of library membership being recorded as middle class. In 1959, in Harrogate, readers were told by a local newspaper that it had 'taken the emergence of an ever-widening stratum of intelligent middle-class people to lift libraries out of a rut characterised by an over-abundance of cheap novelettish literature on their shelves'.[28]

Thus, it is hardly surprising to find Thomas Kelly telling the Library Assocaition in 1966 that: 'Some think we have gone too far and are in danger of converting the libraries into purely middle-class institutions.'[29] In 1976, a report on an outreach project in deprived areas of Nottingham stated that although public libraries started as institutions for the working class, they had 'perhaps become over-responsive to middle-class tastes and demands, and are used by only 25-30% of the population'.[30] By the mid-1970s, therefore, the public library had in a sense reverted to type. It had assumed an unmistakably middle-class identity, in keeping with its historic image as an institution of highbrow culture and social refinement.

The growing awareness of the increasing middle-class orientation of public libraries provoked a reaction in the library profession. A number of socially-aware librarians and library educators began to call for the abandonment of middle-class domination of the public library and a return to what they saw as the institution's roots as a 'popular' institution. To bring this about, priority in service provision had to be given to the socially deprived. At a time when popular culture was flourishing but the level of poverty remained stubbornly high, the moment appeared ripe to reinvigorate working class culture through the instrument of the public library. In 1978 the influential government report *The Libraries' Choice* observed that in the 1950s and 1960s, 'libraries went from strength to strength ... attracting the middle classes in ever-increasing numbers'. The report noted that the middle classes, who made up less than 20% of the population, accounted for 50% of library membership; and so it was deemed necessary to 'counter such a "drift" to the middle classes' by appealing more to the disadvantaged.[31]

Librarians began to express guilt over the exclusion of lower socio-economic groups from the public library. These groups included the unsuccessful ethnic minorities.[32] In 1972, for example, in considering services to immigrant groups, Westminster City Libraries admitted that that 'public libraries are continuing to serve their communities as they existed 10-15 years ago, oblivious to the changes that have taken place in the intervening period'.[33] Six years later, the chair of the Commission for Racial Equality wrote that an inadequate provision of books in public libraries *about* the ethnic minorities, as well as *for* them in their vernacular languages, represented ' a hole in the multi-cultural fabric of our contemporary society'.[34] Such detachment pervaded the service provision of the 'welfare state' public library. 'When and by whom was it decided that public libraries should cater primarily for the middle classes?', asked a contributor to the *Assistant Librarian* in 1975.[35]

Searching their consciences – 'How little we really do', lamented Joe Hendry in 1981[36] – librarians were at least consoled by the fact that the exclusion they identified had happened elsewhere. A decade earlier, American public librarians had experienced a similar period of soul-searching concerning the partiality of the services they were operating. They emerged from their introspection with strategies designed to rescue the disadvantaged from 'library oblivion'.[37] Drawing on this example, as well as their own tradition of social idealism, many British librarians similarly embarked on a new course of action, one which discriminated in favour of the socially and economically deprived. This mode of service came to be known as 'community librarianship'. It embodied 'a recognition that public library services are for all, not only for the better educated, more affluent "middle class" minority from whom the service has tended to draw its clientèle, but also for the less literate, the disadvantaged, those who are perhaps less book-oriented but whose need for information and for life-enrichment may be greater'.[38] It entailed a focusing of resources on the vulnerable and the needy, not least the rising army of unemployed.[39] Moreover, authentic community librarianship demanded not only sophisticated, qualitative research into the complexion and needs of local communities (community profiling), but also the pro-active involvement of librarians in these communities, along the lines of contemporary practice in community work.[40]

Eventually, from the mid-1980s, community librarianship lost momentum and support. Against the backdrop of political hostility and cuts in public services, librarians began to believe that its expense could not be justified. Thus, in the 1990s, once the programme of special support by the Home Office for ethnic minority provision ('Section 11' funding) came to an end, it is noticeable how the good momentum that had been built up in this particular area quickly fell away. Criticised as a vehicle of political correctness, the ethos of community librarianship was questioned by the library establishment on the grounds that it had infringed the noble tradition of neutrality within librarianship. One London librarian announced angrily in 1984 that 'libraries are becoming a political adjunct – we are being used as a noticeboard for a political controlling group'.[41] Similarly, a reader in a north London borough in 1988 complained of 'too many feminist and pseudo psychology books' in his local library, which was 'plastered with leaflets on people's rights etc. and campaigning type posters' and whose staff constantly kept on the counter 'some petition they want you to sign'.[42] Thus, with certain aspects of recent community provision no doubt in mind, W.J. Murison wrote in the third edition of his enduring book *The Public Library: its Origins, Purpose, and Significance* (1988) that: 'Personal involvement with particular causes may raise difficulties which may have dire consequences for the whole of their [librarians'] library service.'[43] Community librarianship also required a reorientation of the librarian towards community work, a trend which some viewed as a threat to professional status: 'There is no doubt that some of the activities engaged in by librarians in the course of community librarianship were not entirely appropriate', remarked one of the pioneers of services to the disadvantaged in the early 1990s.[44] Further, the targeting of the disadvantaged in preference to other user groups – often encouraged in fact by central government spending restrictions and the consequential desire of librarians to protect vulnerable groups even more – appeared to counter the welfarist creed of universalism to which many public librarians felt deeply attached. Whereas equality of opportunity has been an unassailable tenet of public library philosophy, community librarianship's pursuit of *equality of outcome*, where intervention is based on positive discrimination in an attempt to raise the disadvantaged to a level and quality of use commensurate with that experienced by users in the middle of the social scale, was difficult for many to swallow.[45]

The public library in Britain has always displayed a democratic ethos. Yet in the late-twentieth century, the majority of library users were being drawn from middle-class groups, even though these groups represented a much smaller proportion of the population.[46] Thus, as with many public services, the universal provision of public libraries has in effect redistributed resources to the better-off, to an articulate middle class better placed to exploit the cultural-educational infrastructure provided by the state.[47] This fact gave impetus to a new attempt to render the British public library more inclusive: the 'Libraries for All' policy promoted by the Department of Culture, Media and Sport.[48] As community librarianship became de-radicalised from the mid-1980s onwards, its content being devalued in many places into a mere slogan standing for little more than a combination of community information, customer care and traditional outreach and extension services, a more palatable initiative aimed at addressing the class issue appeared in its place. However worthy this initiative (continuing as I write) may be, it is a sobering thought that its objectives largely fly in the face of 150 years of relative indifference on the part of librarians and library providers to the very poorest in society – previously referred to as the 'undeserving' poor, and now termed the 'underclass'.[49] This group, as well as large swathes of the respectable working class, have never looked to the public library as a potential source of improvement.

This process of exclusion is recognised by the general public. 'I think that perhaps middle class people are more likely to use libraries than working class people', remarks one Mass-Observation volunteer. There is an awareness that: 'Where libraries really fail is in reaching out to those who don't already use them.' People least likely to use libraries are seen as the inarticulate and poorly educated, those 'nervous of forms to fill'. Those without fixed address are also seen as lying outside the 'official' orbit of the public library. Another Mass-Observation volunteer reminisces that people who shun libraries are like those who, when he was in Manchester after the war, 'referred to "boowks" when they meant a magazine and a "library boowk" when they meant a book with a hard cover. The operation of a cycle of deprivation is widely acknowledge by users: 'The most likely users are people whose parents took them there as children.'[50]

Corporate Culture

In 1941, James Burnham's book *The Managerial Revolution* showed that modern, industrialised states, whatever their ideological or political orientation, are characterised by the pursuit of rational efficiency.[51] Developing the thesis that the ownership and control of capital were becoming increasingly separated, Burnham declared that managerialism was now sovereign, that 'the ruling class of the new society now being born is the managers'[52] – a techno-bureaucratic officialdom of experts which, as Max

150   *The Public Library in Britain*

Weber argued, is rule-bound, records-oriented, systems based and knowledgeable of the files.[53] These traits are common to managerial bureaucracies everywhere and they are also seen in the modern professions. In modernity, professional groups have attained a considerable amount of power and influence, prompting Harold Perkins to identify the 'rise of professional society' as a major feature of twentieth-century history.

Nowhere has the techno-bureaucratic dimensions of professionalism been more evident that in librarianship.[54] Despite its relatively low status in respect of financial reward, and the lack of influence this has meant, the occupation of librarian is rich in the professionalism which modern society has admired. (Postmodernists would argue, of course, that as modern society passes, the structures and power of the professions weaken, trust in the expert dissolves and professionals themselves are proletarianised by flexible modes of production.) Belying their image as informal, sleepy hideaways, libraries have always been highly formal, busy and bureaucratic institutions. Librarians have always been administrators (the term administration being closely tied to bureaucratic activity in government and public services). In recent decades, however, librarians have taken advantage of the fact that management increasingly serves as a *synonym* for administration. Librarians are now management oriented: 'I see my major role as a MANAGER: of people, of materials, buildings, resources generally and money', announced a chief librarian in 1985.[55]

Public librarians have explored, absorbed and deployed all the major management theories of recent decades: corporate management, management by objectives, total quality management, knowledge management, to name but a few. It is not appropriate here to discuss the efficacy of these various modes of management; but the function they have served in changing the identity of the public library and its professionals, and the way their implementation may have been indirectly sensed by the public, is altogether a different matter. Acronyms like MbO (management by objectives), TQM (total quality management) and, most recently, KM (knowledge management) have been bandied about by the profession with the obvious objective of improving service provision; but also, one senses, because of the indirect, added dimension they might bring to professional authority: being knowledge-rich in management theory displays a certain modernity and relevance. At times, however, it is difficult to extract any real focus from 'management-speak' designed to mean all things to all people. Library staff in Newcastle upon Tyne, in 1995, for example, were notified of forthcoming research involving staff and users, aimed at developing TQM – described as a management philosophy 'embracing all activities through which the needs of the customer and the community, and the objectives of the organisation, are satisfied in the most efficient and cost effective way by maximising the potential of all employees in a continuing drive for improvement'.[56]

These objectives, were it possible to transport them back in time, would have appeared quite familiar to librarians of a century – and certainly three quarters of a century – ago. The origins of the new managerialism in librarianship pre-dates the period covered by this chapter.[57] For example, librarians have long been keen on evaluating their services.[58] Even in the 1960s, librarians were busy learning to speak the language of the accountant and explore the meaning of 'cost-benefit analysis'.[59] By the 1970s, they were ready to speak about 'output measurement';[60] as well as about 'productivity', even in the context of the cosy branch library.[61] But the real injection of management ideology into library work came with the 'Thatcherite revolution' and the growth of the enterprise culture in the 1980s. The pragmatic tradition within public librarianship had always been fairly strong. For example, the 'library manager' in Nottingham who told staff in 1971 that management was suffering from the attentions of 'the management consultants, and professionals at the [management] game, who are likely to destroy credibility by the sheer quantity of studies, courses, seminars, reports, articles and books', undoubtedly represented a strain of opinion which survives to this day.[62]

However, it was in the 1980s that many librarians found themselves seduced by the managerial revolution which accompanied the revival of the commercial spirit and the philosophy of go-getting. Spurred on by a virulent and irresistible enterprise culture, and because new styles of management were becoming widespread in local government at the time, librarians often chose to 'go with the flow' of the corporate management culture of the day. Many librarians, armed with the latest management jargon, became managers first and librarians second. Thus, far from being 'out of touch' with up-to-date ideas, as an influential report on public libraries suggested in the early 1990s,[63] many librarians lined up with key aspects of the entrepreneurial culture of the day.

However, the other main aspect of the corporate culture revolution of the Thatcher years, namely the privatisation and commercialisation of public services, held much less appeal for librarians. Public libraries are grounded in the public service ideal.[64] This itself is rooted in the notion of the public sphere – as explored by Habermas[65] – which comprises non-interested, accessible, open institutions dedicated to rational debate, cultural enlightenment and the free exchange of knowledge and ideas. Frank Webster has correctly pointed out that libraries are public sphere institutions *par excellence*.[66] They were 'formed and developed on the basis of a notion that information was a resource which belonged to everyone'.[67] However, like much of the public sphere, Webster argues, libraries are being eroded by sectional commercial interests. Although Webster's notion of a golden age of the public library in terms of its 'public sphere' status might be viewed as romantic, ignoring as it does the controlling, censorious and 'excluding' aspects of past provision, his assessment that what status in this regard it does possess has in recent years been under threat, and continues to be so, is thoroughly convincing.

The greatest threat to the public library as a public sphere institution came in the form of a government Green (consultation) Paper in 1988.[68] Set against a background of anxiety over declining standards of literacy and a stagnating public library service, a complete revamp of the public library was advocated. The renaissance was to be market led. The major policy shifts advised were the introduction of charging for, and the contracting-out of, services. The Paper explained that charging in public libraries was hardly new: rates had long been levied for borrowing audio-visual items, making a reservation, or requesting extensive searches in business and local studies libraries – and so asking customers to pay for core services, like borrowing books and using reference facilities, was logical and not out of keeping with past provision. A similar argument was employed in respect of sub-contracting: support services such as cataloguing, labeling and jacketing were mostly provided by outside contractors. Thus, contracting-out services to various client groups (like the elderly), or video services, or the work of an entire branch or system would merely be to extend an established principle. The market solution to the problems faced by the public library found support outside government. The right wing Adam Smith Institute asked why tax payers should subsidise 'a system which largely supplies free pulp fiction to those who could well afford to pay for it'.[69] Charging in public libraries, argued the Institute, would provide the public library system with the cash needed for an extensive programme of renewal. It would also trigger a renaissance in the fast disappearing private subscription library sector.

These were fresh and powerful arguments, as their repetition and coverage in the 1990s by a variety of commentators and journalists demonstrated.[70] Most public librarians reacted angrily to the idea of charging for core services. Promoters of commodification were belittled as knowing 'the price of everything and the value of nothing'.[71] In response to the Green Paper librarians organised protest and discussion forums up and down the country.[72] The public library duly survived the mercantile onslaught and in 1995 a line was drawn under the charging issue – for the time being at any rate – by a major review of public libraries sponsored by the Department of National Heritage.[73] Among its recommendations was the maintenance of public library services, including the Internet, free at the point of delivery; moreover, where circumstances allowed, this principle should be extended, it was advised, to other services and materials.[74] Although librarians largely recoiled from the suggestion that they should charge for the core services they provided, they were less hostile to the idea that services be contracted-out (submitted to market testing or compulsory competitive tendering). But while this approach to service provision has been seen in places, it has not become widespread. Thus, the concerns of some regarding 'the appropriateness of certain types of commercial organisations as providers of a whole public information service' were, on the whole, if not misplaced, then perhaps exaggerated.[75]

Full-blown commercialisation might have been kept at bay, but the lure of the corporate culture in terms of looking upon users, readers or borrowers as *customers* pervaded the public library scene: by the mid 1990s half of library authorities were using the word 'customer' to describe their users.[76] In 1989, a discourse on the planning library services stated that: 'A key element in the marketing approach is the definition of customer requirements and preferences – the demands, wants and needs of particular sectors of the customer community.'[77] The most common use of the word 'customer' by librarians in the 1980s and 1990s was as a prefix to the word 'care'. Customer care programmes became the latest manifestation of librarians' historic, declared intention to move ever closer to their clients; 'library publicity' and 'public relations' being terms used earlier in the century. But such programmes were much more sophisticated than previous incarnations, and were based on careful research into the librarian-public interface and the skills required to improve it.[78] That this interface needed improving is illustrated by Ken Hornsby's humorous autobiographical account of the lot of a lowly assistant in a London public library in the 1970s: 'I was not yet used to the idea', he recalled, having recently joined the library staff, 'that the public were a race apart; strictly over-the-counter people who did odd things and asked odd questions'; while later, after gaining much more experience in the job, he was confirmed in the belief that 'the public are exhausting, belligerent, hard work, and not to be put off. You enter the [staff] tea room with the air of someone who has successfully fought several bulls and needs to get his breath back before he fights several more'.[79]

Prioritising the customer struck a chord not only among public library managerialists who had bought into the corporate culture, but also appealed to populists who sought a more 'democratic' library service, responding to a plurality of cultural demands. Irritated by what they saw as the public library's traditional bias towards highbrow and mainstream culture, populists were eager to let customers tell librarians what they needed, not *vice versa*. This 'give them what they want' philosophy, although on the surface appearing to build a consensus in librarianship by uniting its corporate and radical wings, merely served to open up the age old fissure between what one might crudely call the 'educationalists' and 'recreationalists', which cut across the corporate-radical divide. In particular, some were incensed that deferring to users as customers in all aspects of provision endorsed the postmodern disease of cultural relativism. In librarianship this meant robbing the profession of the ability to make value judgements, the absence of which, in the words of Richard Hoggart, 'runs through open commercial societies like dry rot through once sound timber'.[80] Such was the climate of fear created among the anti-postmoderns that one commentator was prompted to announce the imminent 'dissolution of the libraries', in the context of an emerging semi-literate society.[81]

Whereas the implementation of customer care programmes and the like were surely good for the public library user, the overall drift towards a commercial mind-set in public librarianship has troubled those wishing to defend the public library's public service ethos. Bob Usherwood, Britain's leading commentator on the public library over the last quarter of a century, in considering the effects of new modes of management on the institution's public service orientation, asked in 1996 'What have we done ...?' Usherwood writes of 'sins that have been committed in management's name', believing that 'some of the new managerialist ideas had been introduced because of a dogmatic disbelief in any kind of delivery of public service'. He is wary of some librarians' 'uncritical acceptance of the enterprise culture' and senses a 'distinct feeling of disquiet among a number of library professionals' about this. Some managerialist librarians, he observes, have adopted the language of the market trader, junior professionals, in particular, welcoming the importation of commercial values which their more senior colleagues, who learnt their trade in an era of unquestionable loyalty to the public service idea, view with deep suspicion.[82]

Commentators outside the library world generally see the institution as a neutral, democratic territory where people can 'experience their identity as citizens rather than as consumers'.[83] Evidence from people using public libraries in the 1980s and 1990s would appears to support this view. Ordinary people see public libraries as 'public sphere', non-commercial places, in which library professionals *should* operate according to traditional public service ideals. In 1988, one public library user proclaimed that:

On the whole, my library withdrawals are merely political acts. I use my library to defend the principles against those Philistines in the [Conservative] government who would say that the public library system is not being used by sufficient numbers to warrant public subsidy.

Another stated that: 'Our libraries are a great heritage and I DO hope that the Thatcher revolution will not do anything to remove universal FREE libraries.'[84]

A decade later, users' dislike of the corporate culture of public libraries, certainly in terms of charging for services, was still very much apparent. 'I am a firm believer', states one Mass-Observation volunteer, 'in the valuable contribution the public library has made in widening people's horizons by making the world's literature available to them free. I would strongly resist any suggestion that libraries should ever charge for their basic service – book loan.' A pensioner who recently lost his concession for borrowing tapes and CDs free of charge felt he did not wish to complain as the public library 'was a costly service to establish and maintain'. Further, many users are clearly voracious readers and make it clear that they would not be able to sustain their reading if charges were imposed.

Regarding the public library's corporate image, some 'customers' appear to appreciate the efficient, modern buildings often provided for them. Others question the appropriateness of modern designs for libraries: 'New modern buildings don't seem quite right to me'. For one woman, her local library still gave 'a very strong impression of nineteenth century municipalism', a sentiment echoed by another critic who states that most librarians 'retain at least a trace of the aura surrounding that elderly public servant', although, he concedes, 'they have gained in approachability as they get continually younger'. The majority generally acknowledge the helpfulness of staff, but not without the occasional reference to rudeness and officiousness.[85]

Computers

As the previous Chapter showed, computer technology was embraced by public libraries as early as the 1960s. By the 1980s, a combination of automated circulation systems, electronic information services via the 'Prestel' system,[86] online catalogues and local information at the push of a button was making computer technology a highly visible feature of public library use.[87] The 1990s saw the emergence of Internet provision and facilities for undertaking word processing. A classic example of a state-of-the-art 'cyberspace' public library environment was the refurbished Croydon Central Library, opened in 1993. This new library boasted the largest public access CD-Rom network in any UK public library; public access personal computers for private hire; CD-Roms for loan; Internet access, including email facilities; a database linking resources in the local studies library and the borough's museum; and the networking of electronic services to schools and other libraries.[88]

In 1986, Theodore Roszak, questioning the ability of libraries to be seen as places likely to accommodate the new electronic technologies, found it curious 'that the contemporary discussion of information so rarely touches upon the library'.[89] Whereas 'outsiders' may not have appreciated the depth of the interface, both real and potential, between libraries on the one hand, and information and communication technologies on the other, those inside or close to the library world were increasingly enthusiastic in the 1980s and 1990s about the role such technologies could play in developing services. By the late 1990s, librarians and government were encouraging public libraries to be in the vanguard of the digital revolution, urging them to 'work day and night for [a] high-tech future'.[90] The vision was one of a public library without walls.[91] Strategists hoped to fashion a 'new library', a computer-mediated people's network, from the white heat of the information technology revolution.[92]

During this period librarians were by no means prepared to relinquish their anchorage in print culture, or in the *modern* ethos of learning and progress associated with it. To the untrained eye, a strange contradiction in the library world in the 1990s was the take-up of digital technologies in parallel with the opening of new accommodation for two of the world's richest collections of printed material: the British Library in London and the Bibliothèque Nationale de France in Paris.[93] But despite remaining loyal to the print tradition, late twentieth-century librarians increasingly defined themselves in the context of an emerging information society.[94]

An appropriate and scholarly scepticism concerning the existence of an information society fundamentally different from the industrial society that preceded it, is now a firmly established theme in the discipline of sociology. The critique of the information society idea is multi-faceted, theorists viewing as problematic the various propositions which constitute its discourse. Information society enthusiasts believe that: information is now the key economic resource; the information occupations now dominate the workforce; technology, most obviously information technology, is the driving force behind social change; increased access to information has expanded political participation, widened opportunities for social emancipation and inclusion, and considerably reduced class divisions; and quantity of information and the multiplicity of signs are the major determinants of our information culture. Information society sceptics oppose these propositions, arguing that: capital remains the key economic resource; the notion of the information professions is open to wide interpretation; human needs and aspirations remain the informer of technological change; problems of information poverty and exclusion have barely been addressed; and the true value of information lies in its quality and meaning, the latter having been diluted by information overload. Sceptics also question the novelty of the information society, proposing that past information revolutions within modernity – in respect of surveillance, bureaucracy and earlier communication technologies, such as the telegraph or television – were possibly more significant than the recent digital explosion.[95]

Despite these warnings, many late-twentieth century librarians appeared to internalise the idea of a new age, an information society, listening attentively to its utopian protagonists.[96] Mostly, the library community was either unaware of the information society critique or readily turned a blind eye to it, choosing instead to regurgitate the rhetoric of government,[97] or of those who Roszak[98] has referred to as 'the data merchants'. Librarians treated the arrival of an information society as a 'given' social phenomenon. 'We have grown accustomed to speaking of an Information Society, even where we are not quite sure what this means', observed a commentator on libraries in 1998.[99] Librarians asserted that they 'should be in the business of promoting the information society',[100] and presented and marketed themselves as key players in the emerging new age. It is not easy to identify the reasons for this ready acceptance. But there is little doubt that 'information age' librarians were confronted by a series of technological and social developments – new information and communication technologies, the increasing commodification of information, competition from other information occupations, and the emergence of postmodern diversity – which created uncertainties concerning their professional jurisdiction, identity and status, as well as their self-image. The withering of libraries has for some time been seen as a real possibility, with librarians appearing alongside other white collar occupations as prime candidates for extinction as traditional work patterns are shattered. In an effort to defend their professionalism, therefore, librarians perhaps not surprisingly embraced the information society idea as a means of buttressing their precarious occupational position.

It would be wrong to assume, however, that librarians have in recent years been entirely insincere in the digital-utopian zeal they have displayed, promoting the information society vision merely for professional gain. There has been a genuine desire to move with the times, based on a belief among librarians that they can make a significant contribution to the information revolution by exploiting technological opportunities, while at the same time protecting the printed word and avoiding 'the end of the book'. Public librarians, especially, have been keen to stress a natural correlation between their traditional aim of democratising access to knowledge and the widening of access which the digitalization of information promises. One might even go so far as to suggest that the desire of librarians to be pace-setters in the information society – to see their institutions as the 'heart and brain' of a new age[101] – is derived from an historic sense of destiny to be so. Librarianship is conscious of its ancient heritage and thus dismisses the prospect of extinction, preferring to believe that 'for the foreseeable future and for an immense stretch of the past, libraries appear to be very durable institutions'.[102]

Predictions earlier in the century about the state of libraries at the turn of the millennium were less optimistic. In 1932, a dystopian commentator on the public library, looking forward to the year 2000, imagined a society in which: 'Book learning is almost entirely superseded by the radio, the cinema and television, and all public libraries report a steady falling-off both in the number of borrowers and in the average number of books borrowed by each.'[103] Later, in 1977, librarians met to consider the subject of 'Librarianship 1999'. One contributor to the meeting cast doubt on the future of libraries by predicting that:

People will have through their home terminals and television screens access to the majority of information they require. They will not have to go out for it, or even to process it often, for it only has to be dialled for through the telephone linked computer or picked up through direct transmission.[104]

Contrary to such premonitions, the printed word continued to thrive as the second millennium drew to a close. Some commentators have been anxious to point out that the public library's recent interest in information technology, although crucial, has proved to be a dangerous distraction from the problem of low expenditure on book stocks, staffing and other traditional components of service. New technology alone, they argue, will not save public libraries and much more needs to be done to keep the savagery of the cuts in core work, perpetrated in the last quarter of the century, in the public eye.[105] This scepticism has been shared by some librarians. In 1988, Bob Duckett wrote forcefully that:

Messianic talk [about IT in libraries], much in favour today, is part of a new and dangerous imperialism. Like many such progressive/revisionary/radical moves, it contains much that is good ... But like other such ... moves, it overstates the ideal, undervalues the traditional, and departs from reality.[106]

It is apparent that, although recognising its value, the ordinary public library user of the 1990s did not share the same enthusiasm for IT in libraries as librarians, library strategists and politicians. It is not simply that too few, even at the end of the decade, saw libraries as up to date IT-wise;[107] rather that the public was 'not so gung-ho about new technology ... what they really like are more books, longer opening hours, particularly at week-ends, and more sociable facilities'.[108] Regarding the much-discussed information superhighway, for example, the views of many public library patrons diverge from those of public library providers. Whereas users increasingly expect to use the Internet for a wide variety of purposes, including e-mail, e-commerce and recreational use,[109] librarians continued to believe that the technology should be used essentially for information searches.[110]

Planners of the new information-rich public library in the 1990s tended to imbue IT not only with messianic powers, but also with what might be termed 'Victorian seriousness'. A government review of public libraries in 1997 anticipated that information technology 'should help to restore the profound importance of public libraries in our society'. That importance, it was suggested, had been eroded in modern times by over-investment by public libraries in their recreational role. The misguided nature of that investment was partly demonstrated, it was argued, by an unfortunate jettisoning of traditional principles:

The original concept of the British public library system was one of high seriousness and importance. In recent years there has been a shift away from that high seriousness towards entertainment.[111]

Yet public libraries have, ultimately, always (although often after heated controversy) endorsed reading for entertainment and escape. One of the great strengths of the public library, indeed, has been its historic ability to accommodate both utilitarian and idealist perspectives; to provide for the imagination as well as for those seeking 'useful' knowledge. Some providers and strategists of the 1990s, seduced by glittering digital technology, appeared to forget this tradition, wishing instead for a public library future dominated by utilitarian practicality.

The evidence is, however, that the public library *user* does not see the routing of the information superhighway into libraries as a 'saviour' technology, but simply regards it as *another*, albeit important, format – merely in the tradition of the 'highway of culture' which public libraries have provided since 1850.[112] Regarding government 'pronouncements about public libraries getting on-line and so becoming a vital resource in our new knowledge-driven society', one member of the public comments that: 'It might all be so much political hyperbole'. In the context of the public library, this sceptic also compares the 'information present' with the 'mechanical past' of the 1960s:

One of the things I liked best on those childhood visits was the librarians' deft fingering of the rather scruffy index cards in long wooden catalogue drawers, and the readers' little cardboard sleeves with the acquisition details of the books sticking out of them on hand-written tickets. It wasn't so much fun when they brought in computerised scanners with red lights and electronic bleeps.

Generally, new information and communication technologies in libraries – referred to generically by users as 'computers', with little attempt to distinguish between functions – are seen by the public as merely another tool in the public library's armoury. Many retain the belief, in fact, that such technologies, including the Internet, are simply 'peripheral to the main activity which is still the lending of books'. The introduction of computers is seen as the 'most obvious change in libraries over recent years', although often of equal note is 'the increase in items other than books: records, tapes, CD's, CD Rom's, videos etc – very useful'. Notwithstanding some wariness on the part of older users, computers in libraries are on the whole welcomed, but without the 'hype' displayed by providers and strategists. There is an awareness, however, that computer terminals are changing the look and feel of libraries, one user remarking that bookshops were becoming more like libraries, and libraries more like community information centres.[113]

The Public Library and the Postmodern Self

Across the social sciences the proposition has taken root that we have in recent decades entered a postmodern age.[114] Pluralism, fragmentation, dislocation of identity, time-space compression, flexibility and indeterminacy are all features that we recognise and experience, to a greater or lesser extent, in our daily lives. Postmodernism is an 'end of' mode of thought. It stands not just for the culmination or death of modernity in terms of the latter's overarching optimistic and emancipatory impulses, but also for the demise of modernity's constituent elements: that is to say, faith in science, in the knowledge of 'experts', in truth and in the individual as a rational controlling 'actor'. Postmodernity also questions the efficacy of Fordist production, of government economic planning and of world views of, and solutions to, human problems.

Regarding the individual, postmodernity questions the legitimacy of the modern self as essentially self-formed, driven by reason, autonomous and in control of his or her destiny. The postmodern individual, argues Rosenau,[115] is relaxed, flexible, oriented to the emotions and exhibits a 'be yourself' attitude. He or she looks to pleasure and fantasy, prefers the temporary to the permanent and the spontaneous to the planned. He or she is also fascinated by the exotic, the sacred, the primitive and the irrational. In the postmodern world, life changes more rapidly than ever. In the consumption of goods and services tastes are fast-changing, individuals employing their consumer choices as 'do-it-youself identikits'.[116] The postmodern individual, moving between identities and communities as frequently as one changes a shirt and tie or a pair of stockings, is consummate in the 'stage-craft', 'impression-management' skills contributing to what Erving Goffman called the 'dramaturgical process'.[117] People's lifestyles, and hence their selves, 'are continuously remade and reshaped in new and novel ways'; moreover, the postmodern self may be imagined as 'the command centre of a global project, receiving and having to manage response to a vast variety of inputs'.[118]

For the public library to respond to this postmodern, (at times) irrational, image-seeking, emotion-oriented, flexible, human 'command centre' would appear to be asking a great deal of an institution rooted in modernity, characterised as it has been by the technologies of print, by a strong professional culture, by notions of rational knowledge and recreation, by an attachment to highbrow (or at least mainstream) culture and by an ideological commitment to universalism.[119] The institutions of modernity are everywhere under threat, and the public library is no exception in this respect. If, however, the notion of postmodernity and the postmodern self is replaced, respectively, by the notion of late (or high) modernity and the late-(or high-)modern self, then the task awaiting the public library would appear less formidable.[120] Conceptualising modernity as an 'unfinished project' – a 'new modernity' – means that self-realisation (or betterment, -direction, -improvement, -actualisation), within the context of social progress and justice, remain, as they were in classic modernity, crucial to the formation of the self in the late-modern age.[121]

These 'modern' values and aspirations continued to lie at the heart of the public library ethos in the closing decades of the twentieth century. In the tradition of modernity, librarians and library supporters were anxious to advertise the library in terms of social rights. In the 1980s, libraries were said to facilitate – through the development of local information services, for example[122] – the 'right to know'.[123] Information was conceptualised as the 'fourth right of citizenship':

People will not be able to get their due as citizens of present day society unless they have continuous access to the information which will guide them through it ... and unless they get their due they are unlikely to recognize the reciprocal obligation that all citizens have to society.[124]

In the 1990s, the trajectory which government and strategists planned for public libraries was equally 'modern', located deep within the tradition of personal progress which characterised the Victorian origins of the public library. As Chris Smith, Secretary of State for Culture, Media and Sport, declared, the 'future remains true to the core principles that have underlined the service for the past 150 years'.[125] The former Minister for Libraries, Richard Luce, took a similar line:

Nearly 150 years after the first public libraries were set up, there is a need for them to re-establish their role within the contemporary scene. The importance of books and information to *educational self-improvement* [my emphasis] is as strong as ever, and needs to be fostered.[126]

A later Minister for Libraries, Alan Howarth, re-worked the notion of the self-help-oriented 'people's university', proclaiming the transformation of public libraries into 'street corner universities'.[127]

In 1998 government declared the onset of the 'learning age',[128] in which lifelong learning for the individual, aided by public libraries, would be a prerequisite of participation. A contributor to this strategy correctly observed that, in terms of both individual and social progress (as opposed to social control), this was a 'concept relating back to the spirit of Chartism', one of the main catalysts of the public library movement in the 1840s, when workers began to more fully realise the link between politico-economic emancipation and education.[129] In the 1990s, public libraries were allotted a prominent place in the National Grid for Learning – an initiative reminiscent, of course, of the library grid proposed in the 1930s (see Chapter 3), as well as being an expression of faith in modernity if ever there was one. Finally, although focusing on the future and on new information and communication technologies in public libraries, the initiative *New library: the people's network*[130] was saturated with the vocabulary of modernity, most obviously in respect of learning, training and education for citizenship for the individual.

Librarians, too, echoed the modernist belief in individual self-betterment. In South Ayrshire, library-based Cyber-Centres were set up in the late 1990s to give access to the internet and to CD-ROMS, these facilities being integrated with existing open learning resources to give a dynamic service to the *independent learner*. Although clearly postmodern in respect of the distance, flexible learning on offer, this initiative was ideologically rooted in modernity, being described as in the tradition of the 'people's university' and its commitment to informal self-education.[131] Libraries continued to be institutions which challenged the individual to develop and adopt new ways of thinking. As one supporter theorised, libraries are 'dangerous places' that nurture the critical spirit: 'They have presented myself and millions of others with dreams and ideas. They open up a world of education and promises.'[132]

In the late-twentieth century, belief in the inevitability and efficacy of social atomism was resurrected – as Margaret Thatcher's assertion that 'there is no such thing as society' illustrated. Social atomism should not be confused, of course, with the pursuit of self-help. To their credit, public librarians rejected materialistic individualism, continuing to stress the importance of self-help via the informal education, enlightenment and imaginative recreation that people gave themselves via the public library. Moreover, users continue to respond to libraries' endorsement of the modern, progressive self by demanding material which, in the vocabulary of Anthony Giddens, provided 'reflexive' knowledge for self-betterment: from books about the body and manuals on DIY (home improvement), to business texts and information on legal rights.[133] In short, guides to individual emancipation, the literature of self-help.[134]

If the public library's on-going association with independent learning reflected a deep commitment to the modern self, to what extent did its growing fascination with information technology (IT) in the late-twentieth century endorse the notion of the postmodern self? In the postmodern social model people increasingly pursue products and services less for reasons of 'security', for physical need, and more for their value as a sign. Both material and non-material consumption (whether the purchase of a car or going on a certain kind of holiday) is saturated with signification. We have entered the 'society of signs',[135] where the value of a product is determined by its cultural component. The take-up of IT by public libraries, and the use made of it by the public therein, might thus be considered to be, irrespective of the value of the information conveyed, merely a new signifier in transforming the identities of both public libraries themselves and their patrons. Knowledge delivered by IT systems might also be seen as a means of satisfying the aspirations of individuals and the public library system alike to negotiate 'identity changes'.

According to Castells, democratic technologies like the Internet are productive of new 'cultural communes' formed around issues which attract shifting allegiances that cut across the traditional, staple identity of class. Individuals act collectively as agents of social transformation, drawing their personal identities from the range of 'communal heavens' – often taking the form of 'virtual communities' – that they choose to inhabit. Castells refers to this type of self-consciousness as 'project identity' or, when 'communities of resistance' are involved, 'resistance identity'. IT-mediated knowledge clearly has an important part to play in shaping identities. But its power in this respect cannot be assessed properly until the passage of time permits objective judgement to be passed. Moreover, history tells us that whereas some communities of resistance have in the past been able to mount successful challenges to authority, major powerholders have mostly maintained their hegemonic positions. To suggest that information technology, embraced by the people either in or out of public libraries, will act as a corrosive agent on the uneven distribution of wealth, power and influence is surely both romantic and premature.

But a more pressing issue as far as the public library is concerned, is whether IT-literate, postmodern individuals, in search of a 'portfolio identity', choose to explore their consciousness or identity in a public library environment (including librarian-authored websites) or simply opt to by-pass the public library in favour of other access points (the home included) because of the inflexibility or paucity of the public library's electronic services. The public library's historic conservatism, real or perceived, presents a further problem in this regard. The disorganised society that is postmodernity is replete with the type of marginal groups and alternative issues which, for all its commitment to emancipation, the modern public library, used to supporting 'acceptable', 'recognisable' socio-political agendas, may find difficulty in accommodating. In short, the public library is perhaps much more accustomed to serving the predictable than the unpredictable self.

Despite the supposed degeneration of society in a postmodern direction – for example, in terms of an impulse for the immediate, the consumption of mere surface messages and knowledge and a decline in concentration spans and reflective thought – people appear to have shown no desire to abandon the public library as a site of spiritual peace. Most public libraries remain busy places; hardly the sleepy backwaters stereotypically depicted in popular myth. A recent novel, with a female librarian as its central character, testifies to the public library's continuing liveliness: 'The library was frightful today', she remarks. 'Hordes of people from the moment we opened to the moment we closed – and as most of the day was wet we seemed to be permanently surrounded by dripping bodies, damp books and general sog.'[136] In the rush and confusion of a de-centred, fragmented and identity-rich postmodern (or late-modern) world, public libraries provide a haven of spiritual rest for their users. According to Miksa, one of the new benefits of the postmodern, IT-rich library is that it provides a 'personal-space' learning and information environment.[137] Yet the 'public-space' library characteristic of modernity, very much still with us, far from providing essentially a social experience, has always offered intimacy and seclusion for the self, a 'sanctity (or romance) of place' for the individual. As a 'private public space', the library, according to Greenhalgh, 'can be an anonymous place and encourages autonomy and self-determination. It is a private place where personal space is not expected to be invaded'.[138] Many continue to see the public library as a means of escape from the real world. When entering a library it is as if a mild primeval-like trance overcomes individuals, propelling them into the spirit world of learning and knowledge. The public library appears always to have fulfilled such a spiritual role, but its capacity to transport people beyond reality has perhaps taken on a new importance as society has become more fractured and uncertain of itself and its future.

Chris Smith, Secretary of State for Culture, Media and Sport, believes that a public library should be 'a welcoming, comfortable place that people feel completely happy about going over the threshold into'. In fact, he continued, the public library *is* 'on the whole a place which people feel very happy about going into'.[139] Evidence from the public supports this observation. Far from being cold and formal places, libraries are seen as cosy – 'warm and safe places for a person to while away a few hours', or 'a comfortable place to be with pleasant likeable people'. They are perceived, in short, as 'havens of tranquillity', often 'light, airy and blissfully silent'. In terms of their attractiveness to the solitude-seeking self, however, a distinction should be made between larger and smaller libraries. One Mass-Observation volunteer notes that the central library she sometimes works in 'has a spacious feel and even if there is someone else working on the same table it rarely bothers me. The staff are quieter too!'; whereas at her local branch library the staff are more in evidence, there is less room, more formality and less opportunity for solitude. Generally, however, in libraries large and small, in all parts of Britain, individuals appear to undergo a near spiritual experience when using libraries:

I cannot speak highly enough of public libraries, – they have informed me, entertained me, inspired me ... Our library looks an interesting and beguiling place ... to me it feels like the best place (apart from my home) to be because it is full of riches; from other people's lives, or their imagination.

The role of the library as a very personal place, as an informer of the self, is summed up in the words of another observer: 'To me a library is a treasure house of knowledge, information and fantasy.'[140]

Notes and References to Chapter Six

[1] Britain's share of world trade fell from 25% in 1950 to 15% in 1962: D. Childs, *Britain since 1945: a political history* (London, 4th edn., 1997), 75.

[2] K.O. Morgan, *The people's peace: British history 1945-1989* (Oxford, 1990), 406.

[3] A. Gamble, *Britain in decline: economic policy, political strategy and the British state* (London, 1981).

[4] T. Nairn, *The break-up of Britain* (London, 1977).

[5] J. Eatwell, *Whatever happened to Britain? The economics of decline* (London, 1982).

[6] Morgan, *The people's peace*, op. cit., 384.

[7] Childs, *Britain since 1945*, op. cit., 205.

[8] R. Bacon and W. Eltis, *Britain's economic problem: too few producers* (London, 1976).

[9] For a succinct account of cuts in public library provision in the late-1970s, see L. Paulin, 'Recent developments in the provision of public library services in the united Kingdom', *Library Quarterly* 48:4 (1978).

[10] E.H.C. Driver and M.K. Wallis, 'Decision making and the cuts', *LAR* 82 (September 1980), 412, 415.

[11] The Library Campaign, *Expenditure cuts in public libraries and their effects on services* (Sheffield, 1985), 2-3.

[12] Ibid., 19.

[13] *Which?* (February 1990).

[14] 'Crisis? What crisis?', *The Bookseller* (6 March 1992).

[15] L. Greenhalgh and K. Worpole, with C. Landry, *Libraries in a world of cultural change* (London, 1995), 37.

[16] I. Edwards, 'The new Cardiff Central Library', *LAR* 92 (May 1990), 331.

[17] 'Fifty libraries face closure', *Sunday Times* (31 January 1999).

[18] In D. Watson, 'A positive weapon for renewal', *LAR* 99 (November 1997), 580.

[19] MOA, Regular Pastimes (1988), R312, W575.

[20] MOA, The Public Library (1999), 02349, S2207, G2089.

[21] P. Jordan, 'Social class, race relations and the public library', *Assistant Librarian* 65:3 (March 1972), wrote of middle-class power in the library context as the power to demand and be given a good service, as well as the power held by white, middle-class librarians who have dominated the management of library services. See also R. Lahav, 'Is class still an issue?', *Public Library Journal* 4:2 (March/April 1989) and J. Pateman, *Public libraries and social class*, Public Library Policy and Social Exclusion Working Paper No. 3, Leeds Metropolitan University (April 1999).

[22] P. Corrigan and V. Gillespie, *Class struggle, social literacy and idle time: the provision of public libraries in England* (Brighton, 1978).

[23] D. Wardle, *Education and society in nineteenth-century Nottingham* (Cambridge, 1971), 183-5.

[24] B. Luckham, *The library in society: a study of the public library in an urban setting* (London, 1971), 5.

[25] Select Committee on Public Libraries, *Report* (1849), xii.

[26] L.S. Jast, *The library and the community* (London, 1939), 46.

[27] MOA, Reading in Tottenham, File Report 2537 (November 1947).

[28] *Harrogate Advertiser* (28 February 1959).

[29] T. Kelly, 'Public libraries and public opinion', *LAR* 68 (July, 1966), 251.

[30] S. Kothari, *Nottingham deprived areas: library outreach project* (1976), Nottingham Local Studies Library.

[31] Department of Education and Science, *The libraries' choice* (London, 1978), 6-7.

[32] Jordan, op. cit., 72. L. Dawes, 'Libraries, culture and blacks', *Assistant Librarian* 66:7 (July 1973).

[33] R. Brown, 'Library services to immigrant groups', *GLC [Greater London Council] Intelligence Unit Quarterly Bulletin* 21 (December 1972), 35. See also, Westminster City Libraries, 'Seminar on services to immigrant groups' (15 November 1977), held by Westminster City Archives. A public library user in Lewisham, in 1961, protested that he had been racially discriminated against when he, unlike others, was not allowed to use a ticket issued by another library authority in the borough's libraries: PRO, ED 171/5, S.K. Chawla to Minister of Education (29 May 1961).

[34] David Lane in Foreword to E. Clough and J. Quarmby, *A public library service for ethnic minorities in Great Britain* (London, 1978), vii.

[35] P. Halliwell, 'Plea for a public library', *Assistant Librarian* 68:2 (February 1975), 25.

[36] J. Hendry, 'How little we really do: library services for the unemployed in the Renfrew district', *Assistant Librarian* (December, 1981), 150-1.

[37] J.N. Berry, 'Getting into the ghetto', *Library Journal* 91:14 (August 1966). L.L. Sherrill (ed.), *Library services to the unserved* (New York, 1970). D.G. Davies, Jr. and C.K. Malone, 'Reading for liberation: the role of libraries in the 1964 Mississippi Freedom Summer project', in J.M. Tucker (ed.), *Untold stories: civil rights, libraries and black librarianship* (Champaign, IL, 1998).

[38] B. Totterdell, 'Public libraries in a changing society', in K.C. Harrison (ed.), *Public library policy* (London, 1981). For assessments of community librarianship, see J. Vincent, *An introduction to community librarianship* (Newcastle under Lyme, 1986). W.J. Martin, *Community librarianship: changing the face of public libraries* (London, 1989). A. Black and D. Muddiman, *Understanding community librarianship: the public library in post-modern Britain* (Aldershot, 1997). An earlier plea to address the needs of the disadvanataged was made by W.J. Martin (ed.), *Library services to the disadvantaged* (London, 1975).

[39] R. Astbury, *Libraries and the unemployed: needs and responses* (London, 1983).

[40] Pleas for greater involvement were not new. In 1920, it was advised that the librarian in rural areas 'must not be the old-time janitor who kept his books safe in the dusty security of locked-up cases, fading into the darkness behind an impassable counter like that of a bank ... above all, he must travel around the country ... he must awaken and continually test the demand by talking to readers ... and enlisting the support of local residents': 'Books for rural readers', *Daily News* (7 July 1920). In 1937, it was anticipated that 'one of the developments in the future would be not so much an approach to individuals as an approach to groups either through their work ... or through people having particular political and religious beliefs': 'Librarians at Ilkley', *Yorkshire Post* (30 September 1937).

[41] 'The privatisation of reading', *City Limits* (13-19 July, 1984).

[42] MOA, Regular Pastimes (1988), S1540.

[43] (London, 1988), viii.

[44] P. Coleman, 'Past to future – the public library's changing role', in M. Kinnell (ed.), *Informing communities: the role of libraries and information services* (Newcastle, Staffordshire, 1992), 301. See also, P. Coleman, *Whose problem? The public library and the disadvantaged* (Newcastle under Lyme, 1981).

[45] Positive discrimination in community information services was advocated, for example, by J. Ward, 'Equality of information', *Municipal Journal* 82:20 (17 May 1974), 595.

[46] A. Rushbridger, 'Charge of the write brigade', *Guardian* (7 January 1987). Greenhalgh and Worpole, *Libraries in a world of cultural change*, op. cit., 40.

[47] E. Kerslake and M. Kinnell, 'Public libraries, public interest and the information society: theoretical issues in the social impact of public libraries', *Journal of Librarianship and Information Science* 30:3 (September 1998), 160.

[48] Department of Culture, Media and Sport, *Libraries for all: social inclusion in public libraries* (London, 1999). See also, D. Muddiman (ed.), *Public library policy and social exclusion*, Library and Information Commission Report (London, forthcoming); and D. Muddiman, 'Everyone on board?', *Public Library Journal* 14:4 (Winter, 1999).

[49] J. Macnicol, 'In pursuit of the underclass', *Journal of Social Policy* 16:3 (July 1987). L. Morris, *Dangerous classes: the underclass and social citizenship* (London, 1994).

[50] MOA, The Public Library (1999), H2833, S2207, B86, W2731, B1509, B2623.

[51] J. Burnham, *The managerial revolution* (Harmondsworth, 1962).

[52] Ibid., 144.

[53] M. Weber, *Economy and society*, G. Roth and C. Wittich (eds.) (Berkeley, California, 1978, first published in German in 1922).

[54] A. Black, 'The Victorian information society: bureaucracy and public librarianship in nineteenth-century Britain', *Information Society*, forthcoming.

[55] P. Gratton, 'How "public" is the public library', in Public Libraries Group, *Prospects for British public libraries: proceedings of the Public Library Authorities conference* (1985), 9.

[56] Newcastle upon Tyne City Libraries and Arts, Staff circular (14 July 1992).

[57] 'Public library aims and objectives', *LAR* 73 (December 1971).

[58] E.g., P. Morgan, 'Output measurement and libraries', *Assistant Librarian* 68:11 (December 1975).

[59] F. Hogg, 'Cost-benefit analysis: the cost of the public library service in relation to value given', in *Proceedings of the Library Association public libraries conference* (1967).

[60] R. Brown and R. Surridge (eds.), *Output measurement* (Public Libraries Research Group of the Library Association, 1974).

[61] R. Malbon, *Productivity in branch libraries today, and in the future* (Branch and Mobile Libraries Group of the Library Association, 1971).

[62] 'Organize, reorganize, re-reorganize, re-re-re', *Grapevine: Staff Magazine of the Nottinghamshire County Library Service* (Spring, 1971), 3.

[63] Comedia, *Borrowed time? The future of public libraries in the UK* (Bournes Green, 1993). See also, C. Atton, 'The tragedy of Comedia: libraries and the free market', *Assistant Librarian* (September 1993).

[64] G. Mulgan, *The public service ethos and public libraries*. The future of public library services: working paper 6 (Bournes Green: Comedia, 1993).

[65] J. Habermas, *The structural transformation of the public sphere: an inquiry into a category of bourgeois society* (Cambridge, 1989, first published in German in 1962).

[66] F. Webster, *Theories of the information society* (London, 1995), 101.

[67] Ibid., 112.

[68] *Financing our public library service: four subjects for debate*, cmnd. 324 (1988).

[69] Adam Smith Instutute, *Ex libris* (London, 1986), 42.

[70] G. Lord, 'It's time to pay by the book', *Daily Telegraph* (24 March 1993); C. Brockhurst, 'Free library service in question', *LAR* 95 (November 1993); V. Elliot, 'Libraries are urged to charge for more services', *Times* (24 September 1997).

[71] 'The price of everything and the value of nothing', *LAR* 88 (July 1986).

[72] E.g., N. Coe and S. Parsons, 'The post-Green Paper public library service', *LAR* 91 (September 1989), 531, 533-4.

[73] Aslib, *Review of the public library service in England and Wales for the Department of Heritage* (London, 1995).

[74] As explained by R. Shimmon, 'View of the Review', *LAR* 97 (July 1995), 376.

[75] R. Astbury, 'The public library of the twenty-first century: the key information and learning centre in the community', *Libri* 44:2 (1994), 138.

[76] B. Usherwood, *Rediscovering public library management* (London, 1996), 121.

[77] B. McKee, *Planning library service* (1989), 54.

[78] P. Levy and B. Usherwood, *People skills: interpersonal skills training for library and information work*, Library and Information Research Report 88, The British Library (London, 1992).

[79] K. Hornsby, *Is that the library speaking?* (London, 1978), 17, 55.

[80] In E. Dudley, 'Oh, to be in public libraryland', LAR 94 (February 1992), 96.

[81] W.J. West, *The strange rise of semi-literate England: the dissolution of the libraries* (London, 1992).

[82] Usherwood, *Rediscovering*, op. cit., 'What have we done ...?' being the opening chapter to this book.

[83] K. Worpole, 'The future of the public library service', *Public Library Journal* 7:5 (1992).

[84] MOA, Regular Pastimes (1988), W1892, W1893.

[85] MOA, The Public Library (1999), H2637, L2393, A2801, B2728, L2393, B2728.

[86] C. Sullivan, *Impact of Prestel on public library branch services*, British Library Research and Development Report 5694 (1981).

[87] C. Batt, *New technology in public libraries: a survey* (Winchester, 1985).

[88] C. Batt, 'Croydon libraries in Cyberspace', *Streetwise: Journal of Places for People* 8:4, Issue 32 (1997-1998). H.G. Kirby, 'Public libraries and the information society: case study of Croydon Library Service', in J. Thorhauge et. al. (eds.), *Public libraries and the information society* (Luxembourg: European Commission, 1997).

[89] T. Roszak, *The cult of information: the folklore of computers and the true art of thinking* (Cambridge, 1986), 197-8.

[90] 'Booking a stake in the future', *Guardian* (20 February 1997). I. Murray, 'Libraries urged to work day and night for high-tech future', *Times* (20 February 1997). D. Glaister, 'Libraries go on line for high-tech information era', *Guardian* (20 February 1997).

[91] D. Rowan, 'The library without walls', *Guardian* (15 October 1997).

[92] Library and Information Commission, *New library: the people's network* (London, 1997).

[93] H.G.B. Anghelescu, 'Libraries without walls or architectural fantasies: a turn-of-the-millennium dilemma', *Libraries and Culture* 34:2 (Spring 1999).

[94] I. Cornelius, *Meaning and method in information studies* (Norwood, New Jersey, 1996), 55-81.

[95] Authoritative critiques of the concept are given by D. Lyon, *The information society: issues and illusions* (Cambridge, 1988) and F. Webster, *Theories of the information society*, op. cit.

[96] N.W. Horne, 'Information as an asset', *Impact: Journal of the [Library Association] Career Development Group* 2:3 (March 1999) 40, informs librarians that 'we have been in the "information society" for more than thirty years'.

[97] Department of National Heritage, *Reading the future: a review of public libraries in England* (London, 1997). House of Lords Select Committee on Science and Technology, *Information society: agenda for action in the UK* (London, 1996).

[98] Roszak, op. cit., 34-61.

[99] L. Dempsey, 'An occasion for soul and song', *Library Technology* 3:1 (February 1998), 13.

[100] F. Hendrix, 'Public libraries and the information superhighway', *Public Library Journal* 12:1 (1997).

[101] C. Batt, 'The heart and brain of the information society: public libraries in the twenty-first century', in D. Raitt (ed.), *Libraries for the millennium: implications for managers* (London, 1997).

[102] M.F. Winter, *The culture and control of expertise: towards a sociological understanding of librarianship* (New York, 1988), 79.

[103] 'The library service', *Local Government Journal* (23 January 1932).

[104] R. Fothergill, 'New media in 1999', in *Librarianship 1999: Papers read at the one-day conference of the London and Home Counties Branch of the Library Association* (London, 1977), 35.

[105] M. Phillips, 'Books build communities', *New Times* (July 1999). F. Webster, 'Knowledgeability and democracy in the information age', *Library Review* 48:7&8 (1999), 377-8.

[106] B. Duckett, 'The relevance of libraries and the presumptions of IT', *REFER: Journal of the ISG* 5:2 (Autumn 1988), 8.

[107] 'More IT, vicar', *LAR* 101 (June 1999), 327.

[108] S. Montford, 'A new library and public participation', *Streetwise: Journal of Places for People* 8:4, Issue 32 (1997-8), 1, quoting the *Guardian* (16 October 1997).

[109] I. Morson, J. Harrison and D. Cook, 'Boldly venturing into cyberspace', *LAR* 98 (March 1996), 151, found that outside the traditional public library environment 79% of Internet use was classed as 'general interest' or 'leisure'.

[110] R. Newton, A. Maclennan and J.D. Clark Allison, 'Public libraries on the Internet', *Public Library Journal* 13:1 (January-February 1998), 4.

[111] Department of National Heritage, *Reading the future*, op. cit., 3, foreword by V. Bottomley and I. Sproat.

[112] The term 'highway of culture' is used, for example, in 'Famous authors praise city's library progress', *Nottingham Guardian* (26 October 1932).

[113] MOA, The Public Library (1999), O2349, B2728, S2207, A1706.

[114] For authoritative accounts of postmodernism, see P.R. Rosenau, *Post-modernism and the social sciences: insights, inroads and intrusions* (Princeton, NJ, 1992), and D. Harvey, *The condition of postmodernity: an enquiry into the origins of cultural change* (Oxford, 1989).

[115] Rosenau, op. cit., 14, 53.

[116] Z. Bauman, *Thinking sociologically* (Oxford 1990), 205.

[117] E. Goffman, *The presentation of self in everyday life* (Harmondsworth, 1969), 26.

[118] J.R. Gibbins and B. Reimer, *The politics of postmodernity: an introduction to contemporary politics and culture* (London, 1999), 4.

[119] For a professional training perspective on the difficulty of this task, see D. Muddiman, 'Towards a postmodern context for information and library education', *Education for Information* 17 (1999).

[120] A. Giddens, *Modernity and self-identity: self and society in the late modern age* (Cambridge, 1991).

[121] The idea of modernity as an 'unfinished project' is also promulgated by U. Beck, *Risk society: towards a new modernity* (London, 1992).

[122] Library Association, *Community information: what libraries can do* (London, 1980). A. Bunch *Community information services: their origin, scope and development* (London, 1982).

[123] National Consumer Council and National Council of Social Service, *The right to know: a review of advice services in rural areas* (1978).

[124] National Consumer Council, *The fourth right of citizenship: a review of local advice services* (London, 1977).

[125] C. Smith, 'Our oyster', *Public Library Journal* 12:6 (November/December 1997), 117.

[126] R. Luce, 'Libraries: a ticket to civilization', *Independent* (27 October 1993).

[127] 'Britain's libraries: our street corner universities', *Parliamentary Monitor, Supplement 2: 'L' is for learning* (March 1999).

[128] *The learning age: a renaissance for a new Britain*, cmnd. 3790 (1998).

[129] B. Fryer, 'Reviving the spirit of Chartism', *LAR* 100 (January 1998), 8.

[130] Library and Information Commission, op. cit.

[131] A. McCormick and A. Sutton, *Independent learning and the Internet in public libraries*, Library and Information Briefings 84 (October 1998).

[132] A. McCann, 'Libraries: are they dangerous places?', *Assistant Librarian* (May 1994), 70.

[133] A. Giddens, *The consequences of modernity* (Cambridge and Oxford, 1990), 38, argues that the reflexivity of modern life consists of social practices which are constantly examined and reformed in the light of incoming information about those practices; knowing 'how to go on' remains a core characteristic of life.

[134] Giddens, *Modernity and self-identity*, op. cit., develops an assessment of individual 'political' action which he calls 'life politics', whereby individuals engage in lifestyle choices to construct dynamic self-identities.

[135] D. Harris, *A society of signs* (London, 1996).

[136] T. Joseph, *The diary of April March* (Bristol, 1997).

[137] F.L. Miksa, *The DDC, the universe of knowledge and the post-modern library* (Albany, New York, 1998), 84-5.

[138] L. Greenhalgh, *The place of the library*. The future of public library services: working paper 2 (Bournes Green: Comedia, 1993), 12.

[139] In D. Watson, 'Man of the people's university', *LAR* 100 (March 1998), 141.

[140] MOA, The Public Library (1999), D2839, G2134, H1543, G226, K310, A1706.

Conclusion

Rediscovering the Public Library Self

Although viewed by most as an uncomplicated, commonplace and 'everyday' ingredient of British life, public libraries are also, contrary to the general perception, sociologically and historically intriguing and worthy, therefore, of serious research and analysis. This study has attempted to challenge the popular myth of the public library as an uncontroversial, taken-for-granted institution without a history.

Libraries are notable features of the modern society that has been emerging in Britain since the eighteenth century. They mirror many of the characteristics of modernity – *public* libraries, by virtue of their public-sphere credentials and tradition, even more so. At a time when we are urged to embrace a postmodern and increasingly print-free information future, looking back in this way, to remind ourselves of the essence of the public library tradition, verges on the heretical. Yet we should be neither ashamed of investigating the public library's past nor of making use of the lessons drawn from its history in order, amongst other things, to declare our modernity.

The public library encapsulates the aspirations of the modern self: a liberal desire for progress, self-realisation, social emancipation, freedom of thought, the questioning of 'things established' and, although respectful of tradition and history, for release from the chains of custom. The public library has also been, enduringly, 'a place of quiet joy', a spiritual haven for soul and self. But modern selves are not atomistic; they are social. The social self too is reflected in the ethos of public libraries, in that they are communally funded, provide stimulating arenas for social interaction, contribute to the common good and contain books and other information formats which represent a shared store-house of the cultural record (the 'wisdom of the ages' as various Victorian library promoters would have put it) into which individuals can (mostly) freely tap.

Thus, in all its dimensions the self lies at the very heart of the public library philosophy. The need to keep it there becomes even more pressing as society enlarges, globalises, quickens and fractures into a multiplicity of identity options. Public librarians must clearly respond to such changes. This means listening to their public; but not simply in the 'customer care' sense or by buying into the hype of technological advance merely to court popularity. It means becoming more socially aware, more sociological. Public librarians need to be sociologists as much as technicians, technicians of enlightenment as much as enlightened technicians.

To become more self-conscious of its social responsibilities and more aware of the complexities of modern society, the public library world must surely relinquish the conservatism that has plagued its past. From Victorian-style moralising and control to Masonic meetings, from the censoring of 'inappropriate' literature to the celebration of techno-bureaucratic, municipal red-tapism and the managerialist, entrepreneurial spirit, the public library profession, despite its public service tradition and its radical elements, too often trod a conservative path.

The romanticising of community contributed considerably to the twentieth-century public library profession's 'establishment' frame of mind. In the twentieth century, as in the Victorian age, at times of social tension the spirit and vocabulary of community – involving an overblown rhetoric of classlessness and an over-anxious striving for social consensus – was frequently invoked by public library promoters to help steer society towards social calm and away from turbulent storms threatening to bring what they saw as abrupt and distasteful change; towards safer solutions to society's problems and away from radical prescriptions for social and cultural renewal.

Thus, in the First World War the public library championed the revival of the notion of 'good citizenship' designed to 'heal', on liberal-reformist terms, a society riven by strife and susceptible to Bolshevik-style unrest. Between the wars, the public library struck a national pose, mobilising the vocabulary of community to enlarge its status and efficiency. This allowed it, at the same time, to attempt to dampen the social disaffection accompanying mass unemployment, partly by claiming to have taken on a socially healthy, classless image.

The Second World War offered the public library the opportunity of stating its democratic credentials as an agency of free thought, open to all. By virtue of the reading boom of the time, the war enabled the public library to re-emphasise its supposedly classless appeal within a community stirred by 'equality of sacrifice'. The image of classlessness was re-stated with even greater force in the era of the classic welfare state. Despite the opposition (boosted in the war) of die-hard parochial-minded librarians to the formation of larger library authorities, and their hesitation concerning increased state intervention, central funding and government inspection, the post-war decades witnessed a significant shift towards a universal library service. However, the mirage of universal inclusion was in the end dissolved by the realisation that welfarism, including public library provision, was doing little to redistribute wealth, favouring in fact the middle layers of society more than the deprived. For all its benefits, the 'community of welfarism', in which the public library invested with great passion after around 1942 (the year of the McColvin Report), did little to affect the distribution of opportunity in society.

Some librarians came to acknowledge this and worked hard to discriminate positively in favour of the socially disadvantaged. However, the (in many respects) innovative and challenging 'community librarianship' model of service they fashioned in the 1970s and 1980s eventually became the target of a conservative and romantic interpretation of 'community', a combination of traditionalists within the profession and political opponents outside it overseeing the model's demise, yet turning elements of its vocabulary to their advantage.

For many, the 'community' that community librarianship championed proved unpalatable, positioned as it was at the margins of society. Community librarianship was seen to be part of the problem of decline in Britain, not a solution to it. Thereafter, greater faith appeared to be placed by librarians in technological remedies to the poor access and information poverty which continued to deny the attainment of 'true' community. Fresh dreams of social consensus were underwritten by the emergence of new information and communication technologies promising a networked, wired society in which autonomous communities, albeit of the virtual kind, could thrive in an age of intense social uncertainty.

Throughout the twentieth century the threat of radical social and cultural change disturbed the public library world and pushed it towards a safe, conservative community-oriented middle way. None of this drives one to conclude that public libraries have not been a good thing; merely that they have not been unquestionably so. It would be unhealthy, after all, to accept and endorse *uncritically* the purpose and nature of any social institution, let alone an institution, like the public library, whose history is so crammed with cultural conflict. 'Community', like public libraries, is also a good thing. But it can all too easily be high-jacked to defend 'normality', resist the imaginative and defer the 'new'. Becoming more sensitive to the hidden, regressive meaning of community rhetoric will enable the public library to resurrect the true, radical essence of its philosophy: the enhancement and emancipation of the self within the context of progress and social justice.

Select Bibliography

Adam Smith Instutute, *Ex libris* (London, 1986).

Adams, W.G.S. *A report on library provision and policy to the Carnegie United Kingdom Trust* (Dunfermline, 1915).

Addison, P. *The road to 1945: British politics and the Second World War* (London, 1975).

Aitken, W.R. *A history of the public library movement in Scotland to 1955* (Glasgow, 1971)

Andrzejewski [or Andreski], S. *Military organisation and society* (1954).

Anghelescu, H.G.B. 'Libraries without walls or architectural fantasies: a turn-of-the-millennium dilemma', *Libraries and Culture* 34:2 (Spring 1999).

Aslib, *Review of the public library service in England and Wales for the Department of Heritage* (London, 1995).

Astbury, R. *Libraries and the unemployed: needs and responses* (London, 1983).

Astbury, R. 'The public library of the twenty-first century: the key information and learning centre in the community', *Libri* 44:2 (1994).

Audit Commission, *Due for renewal* (London, 1997).

Barbalet, J.M. *Citizenship* (Milton Keynes, 1988).

Barnet, C. *The audit of war: the illusion and reality of Britain as a great nation* (London, 1986).

Batt, C. *New technology in public libraries: a survey* (Winchester, 1985; and subsequent editions).

Batt, C. 'The heart and brain of the information society: public libraries in the twenty-first century', in D. Raitt (ed.), *Libraries for the millennium: implications for managers* (London, 1997).

Beck, U. *Risk society: towards a new modernity* (London, 1992).

Benge, R.C. *Libraries and cultural change* (London, 1970).

Billington, R., J. Hockey and S. Strawbridge, *Exploring self and society* (London, 1998).

Black, A. *A new history of the English public library: social and intellectual contexts 1850-1914* (London, 1996).

Black, A. 'Lost worlds of culture: Victorian libraries, library history and prospects for a history of information', *Journal of Victorian Culture* 2:1 (Spring 1997).

Black, A. 'New methodologies in library history: a manifesto for the "new" library history', *Library History* 11 (1995).

Black, A. 'New times for library history', *Librarians' World* 7:3 (1998).

Black, A. 'The Victorian information society: bureaucracy and public librarianship in nineteenth-century Britain', *Information Society*, forthcoming.

Black, A. and D. Muddiman, *Understanding community librarianship: the public library in post-modern Britain* (Aldershot, 1997).

Board of Education, Public Libraries Committee, *Report on public libraries in England and Wales* [Kenyon Report], Cmnd. 2868 (1927).

Bunch, A. *Community information services: their origin, scope and development* (London, 1982).

Burkitt, I. *Social selves: theories of the social formation of personality* (London, 1991).

Calder, A. *The myth of the Blitz* (London, 1992).

Childs, D. *Britain since 1945: a political history* (London, 4th edn., 1997).

Clarke, P. *Hope and Glory: Britain 1900-1990* (London, 1996).

Clough, E. and J. Quarmby, *A public library service for ethnic minorities in Great Britain* (London, 1978).

Coleman, P. *Whose problem? The public library and the disadvantaged* (Newcastle under Lyme, 1981).

Comedia, *Borrowed time? The future of public libraries in the UK* (Bournes Green, 1993).

Commission of Enquiry into Industrial Unrest, *Summary of the reports of the Commission*, Cmnd. 8696 (1918).

Cooke, P.N. *Back to the future: modernity, postmodernity and locality* (London, 1990).

Cornelius, I. *Meaning and method in information studies* (Norwood, New Jersey, 1996).

Corrigan, P. and V. Gillespie, *Class struggle, social literacy and idle time: the provision of public libraries in England* (Brighton, 1978).

Department of Culture, Media and Sport, *Libraries for all: social inclusion in public libraries* (London, 1999).

Department of National Heritage, *Reading the future: a review of public libraries in England* (London, 1997).

Duckett, R.J. 'Subject departments: their rise and fall at Bradford Metropolitan Libraries', *Art Libraries Journal* (Summer, 1985).

Duckett, B. 'The relevance of libraries and the presumptions of IT', *REFER: Journal of the Information Services Group* 5:2 (Autumn 1988).

Ellis, A. *Library services for young people in England and Wales 1830-1970* (London, 1971)

Ellis, A. *Public libraries at the time of the Adams Report* (Stevenage, 1979).

Ellis, A. *Public libraries during the First World War* (London, 1975).

Ellis, A. *The development of public libraries in England during the First World War*, unpublished PhD thesis, Council for National Academic Awards (1974).

England, L. and J. Sumsion, *Perspectives of public library use: a compendium of survey information* (Loughborough and London, 1995).

Evans, G. 'Welsh public libraries 1914-1994', in P.H. Jones and E. Rees (eds.), *A nation and its books: a history of the book in Wales* (Aberystwyth, 1998).

Everitt, J. *Co-operative society libraries and newsrooms of Lancashire and Yorkshire from 1844 to 1918*, unpublished PhD, University of Wales, Aberystwyth (1997).

Faulks, K. *Citizenship in modern Britain* (Edinburgh, 1998).

Financing our public library service: four subjects for debate, cmnd. 324 (1988).

Foucault, M. *Discipline and punish: the birth of the prison* (London, 1991, first published in French in 1975).

Gamble, A. *Britain in decline: economic policy, political strategy and the British state* (London, 1981).

Gibbins, J.R. and B. Reimer, *The politics of postmodernity: an introduction to contemporary politics and culture* (London, 1999).

Giddens, A. *Modernity and self-identity: self and society in the late modern age* (Cambridge, 1991).

Giddens, A. *The consequences of modernity* (Cambridge and Oxford, 1990).

Goffman, E. *The presentation of self in everyday life* (Harmondsworth, 1969).

Greenhalgh, L. *The place of the library*. The future of public library services: working paper 2 (Bournes Green: Comedia, 1993).

Greenhalgh, L. and K. Worpole, with C. Landry, *Libraries in a world of cultural change* (London, 1995).

Grenz, S.J. *A primer on postmodernism* (Grand Rapids, MI and Cambridge, 1996).

Habermas, J. *The structural transformation of the public sphere: an inquiry into a category of bourgeois society* (Cambridge, 1989, first published in German in 1962).

Harris, D. *A society of signs* (London, 1996).

Harris, J. 'Political thought and the welfare state, 1870-1940: an intellectual framework for British social policy', *Past and Present* 135 (May 1992).

Harrison, K.C. *The library and the community* (London, 1963).

Harvey, D. *The condition of postmodernity: an inquiry into the origins of cultural change* (Oxford, 1989).

Hoare, P.A. 'Library history', in L.J. Taylor (ed.), *British Librarianship and Information Science 1976-1980. Vol. 1* (London: 1982).

Hoare, P.A. 'The development of a European information society', *Library Review* 47:7&8 (1998).

House of Lords Select Committee on Science and Technology, *Information society: agenda for action in the UK* (London, 1996).

Hung, M. *Change and resistance: public libraries in the Second World War*, unpublished MA dissertation, Thames Valley University (August 1999).

Jast, L.S. 'Public libraries', in H.J. Laski, W.I. Jennings and W.A. Robson (eds.), *A century of municipal progress 1835-1935* (London, 1935).

Jast, L.S. *The library and the community* (London, 1939).

Jefcoate, G. 'Democracy at work: the Library Association's "centenary assessment" of 1950', *Library History* 15 (November 1999).

Jefcoate, G. 'Roll of honour: the librarians' war memorial and professional identity', in K. Manley (ed.), *Careering along with books* (London, 1996).

Jefferson, G. *Libraries and society* (Cambridge, 1969).

Jenkinson, P. *Heritage and the public library*, unpublished PhD, Leeds Metropolitan University (1999).

Jolliffe, H. *Public library extension activities* (London, 1962).

Jones, P.H. 'Welsh public libraries to 1914', in P.H. Jones and E. Rees (eds.), *A nation and its books: a history of the book in Wales* (Aberystwyth, 1998).

Jordan, P. 'Social class, race relations and the public library', *Assistant Librarian* 65:3 (March 1972).

Keeling, D.F. (ed.), *British Library History Bibliography* (London, 1972, 1975, 1979, 1983, 1987; Winchester, 1991).

Kelly, T. *A history of public libraries in Great Britain 1845-1975* (London, 2nd edn., 1977)

Kelly, T. *Books for the people: an illustrated history of the British public library* (London, 1977).

Kerslake, E. *A history of women workers in English libraries, 1871-1974*, unpublished PhD, University of Loughborough (1999).

Kerslake, E. and M. Kinnell, 'Public libraries, public interest and the information society: theoretical issues in the social impact of public libraries', *Journal of Librarianship and Information Science* 30:3 (September 1998).

Kinnell, M. (ed.), *Informing communities: the role of libraries and information services* (Newcastle, Staffordshire, 1992).

Kirby, H.G. 'Public libraries and the information society: case study of Croydon Library Service', in J. Thorhauge et. al. (eds.), *Public libraries and the information society* (Luxembourg: European Commission, 1997).

Lahav, R. 'Is class still an issue?', *Public Library Journal* 4:2 (March/April 1989).

Library and Information Commission, *Building the new library network* (London, 1998).

Library and Information Commission, *New library: the people's network* (London, 1997).

Library Association, *A century of public libraries 1850-1950* (London, 1950).

Library Association, *Community information: what libraries can do* (London, 1980).

Linley, R. and B. Usherwood, *New measures for the new library: a social audit of public libraries*, British Library Research and Innovation Centre Report 89 (1998).

Luckham, B. *The library in society* (London, 1971).

Lyotard, J-F. *The postmodern condition: a report on knowledge* (Manchester, 1984, first published in French in 1979).

Macnicol, J. 'In pursuit of the underclass', *Journal of Social Policy* 16:3 (July 1987).

Manley, K.A. 'Sunshine in the gloom: the study of British library history', *Libraries and Culture* 25:1 (Winter, 1990).

Martin, L. 'The American public library as a social institution', *Library Quarterly* 7:4 (October 1937).

Martin, W.J. *Community librarianship: changing the face of public libraries* (London, 1989).

Martin, W.J. (ed.), *Library services to the disadvantaged* (London, 1975).

Marwick, A. *Britain in a century of total war* (London, 1968).

Marwick, A. *War and social change in the twentieth century* (Basingstoke, 1974).

Matarasso, F. *Beyond book issues* (London, 1998).

McColvin, L.R. *The public library system of Great Britain: a report on its present condition with proposals for post-war re-organization* [The McColvin Report] (London, 1942).

McKee, B. *Planning library service* (1989).

McKibbin, R. *Classes and culture: England 1918-1951* (Oxford, 1998).

Mead, G.H. *Mind, self and society* (Chicago, 1962, 1st published 1934).

Miksa, F.L. *The DDC, the universe of knowledge and the post-modern library* (Albany, New York, 1998).

Ministry of Education, *Inter-library co-operation in England and Wales* [Baker Report] (1962).

Ministry of Education, *Standards of public library service in England and Wales* [Bourdillon Report] (1962).

Ministry of Education, *The structure of the public library service in England and Wales* [Roberts Report], Cmnd. 660 (1959).

Ministry of Reconstruction, Adult Education Committee, *Final report*, Cmnd. 321 (1919).

Ministry of Reconstruction, Adult Education Committee, *First interim report on industrial and social conditions in relation to adult education*, Cmnd. 9107 (1918).

Ministry of Reconstruction, Adult Education Committee, *Second interim report on education in the army*, Cmnd. 9229 (1918).

Ministry of Reconstruction, Adult Education Committee, *Third interim report on libraries and museums*, Cmnd. 9237 (1919).

Minto, J. *A history of the public library movement in Great Britain and Ireland* (London, 1932).

Mitchell, J.M. *The public library system of Great Britain and Ireland 1921-1923* [Mitchell Report] (Dunfermline, 1924).

Morgan, K.O. *The people's peace: British history 1945-1989* (Oxford, 1990).

Morris, L. *Dangerous classes: the underclass and social citizenship* (London, 1994).

Morris, R.J.B. *Parliament and the public libraries: a survey of legislative activity promoting the municipal library service in England and Wales 1850-1976* (London, 1977).

Muddiman, D. 'Everyone on board?', *Public Library Journal* 14:4 (Winter, 1999).

Muddiman, D. (ed.), *Public library policy and social exclusion*, Library and Information Commission Report (London, forthcoming).

Mulgan, G. *The public service ethos and public libraries.* The future of public library services: working paper 6 (Bournes Green: Comedia, 1993).

Munford, W.A. *Penny rate: aspects of British public library history 1850-1950* (London, 1951).

Munford, W.A. *Who was who in librarianship* (London, 1987).

Murison, W.J. *The public library: its origins, purpose and significance* (London, 3rd edn., 1988).

Nairn, T. *The break-up of Britain* (London, 1977).

Ollé, J.G. *Library History* (London, 1979).

Ollé, J.G. 'Portsmouth public libraries: the last forty years', *Library History* 15:1 (May 1999).

Orton, G. *An illustrated history of mobile library services in the UK* (London, 1980).

Pateman, J. *Public libraries and social class*, Public Library Policy and Social Exclusion Working Paper 9, Leeds Metropolitan University (April 1999).

Paulin, L. Recent developments in the provision of public library services in the United Kingdom, *Library Quarterly* 48:4 (1978).

Pemberton, J.E. *Politics and public libraries in England and Wales 1850-1970* (London, 1977).

Phillips, M. 'Books build communities', *New Times* (July 1999).

Pimlott, B. 'Is the post-war consensus a myth?', *Contemporary Record* 2:6 (1989).

Pope, R. *War and society in Britain: 1899-1948* (Harlow, 1991).

Proctor, R. 'People, politics and hard decisions', *Public Library Journal* 14:1 (Spring 1999).

Ring, D.F. 'Some speculations on why the British library profession didn't go to war', *Journal of Library History*, 22:3 (1987).

Robson, A. 'The intellectual background of the public library movement in Britain', *Journal of Library History* 11:3 (July 1976).

Rosenau, P.A. *Post-modernism and the social sciences: insights, inroads and intrusions* (Princeton, New Jersey, 1992).

Roszak, T. *The cult of information: the folklore of computers and the true art of thinking* (Cambridge, 1986).

Russell, D. *A social history of public libraries in London 1939-45*, unpublished MA dissertation, University of North London (May 1995).

Russell, D. 'The promotion of public libraries in the Second World War', *Library History* 15 (May 1999).

Snape, R. *Leisure and the rise of the public library* (London, 1995).

Stockham, K.A. *British County Libraries 1919-1969* (London, 1969).

Sturges, P. 'The place of libraries in the English urban renaissance of the eighteenth century', *Libraries and Culture* 24:1 (Winter 1989).

Sturges, P. 'The public library and its readers 1850-1900', in K. Manley (ed.), *Careering along with books* (London, 1996), a special issue of *Library History* 12.

Sydney, E. and R.F. Ashby, *The library in the community* (London, 1956).

The learning age: a renaissance for a new Britain, cmnd. 3790 (1998).

Titmuss, R.M. *Problems of social policy* (London, 1950).

Turner, B.S. *Citizenship and capitalism* (London, 1986).

Usherwood, B. *Rediscovering public library management* (London, 1996).

Vincent, J. *An introduction to community librarianship* (Newcastle under Lyme, 1986).

Webster, F. 'Knowledgeability and democracy in the information age', *Library Review* 48:7&8 (1999).

Webster, F. *Theories of the information society* (London, 1995).

West, W.J. *The strange rise of semi-literate England: the dissolution of the libraries* (London, 1992).

Whiteman, P. *Public libraries since 1945: the impact of the McColvin Report* (London, 1986).

Wiegand, W.A. *'An active instrument for propaganda': the American public library during the First World War* (New York, 1989).

Winter, M.F. *The culture and control of expertise: towards a sociological understanding of librarianship* (New York, 1988).

Worpole, K. 'The future of the public library service', *Public Library Journal* 7:5 (1992).

Index